The Daily Telegraph

Gone fishing

The Daily Telegraph

Gone fishing

Adventures in Pursuit of Wild Trout

JON BEER

AURUM PRESS

First published in Great Britain 2002 by Aurum Press Ltd
25 Bedford Avenue, London WC1B 3AT

A catalogue record for this book is available from the British Library.

ISBN 1 85410 870 0

10 9 8 7 6 5 4 3 2 1
2006 2005 2004 2003 2002

Designed by James Campus
Typeset by M Rules
Printed and bound in Great Britain by
MPG Books Ltd, Bodmin

Contents

Introduction

There are two sorts of book about trout fishing. One sort has titles like *How to Catch Lots of Very Big Trout*. This is not that sort of book. But in case you didn't realise that when you bought it, I will tell you How To Catch Lots of Very Big Trout anyway. It is very simple. You have to go to waters that contain lots of very big trout and then fish there. It is really the only way to do it. This is the other sort of trout-fishing book.

I will not tell you much about the author in this introduction. I suspect that by reading the book you will discover far more about me than either of us will really be comfortable with. Last week I met a man who had just retired from his job in Zimbabwe. He was an avid fisherman and throughout his years in Africa he had kept in touch with his fishing roots by subscribing to *Trout & Salmon* magazine. He had devoured every word. He recounted anecdotes from my childhood and past fishing trips that I had all but forgotten myself. In fact, he seemed to know more about me than my wife did. Judi, who has never read anything I have written about fishing, is now threatening to read this book to find out about the bloke she married thirty years ago.

You will also meet some of the blokes I go fishing with. Paul ('Fishing with Mr Crabtree') and I were at school together and later started a jug band called Garibaldi's Band of Hope. He is now a stipendiary magistrate and still plays in a jug band. He first taught me to fish with a fly. All this is his fault.

Douglas ('Educating Douglas') and I met at college when I used to watch him play rugby for Oxford and the army. Seventeen years later, we met again when he turned up as a doctor in our small Oxfordshire village.

Philip ('Just a Closer Walk with Three') runs a clothing company in Duns Tew, a few villages south of us. We met when I went to buy stuff for my little daughter. He had a stuffed trout in the office which was a bit of a giveaway. Philip has an unfortunate addiction to Whisky flies but he is slowly responding to treatment for this.

Alice ('Fishing with Alice') is the smaller of my two daughters. For the moment. Her fishing was ruined at the age of four when she caught a salmon, something her father did not achieve until several years later, thus making her insufferably blasé about such matters.

'Fishing with Father' was written ten years ago. My father now lives in the cottage next door to us in Cropredy. Which is terribly convenient when the urge to go fishing with a friend comes over me. He still has the camper van. Which is also very convenient.

Much of what follows first appeared in the pages of *Trout & Salmon* magazine, whose editor, Sandy Leventon, must bear some of the blame for all this. Without his support and encouragement – sometimes heavily disguised as pungent abuse – over many years, none of this would have happened. Thank you, Sandy.

1

Fishing With Mr Crabtree

There's something mystical in it, I fancy. A bit like installing bishops by the laying-on of hands, back through the centuries, right back to the disciples. Something like that.

Fly-fishing, I mean: it seems to me you have to be shown in the first place. Not so much the technicalities, casting and so forth, although it helps to be taught that, but rather the fact that fish can be caught on a fly at all. It never seemed very likely to me. Still doesn't, from time to time. Someone has to show you that it can be done. Someone has to pass on the passion of the thing.

If you came from a fly-fishing family then you would have drunk it in with mother's milk, and the feel of the tackle, the smell of dampish canvas and the sight of a box of flies would have all been there from the start, the baton passing smoothly from one generation to another. But if you came from a coarse-fishing family, or a family devoid of fishing, then there was a moment when the flame was transferred. And there was a hand to light the touch paper. With me the hand was Paul's, and it involved a Tups and a grayling on the Derbyshire Derwent in high summer twenty-something years ago.

We had known each other for about ten years. Not friends, exactly, not at first, but we went to the same school and caught the same bus back home and so on. If it took some time to become friends then it was perhaps because we were so different. Nature had fashioned Paul for a prefect. He was decent. In fact, he was so decent that he couldn't understand why everyone else wasn't just as decent. When, years later, I broke up with my girlfriend, he telephoned to ask whether I'd mind if he asked her out. That decent. I sometimes think I might have been a much better person if I had never known him; perhaps I might have developed more of a conscience. But with Paul as a friend I have never really felt the need for one.

To look at him you would think that Paul had always been a fly-fisherman. He wears that sort of check cloth cap and corduroys and he smokes a pipe which he fills from one of those squashy leather pouches polished smooth in a back pocket. And he looked that way in school. Only without the pipe. But Paul did not start out as a fly-fisherman. His own benediction into the brotherhood had come from an ancient ghillie at the junction of the Exe and the Barle in Devon. It was 1960, Paul was eleven, the ghillie was eighty-two.

I wonder how many fathers today would take a young son, crammed to bursting with visions of Mr Crabtree and Peter, for a week's fishing holiday in a West Country hotel. Blessings upon the man, for Mr Richardson, as I recall, had not the slightest interest in fishing. Perhaps it was not all self-sacrifice; the hotel had – and still has – a splendid snooker room where Mr Richardson spent the days in a haze of blue cigar smoke whilst Paul was handed over to the charge of Bill Thorn. I would love to know what the eighty-two-year-old Bill thought of landing the tuition of an eleven-year-old schoolboy, even one as squeakily decent and apple-cheeked as Paul. But then it is hard to know what old ghillies are thinking at the best of times.

Paul had a rod, split cane, with two tops and a silk line. Bill provided a March Brown and showed the lad the rudiments of casting in the weir pool of the River Barle across the fields from the hotel. Then he took the lad to swing the wet fly through the pools and runs towards the junction with the Exe. Imagine this: Paul caught eight fish that first day. That evening they were displayed in triumph on the big plate in the entrance to the hotel. I envy Mr Richardson the sight of his son's face that evening. Paul is human. Probably by the next day he was advising the other fishermen on their choice of fly. Certainly an elderly guest, a judge no less, showed him a fly-box for the first time, a wondrous sight to a young lad, and invited him to pick out a selection from the magical ranks of furs and feathers. Do judges still do things like that these days? There were six fish that second day, suspiciously similar to those of the day before, all at 8 inches – the legal limit then, and now, on these waters. And four the day after. And one grayling of a pound.

* * *

I know all this because the other day Paul happened to ask me where I planned to go fishing. I said that I was just off for a day's trouting at the Carnarvon Arms Hotel. It is quite possible to hear a fisherman's eyes go misty over the telephone. And then it all came out: the rod; the snooker table; old Bill; those first fish; the triumph; the judge and the fly-box; the shock of seeing an ancient and revered ghillie peeing beside the river. Everything.

Now, I am a sucker for a story. Show me the spot where G.E.M. Skues first pulled the wings off his dry fly and called it a nymph and I will be there on the bankside thinking noble thoughts of something-or-other and communing with the shades and what-have-you. I have fished the Aclou beat of the River Risle that Charles Ritz considered 'the finest in the world and better than the finest reaches of the Test, the Itchen and the Wylye'. He was dead wrong: it isn't. But I have fished there, and if someone would point me to the canyon where Clementine caught a foot against a splinter and fell into the foaming brine, I will happily fish there too, walking in the very footprints of that poor girl (which, by a curious coincidence, were the same size as my own – although not, it seems, the same shape). I do love a bit of fishing history.

Mentally, then, I was a small, clean schoolboy in grey flannels and jacket and a blue-and-black tie as I made my way past Tiverton from the M5 and followed the narrow, wooded valley of the Exe north towards Exmoor. At Exebridge the small road to Dulverton lurches over the river beside the Anchor Inn and the small boy would have watched the railway approach the lane from the east. The railway track is gone now but some unmistakable station buildings still stand beside the road and form the first outbuildings of the Carnarvon Arms Hotel. A tennis court now stands alarmingly where the trains would have shot beneath the old road bridge, and just beyond lies the hotel itself.

The Carnarvon Arms was a product of that railway, built by the fourth Earl of Carnarvon to accommodate the solidly tweeded sporting Victorians that the railways brought to the less accessible bits of Britain in order that they might shoot, hunt or hook whatever moved in those parts. And they still do.

I don't know what it was like in 1960, but it had been dry for weeks when I tackled up on a warm day in early summer. The Exe hereabouts has left the moors and flows confidently, swinging round between sandy banks where the martins nest. If the trout streams of the south are gin-clear then those of the southwest are more like old malt, stained with the peat of the moors above. We walked upstream from the old railway bridge towards the junction of the two rivers: the Exe and the Barle. I don't know exactly what I expected at the junction of these two quietly famous little streams. The junction of the Exe and the Barle that day was no Khartoum. The Exe swept by serenely enough, but the Barle, the stream I had come to fish, hardly seemed to be pulling its weight.

It lay in a series of rocky pools, linked by small stickles, each petering out a few feet into the next pool as if that was all it could be fagged to do. A sad sight. It was a warm day but there was plenty of shade under the tall trees on the far bank. There was little more than a twiddle of a small fish or two in the shallow tails of the pools. These were the same lively runs where the eleven-year-old Paul had taken eight fish on a March Brown swung across the current. Where had the water gone? It had been dry, certainly, but not that dry, surely? The answer lay around the next bend. Paul had been taught to cast in the unencumbered waters of the weir pool. It is still there, now with small pontoons built out over the current, the legacy of a game fair but useful for instruction. At one end of the weir the ponded water of the pool slips through an ancient sluice and into a narrow channel which leads away across the meadow. It is an old mill leat. Most of the waters of the Barle were heading out across that meadow towards the old railway line.

We had been warned about the mill leat by Mrs Toni Jones who owns and runs the Carnarvon Arms (incredibly she was doing just that the Easter of 1960 when Paul and his father arrived). The mill has long gone but its ancient right to siphon off the waters of the Barle has been taken over by the Exe Valley Fish Farm. That too has been there since Paul's visit, so it is hardly a new problem. Indeed, when there is plenty of water in the West Country, it is no problem at all. Then, most of the water sweeps over the weir and on down to join the Exe, the trout thrive and the salmon flock into beat C and everything is oojah-cum-spiff. But the flow down the leat is more or less constant and in the summer of a drier season most of the water of the Barle can be led away to rejoin the Exe at Exebridge, leaving the last quarter-mile of the Barle a sorry sight and the fisherman on that beat feeling a bit gloomy.

Unless, of course, he takes a careful look at the mill leat. I doubt whether the salmon fishers who come to the hotel have given it a glance. Salmon fishers are strange, haughty creatures with their minds on grander things: the leat is just something to step over between beat B and beat C. And to many trout fishers, used to the broad and lively waters of the West Country and the livelier stuff of the Barle above the weir, the leat just looks like a disaster, ruining, for the time being, the bottom bit of the Barle. But for the man who spends his time fossicking about on the unlikelier headwaters of the Thames, the small streams of the Welsh borders and waters of little consequence anywhere else, that leat leading out across the meadows looks like the business.

It is small, certainly. But then it has never suffered the whims of the West Country weather, scouring a broad bed down to the rock in times of flood and then shrinking to a trickle in drought. When the Barle floods, the stuff just pours over the weir; when the Barle shrinks, the weir keeps the flow trotting down the leat, day after day, season after season. This stability of flow is why fishermen make such a fuss about the chalkstreams. The fauna flourishes. And so do the trout.

We followed the water rushing down the leat from the weir. It is a narrow little stream, but there is plenty of water and it flows deceptively quickly with none of the rocks and boulders of the river to slow things up and provide the sights and sounds of fast water. And it is deep. Too deep for thigh waders in spots, shallow and bright in others. And the bottom is clean gravel. There is plenty of shade from the bushes and trees that overhang the stream, sometimes touching from bank to bank. All in all, it is well nigh perfect.

There was nothing rising on that warm morning but on a small water that doesn't seem to matter. I put on a smallish fly, an Easy Rider Dun with its hare's-ear body and mixed grizzle and red hackle: it is what I always put on when I am not sure what they are taking – and often enough when I am. And I flicked it up into the gap between a holly tree on my bank and a hawthorn on the other.

The first cast, like the first pancake, doesn't count. That went into the hawthorn – but it is surprising just how often you can pull a fly out of a hawthorn bush if you don't snatch at the thing. This is just as well because the second cast went in there as well. The third cast fell in the gap onto the pale deep pool beneath the bushes, and a trout who had been waiting all his life for such an eventuality hurled himself on the thing as if the chance might never come again.

It was not a chalkstream trout. It was a trout of the West Country, smaller, fitter and wilder than the trout of most chalkstreams. A little gem. Just like that mill leat.

And there were more of these bright little fish to follow. Each gap in the foliage, each small pool scoured on a bend, produced an eager rise to a careful dry fly all the way down that magical little water that flows between the Barle and the Exe. The mystery of the thing is that hardly a fisherman in that fishing hotel bothers to fish the leat.

*　*　*

There is another mystery. On the last day of Paul's visit, old Bill Thorn let it slip that the trout Paul had been catching so prodigiously had been stocked just a day or so before. But Mrs Jones tells me that her waters were never stocked in those days. She thinks that perhaps the kindly old soul had gone down to the trout farm, come back with a bucket and slipped a few stockies into the pools to encourage the young lad.

Or he may just have told Paul they were stocked to wipe the smug smile off his apple cheeks. You never can tell with old ghillies.

One more thing: that girlfriend. Paul never did ask her out. We got married a month or so later.

Educating Douglas

Listen: it is important, when learning to windsurf, to keep your back straight. You must not bend forward as the sail tugs at your arms. Keep your torso straight and lean back against the pull of the wind in the sail.

I knew all that. I had listened when he told me. I am not an idiot. I understood well enough what was required.

So we can assume that when I bent forwards as the sail tugged at my arms it was not because I had failed to grasp the concept of leaning back. Nor was it because I had simply forgotten his instruction to lean back: my attention span is limited, certainly, but as he was bellowing 'Lean back!' at me from his dinghy every fifteen seconds, there was no real danger of it slipping my mind.

And the thing is, I really wanted to lean back. I just couldn't. If I could have leant back I would have done so and his bellowing 'Lean back!' at me really didn't help much. I told him all this as he steered his dinghy closer to the windsurfer, as once again I heaved myself wearily out of the water onto the unstable board. I was very tired. I told him that too. He said it was because I had been bending forward: he suggested I lean back.

That was five years ago. The man in the dinghy was Douglas. This year it has been my turn. This year I have been teaching Douglas fly-fishing.

Look: I am not a casting instructor. Never have been: never will be. I don't cast well enough for a start. And even if I possessed the skill to place a dry fly onto a sixpence 30 yards upwind, I do not have the skill of imparting this ability to others. But, what the hell, I was willing to give it a bash.

My friend Douglas: what manner of clay do we have here? I first saw Douglas nearly thirty years ago. I was newly arrived at college. Douglas was in his second year with an air of maturity that made one feel slightly frivolous. He had a job: he was in the army. He was not just in the army: he was an officer in the Parachute Regiment, which is the army in its most virulent form. At the end of term, when some of us were hitching down to St Ives, sleeping on beaches, playing guitars and smoking all manner of things, Douglas would rejoin his regiment and practise dropping on people from planes and killing them. Douglas played rugby rather well. He played centre-three-quarter. There were two types of centre in those days. There were the elusive, will-o'-the-wisp sort of centres, the sort that glide silkily through the ranks of the opposition. And there were the other sort, the thrusting, only-girls-do-sidesteps sort that take three men to bring them down. Douglas was that sort and he has three Blues to prove it.

We had little in common, let's face it. We each had a vague idea the other existed. And then, a dozen years ago, I saw a vaguely familiar face moving into a house in the village. It was Douglas. In the intervening years he had left the army, returned to university and medical school and he was now a GP. And a few years after that he was trying to teach me to windsurf off the beach at Budleigh Salterton.

Budleigh Salterton was also the scene for Douglas's first lesson in fly-fishing. The lovely River Otter slips into the sea at the end of the beach. Upstream, where the effect of the tide runs out, there is a stretch of river, heavily wooded on one bank and open on the other. It is the haunt of brown trout, a few sea trout in season, schools of impressive mullet foraging up from the sea and innumerable dog-walkers who spend their time pointing out the mullet to you in the belief that they are trout. They mean well. And the fishing is free.

Remember learning to cast a fly? The difficulty of getting the rod to do the work, loading it against the pull of the line, letting the rod catapult the line high in the back-cast. Remember that? 'No further back than 12 o'clock' you are told, so you stop it there and the line falls limply behind you. So you try harder, thrashing the rod back to 3 o'clock, 4 o'clock – and the line gets caught in the grass behind you. So you wang it forward before the fly can touch the grass and you crack the fly off in a fair imitation of Frankie Laine doing 'Rawhide'.

So when I kept reminding Douglas, that first morning on the Otter, not to let the rod go back beyond 1 o'clock, I was trying to help – but I was think-ing, just a bit, of windsurfing.

He could cast a fly. Not necessarily every time, but often enough. It was time he was casting at something more than mullet.

Our next outing was to the River Coln in Gloucestershire. The Coln bubbles out of the Cotswold limestone and runs crystal-clear down to the infant Thames. At Fairford the fishing belongs to the Bull Hotel, a fine old fishing inn with the nicest landlady I know. Rarest of all, the Bull water is not stocked. All fish are returned to the river to breed with the consequence that the river is stuffed with trout and grayling of all sizes and degrees of difficulty.

Furthermore, the trout of the Coln have grown tolerant of humans on the riverbank: Fairford has even more dog-walkers than Budleigh Salterton. This was important. Douglas is not a small man. You need a certain degree of heft to shrug off a loose-head flanker and he had not grown any smaller in the years since he gave up the game. Also, casting was not yet a thing of economy: Douglas still needed room to operate. With luck and a following wind the trout might mistake him for a man throwing a stick for a dog.

One did.

Douglas was down beyond the bend of the first field. I could see the rod flicking back and forth. And then it was arched. I got to the bank to see a fish larking on the end of the line. Then it was in the net and Douglas was looking down into the net at his first fish. It was a perfect fish: an honest little wild brown trout from a crystal river on a sunny day in spring. It is a privilege to be there when a man catches his first trout.

On the way back home we trout fishermen talked trout fishing. Douglas had been boning up on flies: wet, dry and otherwise.

'How do you know,' said Douglas, 'whether to use a dry fly, a wet fly or nymph?'

It had been easy that day on the Coln. We had been fishing dry flies. The fish had been feeding on something on the surface so we gave them something on the surface. It all made sense – and, what's more, it worked.

'But suppose they had not been rising?' he asked.

'They might still come up for a dry fly – or they might not.'

'And if they don't?'

'Then you have to get the fly down to the fish.'

'And that's when you use a wet fly, is it?'

'Yes.'

'Or a nymph?'

'Yes.'

'So is a nymph a type of wet fly or is a wet fly a type of nymph?'

That is not an easy question to answer. I explained: a nymph looks like a nymph and you usually cast it upstream, like a dry fly – but you don't have to. A wet fly looks more like a dry fly but it is probably taken for a nymph. You usually cast it downstream, that is, across and down the current, unless you are fishing upstream wet fly – which is very effective too. Any more questions?

Douglas, I noticed, was not taking notes. I suggested he read a fishing book, something a little less technical, a little more lyrical: Arthur Ransome's *Rod and Line*. He enjoyed that. Everyone does.

Our third outing was to the River Wylye. I had been fishing more than twenty years before I first threw a fly over one of the classic southern chalk-streams. That was on the River Wylye at Sutton Veney, which is where I was now taking Douglas. The upper Wylye is an intimate little stream, less man-icured than its more prestigious neighbours and all the better for that. It is stocked, certainly, but only with brown trout in recent seasons and there is a good head of native grayling. There are no native dog-walkers.

There is a rule on the Sutton Veny water, as there is on many of these southern streams, that only dry flies and upstream nymphs shall be used. There was a time when I thought I knew the difference between a nymph and an upstream wet fly. Now I wasn't so sure. It didn't much matter to start with: something was rising in the waters of the Wylye.

The waters of the Coln had been crystal clear but the Wylye is clearer. The trout of the Coln are used to folk galumphing along the bank: not so the fish of the Wylye. So on the Wylye you must crouch and sometimes you must crawl. There are two ways to tackle such fishing.

Method 1.   You see a rising fish. You approach as cautiously as may be and, once in range, you cast at the fish. This first cast is your best chance. If the fish does not rise, you cast again. Each wave of the rod, each cast on the water increases the chances of spooking the fish, decreases your chances of catching the thing. After half-a-dozen casts you have scared the fish and you must mooch off to find another.

Method 2.   Similar to method 1 until the moment to mooch arrives. You do not mooch: you stay put. Your friend, who knows more about these things, suggests you try another fish but you ignore him. You continue to cast occa-sionally. Time passes: small climbing plants gain a foothold on your person but you do not move. Eventually, you and your casting become a part of the natural order of things. Also, the fish realises that it feeds with you there or not at all. It commences feeding. And after a while it feeds on your fly. You have bored it into submission.

I am a method 1 man myself. Douglas, on the other hand, favours method 2. He might have invented it. It certainly seemed to work on the Wylye that day. There is a certain smugness about a man who has caught his first grayling.

*   *   *

My last fishing trip with Douglas was a few weeks ago in high summer. Douglas and Anne were on holiday in Devon. They had been there for a few days. He had fished the River Otter again and caught a trout between the cows and the dog-walkers. He had gone to the River Teign and fallen in and fished on through a chill day in sodden clothes. Now he wanted to try the waters of the Arundel Arms at Lifton. I had never visited the West Country waters of the Arundel Arms, so I arranged to meet them for lunch in the bar. We would fish in the afternoon.

I got there at 12.30 p.m. An hour and a half later they had not arrived. I stood in the hall reading the fishing returns and regulations when I noticed the beat allocations for the day. There was Douglas's name under beat 3 on the River Lyd. He had arrived early and gone straight down to the river. He had left a message at the hotel reception but it had not reached me. He would return later for lunch. Really, the man had become a fishing fanatic. I had a glimpse of the sort of things wives have to put up with. That was another thought: Anne is not the sort of wife who takes readily to Putting Up With Things. I wondered how she was taking to Douglas's new passion for rivers. Worse: I wondered who was going to get the blame.

It was a perfect summer's day on the lovely little River Lyd. After lunch we drove back into the Devon lanes to beat 3. We walked through the woods to the riverside meadows. There was not a house in sight, not a road to be heard: a magical valley hidden in the Devon hills. It was hot, the bees buzzed, the bright sun threw the river beneath its trees into dark shadows. It was far too hot to fish. Anne had brought a rug down to the river. She got out one of those huge paperback novels, thicker than it is wide, that fishermen's wives always seem to have about their person. I was beginning to see why.

Douglas was away up the river, striding down to the water's edge at a bend where he had taken trout that morning. There was a sort of look in his eye that boded ill for any trout and salmon in his vicinity. He had become a game fisherman. I felt a mixture of pride and apprehension in equal parts.

A bit like Doctor Frankenstein.

3

March Brown

You know that scene where the escaped prisoner-of-war is just making his way through the last checkpoint? The German officer at the barrier examines the papers that have been cunningly forged by a fellow prisoner with pebble-thick spectacles who doesn't want to escape himself. The officer hands back the papers and opens the barrier.

'Have a good journey,' he says.

'Thank you,' replies the escaper in relief – and realises, way too late, that the German officer spoke in English. *For you, Tommy, the war is over.*

A lot of trout are going to be feeling a bit like that in the next few weeks. These are the fish that are caught on a March Brown fly. They are right to feel a little foolish.

The March Brown is probably the best-known artificial fly in the whole box. Every fisherman knows it and most have used it. It is unquestionably a great fly: it catches trout wherever there are trout to be caught, in rivers, chalkstreams, lakes and little ponds. And this is strange because the natural beast this artificial is supposed to be imitating is rather uncommon. I doubt if one trout in a hundred has ever seen a natural March Brown. So a trout that falls for a fisherman's March Brown in a chalkstream, lake or little pond has no one to blame but himself.

The natural March Brown is a creature of a few rocky rivers of the north and west. You can find them on the waters of the Cheviots and Pennines, on the Tees, Tweed and Eden, but Wales' River Usk is the most famous March Brown water. I saw my first hatch of March Browns on the Usk. It was a cold, grey day in early March, the sort of day best spent in bed. But because it was the opening of the trout season I was beside the cold, grey Usk. I should have been sniffing the March morning air, revelling in the first day of fishing: I should have been thinking noble thoughts. At noon there had been not a sign of life: I was thinking about lunch, which is as noble as I could manage. The change when it came was sudden and remarkable. I did not see a fly emerge: you don't. One minute they are not there, then you see one, and then another and you realise they are everywhere. They burst through the surface in mid-stream and drift down with their mottled brown wings held apart to dry before they launch into the air.

Conventional March Brown wisdom has it that a nymph imitation is more effective than the dry fly during a hatch. Pish and tush! What sort of lumpen soul would pass up the first good hatch of the year in order to catch a few more trout on the nymph?

That first, exhilarating hatch was over in minutes. The first hatch often comes around noon, delayed for an hour or so if there has been a sharp frost the night before. They are brief affairs, the flies coming in concentrated bursts like waves of enemy bombers over a target – and for much the same reason: in a burst some will get through. And so we waited for each bustling, urgent hatch, listening for the first crisp rise, watching for the first waggle of little brown wings. And so we missed lunch and didn't care a jot.

*   *   *

There is no mention of the River Caldew in *Where to Fish*, the bible of the travelling fisherman. I don't know why – it's just not there. I was pottering west from the River Eden and just came across it, a fine rocky river running from the flank of Skiddaw in the northern lakes to join the Eden in Carlisle. At Dalston it runs through a small wooded gorge. It was a hot day in July, the permit from the post office cost £2 and we had nothing better to do than fish that shaded little river. In fact, there *is* nothing better to do on a hot day in July than fish a shaded little river. So we did.

The bottom hereabouts is littered with slabs of red sandstone like the ter-racotta roof tiles from a Roman villa. I picked one of these rocks from the river bed and turned it over. I had never, have never, seen so much life on a single stone. The nymph of the March Brown is a flat, broad beast designed to cling to smooth rocks in fast water. As I turned the rock a wave of these little brown nymphs scuttled round away from the light like an army of bar-nacles on manoeuvres. There were dozens on that rock and under every other rock in the stream. Not just March Browns; there were nymphs of a score of different species. The Caldew teemed with life and I caught my best fish of that season ten minutes later in the pool beneath Dalston Bridge.

Now let me tell you something else about this same River Caldew and its March Browns. Last year a researcher from the Environment Agency was to give a talk on river life to a local school. She went to the Caldew to collect some samples. What she found was disturbing: where there should have been over thirty different families of invertebrate life there were just two or three. Something had wiped out most of the river's food chain over a 30-kilometre stretch – most of the river. There was no sign of dead fish, no visible pollution. The devastation was traced to a sheepdip. The new synthetic pyrethroide sheepdips have been heralded as 'safer' because they are largely non-toxic to shepherds. They are, however, up to a hundred times more lethal to invertebrate life than the organophosphate dips. A few drips from a dipped sheep can wipe out aquatic insect life over a large area. It may not kill trout and salmon. It just starves them.

Timely, then – or ironic – that today sees the launch of another fishing interest group. The Wild Trout Society is concerned with the conservation and management of wild-trout fisheries.

N.B. The Wild Trout Society is now three years into its sterling work and has proved its worth by kick-starting conservation projects on many rivers. To join (£25) write to Wild Trout Society, 92–104 Carnwath Road, London SW6 3HW.

4

Just A Closer Walk With Three

What I had imagined, of course, was a *Shetland* pony. What we had here was a *Highland* pony. It is a mistake anyone could make.

I have, as a policy, steered clear of horses all my life. We have never got on. And a father of daughters quickly learns to change the subject whenever talk of horses occurs because he knows Where Such Talk Can Lead. So I don't think I can be blamed for confusing Shetland and Highland ponies. But it was a shock, I can tell you.

We had a yen, you see, to fish the remote hill lochs of western Scotland. The trouble with these little gems hidden high in the hills is that they are remote: a long walk in and a long walk out. So the idea was to camp up there in the hills, travelling from loch to loch. And the trouble with this is that it takes a lot of stuff to camp in any sort of comfort and I did not fancy lugging a lot of stuff high into the hills. And so we hit on the idea of a horse.

Picture this: two carefree fishermen, striding the high country carrying just a rod and tackle bag, the small willing pony beside us bearing the tent and gear, a happy band of three companions free to roam the hills. Anon, we would come to a small loch where we would fish as the pony rested. Sounds good, doesn't it: we would have a slice of that.

David Hay-Thorburn runs Brenfield Activities from the Brenfield estate near Lochgilphead on the shores of Loch Fyne. The estate is renowned in the horse world for its terrifying trail rides across the wild high country of Argyll, but David will arrange just about any sporting enterprise you care to throw at him. I rang him and laid out our vision of fishing the hill lochs with a pony. In a day or so he had got us permission to fish and camp in a scatter of hill lochs on a remote estate high in the hills where the rugged slopes were still mercifully free from the conifers that have crept over the west. The only access to this Shangri-La is an ancient drovers' trail from Loch Awe to Loch Fyne, the oldest track in Argyll. He had also got us Dougal.

If you are familiar with horses, Dougal is a grey Highland pony. If you are not familiar with horses, Dougal is a huge and alarming creature, a white-washed brick privy of a thing. David's first job was to show us what goes where on a pack pony. I was numbed to find that putting on the bridle involved me putting my thumb into Dougal's mouth. We learnt to lace Dougal into his packsaddle – like rigging a small but complex sailing vessel. Then we unloaded from the car all the gear we had considered necessary for a spell of fishing in the hills. In a heap beside the pony it looked daunting: heaven knows what Dougal thought of it. We stuffed bits into panniers, slid bags into sacks and slung them across his saddle, piling stuff ever higher. Dougal stood stoically in the rain as we suspended buckets and kettles from anything we could tie a rope around. And then it was time to be off, up into the hills that had disappeared in the driving rain.

David walked the first few yards with us down the track. He left us with the helpful advice that Dougal had known these mountains all his life. He would tell us if a piece of ground was too boggy or dangerous for him to cross: he would simply refuse to cross it. That was reassuring. For a while.

Looking back on events, I am not sure it was wise of David to tell us this within earshot of a horse with Dougal's sense of humour.

We were on our own. The track turned up the hill and became a little rock-ier. Dougal stumbled just a little on the wet rocks. Was the load too heavy? It looked huge. Was he trying to tell us something? *Don't worry about me, lads, I'm an old, old horse but you just go on and enjoy yourselves, I'll do my best. How about a mint?* Mints, we had been told, were Dougal's favourite and we had stocked up with several packets of extra-strong mints in Lochgilphead. Dougal was just no good a making a mint last. You could hear him crunch an extra-strong mint across 200 yards of windswept moorland. It put the shivers up the chap who had to put his thumb into Dougal's mouth when bridling.

We climbed gradually past startling banks of bluebells and out onto the rough pasture of the hills. The old drovers' track struck off to the right and we began to climb in earnest. *So this is a hill, is it, lads? Interesting. Tell you what: I'll give it a go for a couple of minutes and if I can't manage it we'll call it a day, OK? How about a mint?* We struggled on for another 100 yards. It was this business about Dougal telling us whether something was safe for him to cross or not that was the problem. As soon as Dougal realised that we had not the slightest idea what a horse could and could not do, he began to enjoy himself.

Sorry, lads, I'm afraid this bit's far too rocky for my old feet. (How about a mint?) So we would find a detour. *Sorry, lads, this is a bit too boggy. (How about a mint?)* So we would find something firmer. Sometimes it was too steep uphill and sometimes it was too steep downhill. We came to the first river. It had been raining all day: it looked as if it had been raining all year. The small stream that came down the valley shared the track for a few yards.

I can't cross that! That's a river, that is! I'm not allowed to cross rivers – I've got a note from my mother.

'It is not a river, Dougal, it is a stream.'

That could be 10 feet deep, that could.

'Dougal, it will not come up to your knees'

You go first, then. If you make it to the other side in one piece, I'll think about it. How about a mint?

And that is what we had to do. We attached a long rope to the reins and I waded through to show him it was safe and after much persuasion from Philip, Dougal came though, muttering to himself about what havoc the water was going to wreak on his old joints. And then the Land Rover jolted around the bend. David had come to see how we were getting on. We explained our concerns about Dougal. Was he really up to such a rigorous journey? David gave us the sort of look reserved for the terminally naive non-horser. Dougal, he said, had pulled a 67-ton fishing boat through the Crinan Canal. Dougal, he said, can drag a tree at a fast trot up steeper slopes and rougher ground than we had seen. Dougal, he said, was having us on. He gave Dougal a resounding slap on his enormous white rump and Dougal was as good as gold after that. More or less.

We climbed on, up beyond the last of the rough grazing into a country of crags and heather and moss. Mostly moss. After four hours of driving rain we arrived beside our first hill loch. We were not a happy band of three companions roaming the hills. We were tired and cold and wet. Mostly wet. For some time we had found nowhere that did not squelch as you trod, nowhere that was not battered by the southerly wind that had white horses dancing up the loch.

First things first. Philip would go off in search of somewhere to put the tent before the rapidly approaching dusk: I would brew a kettle of tea. We had hung the Kelly Kettle on the outside of the Dougal's load for just such an eventuality. Unfortunately the matches were buried in the heart of my bag in the middle of the load. Everything had to come off and in unpacking we made an interesting discovery. The bag containing all the food had been lashed tightly on the top of the pack – so tightly, in fact, that it had exploded a large carton of fresh orange juice amongst all our fresh provisions. Orange was a recurrent motif in much we would eat during our time in the hills.

But we had made three other, happier, discoveries. Philip had found a spot to the north of the track, close to another loch, where there was a tiny patch about five feet in diameter that was slightly less soggy and not very sloping.

And it was sheltered by a shoulder of the hill from the driving wind. I had discovered that dead heather, even when soaked, will eventually boil a kettle: we were not short of heather. And we discovered that it had stopped raining. We drank a cup of tea, reloaded Dougal and retreated to the sheltered spot.

Our camp was at the windward end of the small Loch Tunnaig. It too was sheltered for a few yards, and as we set up the tent there was a miraculous ring of a trout rise in the scatter of thin reeds in the shallows. We had almost forgotten why we had come to these hills. Dougal was tethered and fed. We had wolfed down a huge tin of cassoulet heated on the gas stove and as the light began to leak from the sky we set about fishing our first hill loch.

Before going up the hill we had taken advice from Archie MacGilp of the tackle shop in Lochgilphead. Archie fishes these high lochs and he had supplied us with a selection of the local flies that are used hereabouts and much useful advice. The first bit of advice was that we might have come too early. By the first week in June the fish are usually starting to move in the cold high waters but the season was very late this year. He suggested several traditional flies in red and black: Bracken Clock, Kate MacLaren and a Kehe/Bibio cross of his own devising. It was getting dark as we got down to the lochside. The water was stained brown with the peat of the hills and I fancied something a bit more obvious to liven things up. Now, I am mostly a river fisherman and my fly-box is a thing of quiet restraint in tones of brown and olive. But stuck in the foam lid was a large bright something, a great teddy boy of a fly, that had arrived stuck to the front of May's edition of *T&S*. It positively glowed. It was a Ruane Hothead in Day-Glo green and black. And, by golly, it worked. In the long, low twilight of the Scottish hills we had our first hill trout.

*   *   *

Tuesday morning I woke at 3 o'clock. And at 4.15. And at 4.50 and 5 o'clock. One of the disadvantages of sleeping in your own comfortable bed at home is that you are not awake to enjoy it. This is not a problem in a tent on a lumpy patch somewhat smaller than its two occupants. Philip unzipped the tent. Dougal, the Horse Who Couldn't Climb Uphill, was standing majestically on a crag, as high as his tether would allow. The wind was still stiff from the south and we cooked bacon and sausages *à l'orange* in the tent. We were setting out that morning for a large loch a little to the north. We had decided to leave the tent where it was and to travel light.

Dougal, the Horse Who Couldn't Go Downhill, bounded down from his crag like a chamois at the rustle of an extra-strong mint packet and stood waiting to be saddled. There is a certain irony in taking a horse fishing. Most of the stuff the horse carries is horse stuff. There is a huge steel stake to which he will be tethered. This, of course, needs a heavy lump hammer to bang it into the ground. And a long bar so that the two of us could pull it out again. A long rope to join Dougal to the stake. All this is carried in heavy canvas and leather panniers slung over a wooden packsaddle. His breakfast goes into one pannier and his bucket swings from another. We topped it all off with rain gear, waders, rods and tackle bags, lunch and the kettle. The sky was clear as we set off for Big Tinker Loch. Twenty yards later the whole lot slid off to one side: we had forgotten to re-tighten the cinch straps after loading.

Our hill-loch fishing really started that day on the Big Tinker. There were no rises with the wind still strong from the south. I started with the Ruane hothead and got a pull almost immediately. Philip, who knows far more than I about loch fishing, had put on an intermediate line and was experimenting with weighted flies in the absence of a rise. He had a fish within a minute or so. The fish was typical of the trout of these hill lochs. It was 10 inches long, perhaps 6 ounces, with a deeply forked tail and bold markings. My first fish of the day came a little later, a twin in size and shape but with just a few dark spots on a body of metallic green. Our first brace for supper.

The day went on. We caught fish steadily enough but nothing like the baskets of the warmer weather when twenty or thirty fish are commonplace. By late afternoon I had lost my one Hothead and Philip had found the fly of the moment, a Whisky Fly that took six fish in half an hour and was, in one variation or another, to be the most successful fly throughout our days in the hills. That evening we started back to camp with half a dozen of these small fish for supper and Philip had returned the best fish of day, a beauty of 13½ inches.

We had talked about how such evenings would be on the long drive north: the fish grilling over the glowing ashes, the smell of heather and coffee, perhaps the plaintive sound of a harmonica played in the still of the evening. It can't be that difficult to learn, surely. All you do is blow and suck.

*   *   *

We did not find out whether I could learn the harmonica that evening. The wind shifted and strengthened. The tent was rattling on its moorings. It was to be a long and stormy night.

This tent, which had always performed splendidly at the bottom of our garden, had evidently not been designed for a gale in the Scottish Highlands: this was something of a disappointment in a tent marketed by Millets as the

'Highlander'. There would, I agree, have been problems in calling the thing 'Bottom of Our Gardener', but it would have been less misleading. Philip was particularly disappointed: he occupied the windward half of the tent.

We were perched behind a crag in a sodden wilderness of moss and heather, high in the hills between Loch Fyne and Loch Awe. The wind had been strong from the south since we had arrived several days before but during the night it had shifted, sneaking around the side of the crag which sheltered us, and was now driving the rain through two layers of nylon to emerge as a fine drizzle in Philip's half of the tent. It was nature's way of telling us that it was time to get up.

We wrapped up in waders and waterproofs as best we could and unzipped the door of the tent. Dougal was staring reproachfully from a little way up the hill. The wet night tethered on a windy hillside had left our Highland pack pony in a three-mint mood, a measure of the number of extra-strong mints that would be required before normal relations could be re-established. The bribe and breakfast delivered, we were ready to start fishing.

Our soggy little campsite lay beside Loch Tunnaig. There are twenty or so lochs and lochans on the Ederline estate up in the hills between Loch Awe and Loch Fyne. You can see them on the Ordnance Survey map, scattered amongst the black squiggles that denote rock outcrops and north of the dotted line that is the ancient drovers' track across the tops. They have splendid Gaelic names like 'Loch na Creige Maolaich' and 'Loch Gaineanhach', names redolent with romance and probably resounding with brave feeling if only I knew how to pronounce them. Unlike the Welsh language, which seems to manage with only the most frugal use of vowels – and sometimes none at all, Scots' Gaelic seems to have more vowels than it knows what to do with, and an honest attempt to pronounce them all leaves one sounding vaguely Australian. There is another problem: many of these lochs have the same name. There are at least four 'Dubh Lochs' amongst the Ederline hill lochs alone. It was something of a relief then to find that these fine Gaelic names are only used by the mapmakers: the locals, fishermen and landowners alike, have more prosaic, if less romantic, names for the hill lochs.

So, our soggy little campsite lay beside Duck Loch. It was the first loch we had arrived at on our way up the drovers' track from the west. Over a rise, the wind-lashed expanse of Sandy Loch stretched away a mile or more to the south. It was not an inviting sight. To the east the track climbs steeply up to its highest point, the pass over to the upper lochs. Today we could see only a few hundred yards of the track before it disappeared up into the grey cloud that hid the upper slopes. We didn't fancy that much either.

That left us to explore the lower lochs to the north. At least we would have the wind and rain on our backs to begin with. We trekked north across a low rise to Big Tinker Loch where we had fished the previous day. We fished along the eastern shore, casting up the loch with the wind and getting small tugs and the occasional fish to keep us interested. A small inflow joins the loch at the northwest corner and we followed this up to the smaller, steeper-sided Little Tinker Loch.

Fishing a small stream on a poorish day, the river fisherman explores each bend and run and pool, looking for a spot where, through some quirk of the shade and depth and vegetation, the trout are feeding. More often than not there is such a spot to be found. That has always been the charm of small rivers for me. What I was astonished to find was just that same variation in these hill lochs. Little Tinker Loch did not produce a fish, not a rise, not a tug. It *looked* dour – but I only remember thinking that after I had been fishing it for a while. A second little stream flows into Big Tinker at its southern end. We followed this stream a few hundred yards up to another loch about the same size as Little Tinker. It was steep-to at its windward, fishable end. Philip took one corner, I took the other. Within a couple of casts Philip was into a fish. And then another. I think I might have had a tug. When Philip had his third fish I found myself sort of edging his way. Nothing obvious – just so that I wouldn't have to shout to congratulate him. He had switched from his Whisky Fly to a small Whisky Muddler and now they were hitting it as the fly landed. I did not have a Whisky Muddler nor anything like it, but I could see them rising and I put on a dry fly. I think a fluke of that gusty wind must have caught my fly as I cast because it landed quite close to where Philip was catching all the fish and a trout grabbed it.

It did not last. With two of us lashing the water in that small corner the action soon slowed and then stopped. A steep stream tumbles into this fruit-ful little loch from the west and a stiff climb up the stream brings you to a small, pretty loch with deep water beside a bank of steep rock. It is hard to judge depth in these peat-stained waters: your feet can be out of sight at wader-depth. Three forlorn rowan trees with their toes in the far bank give this loch its local name. It is a beautiful, haunting spot and we fished there for an hour or so without a sign of a fish. Four lochs, all interconnected, three the same size and all within half a mile. Two of these lochs produced no fish. And one of them produced a dozen fine little hill trout from just one small corner. On another day it might be the other way round. I have no idea why.

It was mid-afternoon as we retraced our steps through those four lochs. The rain had stopped some time before but we had hardly noticed. We fished each loch in turn with exactly the same results. As we fished back along Big Tinker the area of calm water at the windward end began to lengthen and stretch up the loch as the wind began to drop.

We had been waiting for that evening since we first thought of walking up into the hills with a pony. It was of the stuff we used to pay one-and-nine to see in the Saturday-morning cinema: dead heather burns every bit as bright as sage-brush and tumbleweed; the smell of grilling trout climbing into the still air and Dougal looking impossibly romantic against a western skyline of granite crags; a pot of coffee bubbling in the embers of the campfire. It was touch and go whether we wouldn't just burst out singing something with 'Kiy-yi-yippee' in the chorus. We might even have set a spell and whittled something if there were any wood nearer than Rowan Tree Loch. As it was, setting down was still out of the question on a soggy Highland hillside, so we left Dougal munching on his hay whilst we walked down to fish Sandy Loch through the long northern twilight. It was still not dark when we came back in sight of the camp. We could make out Dougal against the dark hillside and he could see us. He gave a whinny of greeting across the mirror surface of Loch Tunnaig. It was strangely touching, a welcome home in the emptiness of the hills. But he was probably only asking for a mint.

It was still calm when we woke the next day, our last in the hills. The pass over to the higher lochs was visible for the first time and we were determined to fish at least one of them. Saddling Dougal was a slick operation now, a satisfying buckling of canvas and tightening of leather straps. I bet I could have rolled a cigarette with the other hand if necessary. We packed the panniers with goodies salvaged from the food bag, treats we had been saving, and set off up the track towards the pass outlined against heavy grey clouds.

It was a warm climb. Dougal was rapidly disappearing under a garnish of discarded clothing as we stripped off – first waterproofs, then fleeces and padded shirts. Behind us the pattern of lower lochs was spread out to the west. As the track twists up to the ridge, a small stream tumbles down alongside and a last turn brought us suddenly to its source, a pair of small lochs bisected by the old path. We left the track here and struck north along the shore of Windy Loch, which must be something if it is windier than the others we had fished that week. It was barely ruffled this morning.

Walking the tops was not quite as I had pictured it. I remember seeing Michael Caine in *Kidnapped*, striding through this sort of country in a kilt and a pair of those dinky ballet slippers that Highlanders wear in such films. They didn't seem to inconvenience him at all. I don't recall him going up to his tartan stocking-tops in the stuff. Nor slipping on his kilted backside. Not like me. Dougal, after all the fuss we had had on the journey up into the hills, seemed to have lost the note from his mother that excused him from going across boggy bits. Now he was bounding over them without breaking stride, leaving us hanging on, slithering in his wake.

A little north of Windy Loch lies a small loch with no Gaelic name on our map. It is known locally as Rainbow Loch. Here a fluke of geology has left a seam of limestone, enriching the waters so that a stocked population of rainbows grows wondrous large for a few years and then disappears, as that short-lived species cannot reproduce hereabouts. Good. We were not heading for Rainbow Loch. A little to the east, across a steep gully in the deep layers of peat, lies the Cam Loch.

Cam Loch is not the highest of these hill lochs but it is as near as makes no difference. Where most of the lochs are simple fingers of water pointing roughly northeast, Cam Loch has a tortuous coastline of headlands and bays, beaches and peninsulas, like a miniature mock-up of the Mediterranean. It may even have some of that limestone. It is just perfect.

We unloaded and unsaddled Dougal, plunging his stake up to the hilt in soft peat with a couple of strokes of the lump hammer. We left everything in the panniers and scrambled the fishing tackle together. The sun was out. We were off fishing.

Things had changed. On other days our scramblings along the loch shores had been hidden, or so we supposed, by the wind and the waves. Now as we moved along the shallows, the rises we had seen as we approached slowed and stopped. I climbed over the first heathery headland and a fish, startled in the shallows, bulged away into deeper water. It was a big bulge. It suddenly seemed possible to spook a whole loch. Quite an achievement.

My first Cam Loch trout was my last of this walk in the hills. It was not a huge fish – 12 inches – but like all these wild fish of the cold waters it felt like twice that until it broke the surface. I was mighty pleased with it. Philip thought the fuss I had made catching it would probably have wrecked our chances of another thereabouts. It was gone noon: we would have to leave in an hour if we were to make our way back down to the camp by Duck Loch. There we would have to pack the tent and all the paraphernalia and pile it somehow onto Dougal before setting off back down the track to civilisation and a long, long drive back home. It would be nice to have one last fish.

The sun was high and bright. The movements in the shallows of the bays had stopped. The ways of fish in still water are a mystery to me. Not to Philip. A long peninsula reaches to the centre of Cam Loch, dividing it into a several distinct arms. If any fish were moving between any of these arms they would have to pass the tip of the peninsula. He set off around the indented coastline and some time later appeared a couple of longish casts away from where I stood rebuilding my leader.

I would prefer to gloss over the next half-hour. After a few minutes I looked up and saw an extravagant bend in Philip's rod. A tough little hill trout can do that, so I called over and asked if it was any size.

'Could be,' he said – and there was a sort of something in his voice. Not panic, exactly. And then the thing broke the surface. It looked huge. Now this is a small loch, remember, so things can look huge. I thought 2 pounds: Philip said 1½ (and probably thought 2). And then I did something unforgivable.

'Could you slacken off while I run round to photograph the fight?' I asked. And then Philip did something unforgivable: he agreed to this ludicrous request.

That dash in chest waders through crag, bog and heather took over ten minutes. Michael Caine in his kilt and ballet slippers might have done it quicker but I doubt it. I arrived in a flurry of splash beside Philip and waded out. Philip raised the rod to tighten the line. The top vibrated and jerked down. The fish was still on – but it had somehow become even heavier. I was clicking away as Philip hauled in against increasing pressure until, horribly, everything went solid. He didn't say much. He didn't have to. In the slack of that ten-minute dash the fish had sulked down amongst the boulders of the rocky bottom. The line had snagged on something. He slackened again and pulled. A frayed end came back and Philip reeled in. He still didn't say much.

We climbed round the western shore. Here a heather-studded cliff hangs high over the loch. A fabulous view to the east looks over Horseshoe Loch and on down to Loch Fyne and the mountains beyond. You would give a lot for that view – but not as much as we would have given for that hill trout of a pound-and-something.

It was way past time to go. We made our way round to Dougal and the pack. Dougal stood as far away as his tether would allow. We could see why. In our rush to get fishing we had tied his tether a foot or so too long. The remains of our lunch lay strewn about the panniers and clothing. Dougal had munched his way through two apples and a packet of ginger-nut biscuits. He knew what he liked: he had left a packet of fruit shortcake untouched. He had also unwrapped and taken two large bites from a precious pound of Bleu de Gex cheese brought lovingly from France: he didn't fancy the rest of it.

Frankly, neither did we.

5 𝕃

Hobbs's Leviathans

You know the scene: under the cottonwood trees outside some dusty little one-horse town somewhere west of the Missouri, a small crowd of town folk are gathered around a showman's wagon with 'DOCTOR THEOPHILUS J. GOLIGHTLY' emblazoned on its side. The good doctor is standing on a small makeshift stage in front of his wagon. He wears a monocle, a dapper moustache and a fancy waistcoat. He holds a bottle of 'Miracle Gumbo' aloft in one hand.

'Good friends,' he calls to the scanty gathering. 'Citizens of Hog's Wallow, I am here to tell you a story, a story of high adventure and tragedy . . .'

Well, friends, I am that man in the fancy waistcoat. And I have a story to tell to you. It has everything a story should have. It has triumph and tragedy. It has irony and history. Lots of history. It has a timeless river and it has huge, huge trout. It also involves a lot of beer.

It began, for me, in the last days of last summer. I had hired an ancient Thames camping skiff for a trip down the river from Lechlade to Oxford with my youngest daughter. The Thames was low and clear after a dry summer and flowed serenely between meadow banks of willows and purple tangles of Himalayan Balsam. A statue of Old Father Thames lounges beside St John's Lock, the first below Lechlade, and on the other bank, beyond the weir, stands a lovely old pub. It is the Trout Inn.

It is not the only inn of that name along the river. There is another at Tadpole Bridge, some 10 miles downstream, and a third beside the weir at Godstow as the river swings south towards Oxford. All these Trouts must mean something. They do. You can see what they mean at yet another pub on this stretch of the river. The Swan is a lovely creeper-clad inn beside Radcot Bridge. It takes a minute for your eyes to become accustomed to the cool interior after the brightness of the river. Then you start to notice the mounted fish around the walls. There are the usual Thames species – pike and perch – but dotted amongst them there are some big-shouldered jobs, ugly numbers, some of them, with teeth, and not made any prettier by some horrendous taxidermy. For the most part they were caught in the river hereabouts, in the 1960s. They are Thames trout.

The Thames trout is a legendary beast. It is famous for its size – there have been specimens weighing over 17 pounds and bigger ones have been seen. It is likewise famous for its rarity. They are rare enough to discourage all but a few dedicated souls from searching for them. Thames trout are caught – but rarely by the few, poor benighted souls who were looking for them. And the chance of catching a Thames trout if you are *not* looking for one is even slimmer. Are you getting the picture?

The reason that the trout of the Thames are so big – and so rare – is simple. It is unlikely that trout breed in the Thames. Such trout as are there have slipped down from the troutier waters of the tributaries: the Coln, the Windrush, the Evenlode and, of course, the Kennet. Two things can happen to the innocent immigrant newly arrived in the big, rich waters of the Thames: it can be eaten by the big, rich predators that thrive in such places. This is the easiest thing for the trout to do. The alternative is to join the big, rich predators and feast on the wealth of fodder fish: a six-year-old Thames trout can weigh close to 10 pounds.

I did not know any of this as I stood in the cool of the Swan Hotel gazing up at the brutish specimens around the walls. All I knew then was that I wanted to catch one.

So I phoned Vaughan, who knows a great deal more about such things than I do. Vaughan Lewis runs the Windrush Environmental Consultancy, but he was once a senior fisheries officer with the Thames NRA and knows as much about the fish of those waters as any man has a right to.

'You know, of course, about A.E. Hobbs,' Vaughan said. It wasn't a question. Don't you just hate it when people say things like that? I do. It makes me feel so ignorant. No, I didn't know about A.E. Hobbs. So he told me about Mr Hobbs.

A. Edward Hobbs was perhaps the greatest trouter the Thames has ever seen. He caught his first Thames trout as a boy in 1880. His book, *Trout of the Thames*, was written just after the Second World War, some sixty-five years and thousands of trout later. It is a little gem of a book of the sort we don't get nowadays. A man has something to pass on in the way of fishing. He says what he has to and then stops. It fills around ninety small pages and you could easily lose it in a bookcase. It is the vibrant record of a lifetime in pursuit of Thames trout and you will read nothing in these few pages that you could find in any other book. It is, quite simply, the business.

Trout of the Thames has been out of print for many years. Vaughan did not have a copy but we have a mutual friend in David Reinger, the erudite fishery officer of the Cotswold Flyfishers Club. I have yet to find an out-of-print fishing book David doesn't have. Did David have a copy of *Trout of the Thames*? He had two.

I read the book at a sitting. It is that sort of book.

'You know, of course, that there is a pub called the A.E. Hobbs.' It was Vaughan, doing it to me again. 'I think it is somewhere in Henley.' I was amazed. Offhand, I could think of only one other hostelry named for a fisherman and that was the Izaak Walton Hotel on the Dove. A week later I was driving down to Henley on a warm day of early spring.

There are some lovely pubs in the soft, wooded folds of the Thames around Henley. They nestle. Some are hung with warm red tiles; others peek out of a dense tracery of Virginia creeper. The A.E. Hobbs is nothing like these. It is a creation of the late 1960s, a radical square box looking for all the world like a squash club in the middle of a housing estate. Instead of a traditional pub sign, the A.E. Hobbs has a life-size model of the great man on top of a slim 12-foot pole. Fly-fishing purists will be pleased to know that he is holding a fly rod – although only a handful of the thousands of trout he caught were on the fly ('This mode of fishing . . . for trout on the Thames is not recommended'). And his eyes bulge alarmingly – a perfectly understandable expression for a man who finds himself standing on top of a slim, 12-foot pole.

But do not despair: the A.E. Hobbs is run by Bill Thurston and Bill is a fisherman. Just inside the bar a large poster gives a potted history of Mr Hobbs and his book. The walls of the room are peppered with ancient prints and photographs of the river and what, at first glance, appears to be an illuminated glass case of two monstrous fish. It is a backlit photograph of one of Hobbs's trophies: a pair of Thames trout from 1902 and 1903. Both are over 10 pounds. They were the finest pair of wild trout I had ever seen.

I had read about these very fish in Hobbs's book. From 1890 until 1945 he had kept a meticulous record of his fishing. It is a staggering achievement. 'In fifty-five years . . . it has been my pleasure to catch 878 trout over 3 lb each and a large number over the 16-inch limit and up to 3 lb. Of these I have ten mounted whose average weight was 9¾ lb.'

Those ten fish form the finest collection of Thames trout in history. I had read the stories of their capture in Hobbs's own words. I was looking at a photograph of two of them. Where were these fish now, half a century later? Bill Thurston was way ahead of me. He told me more about A.E. Hobbs.

There is, possibly, another explanation for that look of unutterable horror on the face of Mr Hobbs in front of the unlovely building that bears his name. A.E Hobbs was, by profession, an architect. In particular, he designed pubs.

Henley is remarkably unspoilt. In the heart of this little town beside the Thames there is a brewery that has remained independent for well over two hundred years. Brakspear's brewery has pubs throughout the surrounding parts of Oxfordshire, Berks and Bucks. Some of these pubs are the charming ancient inns that nestle in the countryside and along the Thames itself. Others were built early in this century in the characteristic 'Brewer's Tudor' style: brick and tile with plenty of hipped roofs and dormer windows, oak doors and wrought-iron latches. These were the cosy creations of Brakspear's architect – Mr A.E. Hobbs.

The brewery buildings themselves in the heart of Henley are much, much older. Bill Thurston had kindly arranged for me to visit the brewery. He wanted me to see something. In a company office unchanged for a century, I was introduced to estates director Mr Tony Verey. He too had a tale to tell.

Some time after the death of their former architect, Brakspear's brewery received a strange request. The brewery had an ashpit, a place where the broken bottle glass and general rubbish could be safely dumped. The caller had a quantity of old glass cases and their contents to dispose of. She knew of Brakspear's ashpit because many years ago her father worked for the brewery. Could the glass cases be dumped in the brewery ashpit? A waggonload of hazardous rubbish duly arrived: it was, of course, Edward Hobbs's collection of mounted fish.

We had been following Tony Verey through the labyrinth of the old brewery. We arrived at a small door along a narrow passage. This was the sample room where a small barrel of each brew is held to check its qualities. The small whitewashed room was lined with racks of metal barrels. And high on the walls above the barrels were shelves of stuffed fish. Magnificent specimens of several species: huge pike, chub and golden tench. And trout. The last chapter of *Trout of the Thames* is entitled 'My Most Exciting Catch'. It tells of a cold day in June 1897 – a hundred years ago. It was a hopeless day and he had sent Bob Young, his long-time boatman and friend, down to the Bell for a scotch to ward off the flu. The inevitable happens: a huge trout is hooked above the weir. In the course of the fight the fish runs down through the sluice and Hobbs has to cut the line and re-tie it in order to carry on the battle below. After a long and exciting tussle a magnificent specimen is landed singlehanded through the piles and impediments of Hurley weir. The story ends, 'The inscription on the glass case reads: Thames Trout, weight 9 lb 5 oz. Caught by A.E. Hobbs, June, 1897.' I had just read that same inscription on the glass case above the barrels of the sample room.

It is a strange thing to read a hundred-year-old account of a titanic struggle and to see that same fish in front of you.

There were several other cases, each containing magnificent specimens, in the sample room, but only one other held Thames trout. Only three of Hobbs's original collection of ten had survived. These last two were the terrifying pair of fish whose illuminated photograph I had seen in the pub. They were on the top shelf and I could just make out the inscription – caught May the second and twenty-fifth, 1896.

Hang on, though! The pair in the pub were dated 1903 and 1903. There was a sort of a something in Tony Verey's eye as he led us out into the streets of Henley and round to the old building on the river that once housed the famous boating club. It had always belonged to the brewery and had been a wharf and stables before it was loaned to the boat club. Now it has been restored as a private reception centre for the brewery. On the first floor, overlooking the river, there is a collection of artefacts and pictures from Brakspear's two-hundred-year history in brewing. On the ground floor there is a comfortable private bar.

And around the walls is the world's finest collection of one man's life as a fisherman. It is bewildering. I stared about me at beautiful specimens of perch and bream, pike tench and chub.

And there were the seven missing Thames trout of A. Edward Hobbs.

Troutes Directions

Fish *en France*

All Gaul is divided into three parts, and so is this sampler of things French and fishy.

*   *   *

Stand on the Pont Saint Michel. (Actually, you don't have to do this; I am just establishing Place: we are in Paris.) To your right lies the Isle de la Cité with the Offices of the Police Judiciaire along the Quai des Orfévres where Maigret sat and watched the barges passing up the Seine. To your left, the Rive Gauche (where else?) with its echoes of artists and students in the streets and cafés around La Sorbonne. Before you the River Seine flows downstream past the Louvre and on towards the Eiffel Tower. Behind you is the pale magnificence of Notre Dame and upstream is one of the prettiest trout streams you could find in France. Or anywhere else. Quite a long way upstream though. About 200 miles upstream.

The River Seine rises in the department of Côte d'Or. I don't know if you have a working knowledge of the departments of France. Mine is pretty fair: at school the usual punishment for the usual crimes was not lines or even an essay: it was to draw a map. Exactly which map depended on the nature of the crime and the prosecuting prefect. A fairly minor peccadillo could carry a penalty of 'Map of Australia with all the rivers'. This was a doddle – Australia consisting, as it does, of a coastline, desert and precious little else, especially rivers. Ten minutes, tops. A more serious crime might call for 'South America with all the countries'. Trickier, certainly, but not too taxing. But a major-league crime, a sin of the deepest dye, would be punished by nothing less than 'France with all the departments – named'. I became pretty familiar with the administrative geography of France. Côte d'Or is about a third of the way down on the right.

Around Châtillon-sur-Seine is high, rolling countryside of deciduous forest and pasture. It is not rich land: inches below the topsoil is the limestone bedrock that characterises the streams that feed the infant Seine. The Upper Seine is not a Hampshire chalkstream: it is none the worse for that. It is not manicured and cosseted. It just streams, bank high through beds of ranunculus, over a pale limestone bed. Take a look at the Coln in Gloucestershire or the Wye and Dove in the limestone valleys of the Derbyshire peaks. That sort of thing.

Below Châtillon the river is tamed by many mills and weirs which provide depth despite the recent droughts that have shrunk the rivers of France as much as ours. Above the town the Seine is smaller and faster and, to my mind, more interesting. Follow the river higher still, looking for the smaller, wilder headstreams with the smallest, prettiest, wildest trout and you get a disconcerting surprise. Often as not the valleys steepen and then end in a towering wall of limestone with a fully-fledged (if small) river tumbling out of a cave at the base.

We came at Easter this year. It was cold and grey and the fireplace in the gîte I had booked was 5 feet tall and 6 wide and could take a fairish-sized tree trunk. We piled in a small forest on that first night and kept it going. Next morning we set off to find the fishing. This is not hard to do in France. We had a drink and asked at the first bar in the village of St Marc-sur-Seine, 22 km south of Châtillon. They sent us along the street to a small hotel, Au Soleil d'Or, where a comfortable woman, built along the same lines as our fireplace, was knitting behind the bar and watching television. We had another drink (finding fishing in France can be every bit as enjoyable as the sport itself) and asked, 'Is it possible to buy a ticket to fish here?' This is a phrase I have perfected in several languages. It requires no clever stuff with verbs – two simple infinitives do the job and can be swopped with any number of others to suit the purpose. And the answer is 'Yes' or 'No'. It was 'Yes'. She reached down an old biscuit tin and proceeded to get out bits of paper. French fishing clubs are usually very well-documented, with maps and hints and adverts and all sorts. La Saumonée, the APP (*association de Pêche et de Pisciculture*) of Aignay-le-Duc that has the fishing on this stretch of the Seine, is no exception.

And slowly she explained to the three of us what it would cost for us to fish hereabouts. If sometimes it takes a while it is because I can never quite believe what I hear.

La Saumonée has 48 km of water. The *annual* subscription for the club is 149F. That is around £17.50. All fishermen must also pay the *taxe piscicole* (fishing licence) at 44F. Fishermen who fish on category 1 waters (i.e. salmon and trout waters) also pay a supplement of 91F. A further 76F is charged for '*un accord de réciprocité*'. Look closely at this last bit. We have a lot to learn. French angling associations have long had reciprocal arrangements with their neighbouring clubs: you can fish our waters if we can fish yours. Occasionally this is done in Britain. Very occasionally. In France it goes further. Reciprocal arrangements have been negotiated throughout the Côte d'Or department so that an angler can fish on any club waters throughout the department (almost all rivers are club waters with a few exceptions for conservation and short private stretches). Why stop there? Why indeed. They haven't. Two-thirds of the APPs in seven departments around the Côte d'Or have joined this *accord de réciprocité*. That is unlimited fishing in an area the size of Wales. And even this is peanuts. Two other enlightened confederations of clubs have recently combined to agree reciprocal fishing in a total of forty-seven departments from the Mediterranean to the Channel. Unlimited fishing throughout half of France, including national licence and club membership, for less than £45 a year. Makes you think.

Outside the Soleil d'Or it was still raining. The Seine was tinged with colour. And so, by this time, were we. All that week it rained. Not hard enough to stop you getting up in the morning and thinking the day would be fine, but enough to make you realise that it wasn't. Small damp figures hunched under small damp trees and trundled worms around the eddies in the margins. A few years before I had seen it in June when the mayfly had been coming off in clouds and there were heavy rises between the banks of weed undulating in midstream. For those frantic weeks the upper Seine is a busy place, for universal reciprocity has its drawbacks and many anglers come to sample this splendid fishing. Then is the time to retreat to a nearby tributary, the Ource, a few kilometres to the east where the trout are as good, if less renowned, and the grayling are better.

But for now it was too early, for the grayling and the trout hugged the quieter backwaters. I wanted to photograph the Seine above Châtillon but the sky remained resolutely dark and forbidding. Until the Friday, when the horizon lightened in the morning. Now, Friday is not an ideal time to photograph a category 1 river of the Côte d'Or. These salmonid rivers are closed on Tuesdays and Fridays throughout the department. It gives the fish and the fishermen a rest. But we were leaving early on Saturday and Friday was our only chance. We tackled up beside a pretty mill and Simon stepped up to the stream, working his line out over the water. A small brown van pulled up behind the buildings and two large men in sunglasses and peaked caps

climbed out. They wore guns on their belts. They were the local fishery offi-
cers. Imagine that on the Derbyshire Wye.

*   *   *

Three pages of the atlas to the west is another river in another countryside:
the Loire. The Loire is a sinuous monster of a stream, sliding between shifting banks and islands of sand and gravel around the town of Briare where we
crossed it on the route north along the N7, the old route between Paris and
the South that, in the days before autoroutes, would jam solid with fleeing
Parisians in the first week of August. Now, even in the summer, the N7 is
comfortably quiet. Nine kilometres north of Briare, mercifully bypassed by
the N7, lies the village of La Bussière. And its chateau, Le Chateau des
Pêcheurs.

I am not normally one for chateaux but you have to make an exception for
a Fishermen's Chateau. We had not stumbled on it by chance. I had been
reading one of those guidebooks that disappear from the public library round
about March: a *Guide to the Loire* or some such. Now, there are more
chateaux on the Loire than you can shake a stick at, and usually the guidebooks bang on about additions made in the seventeenth century or Rococo
plasterwork in the salon, but this book kept announcing that such-and-such
tributary, 'an excellent little trout stream', joins the Loire here or there, so the
author seemed to be of the right stuff. 'The Chateau des Pêcheurs,' said the
guidebook, 'is the largest museum of angling in Europe.' Possibly it is.

The chateau at La Bussière has not always been 'des Pêcheurs'. The name
was assumed in 1961 when it was decided to create a museum of things fishy
in the old keep. It could hardly have a fishier setting. The whole chateau is a
series of courtyards surrounded by formal gardens, but at the centre stands
the old keep, approached over a moat and backed by a large lake in which
impressive carp were wallowing at the surface. They were a long way off as
we watched: three years of drought had lowered the water level and drained
the moat. I imagine it will be well and truly filled at the end of this winter. It
is the old keep, an island of turrets and tall towers, that houses the museum.

Inside the walls are bedecked with stuff *de pêche*. I had expected a vast collection of tackle receding into the past with reels and rods, ancient and
modern. There is much of that, although some of what there is has certainly
never caught a fish. One of the more bizarre and spectacular exhibits is a display by Pezon and Michel of multi-section rods and terminal tackle of 1889.
Each float is lavishly gilded and encrusted with the arms of the Russian

Imperial Family. There are displays of flies, ancient and modern, and cases of stuffed fish. Alongside this fishing hardware there is an impressive collection of fishy art: engravings, watercolours, prints and, upstairs, many ceramics and sculptures. The collection is worldwide and many of the more unusual and haunting exhibits are from the Far East. Down in the cellars, the kitchen is preserved and displayed with all the arcane and often inexplicable contrivances for preparing fish dishes. It is well worth a visit. (The 'aquarium', housed in a cellar off another courtyard, is not. It is a dingy display of a few small fish tanks holding a few small freshwater fish that have become almost translucent in their underground home. This aquarium rates alongside Nelson's bloodstained shirt in the National Maritime Museum as the saddest museum exhibit I have seen.)

*   *   *

There is a Law of Nature, like gases of equal volume varying with the square root of something-or-other. That sort of thing. This law states that everywhere with decent trout fishing is three hours' drive away. From me, at any rate.

One day this summer I found a spot, a place of bright little chalkstreams running through lush meadows. And trout: deep, fine fish lying in the channels between weed beds. And not expensive: around £16 for up to two weeks of this sort of fishing. How far does one have to travel to find such a place? About three hours' drive from my place.

Three hours south*east*. I took the M40 towards London. Within an hour I was driving south around the M25. In two hours I was stuck in a traffic jam around Junction 8 and then driving south on the M23 towards Gatwick. In two-and-a-half hours I was in the chalk downland to the east of Brighton. At Newhaven. I was going fishing – in Normandy.

It is not a bad way to travel to the river. A leisurely meal on board the Dieppe ferry and a snoozle in the afternoon sun as we approached France. And within a ten-minute drive of the port there are several of the prettiest chalkstreams you might wish to find.

You will need to find a tackle shop. Dieppe is a charming old town, crammed with seafood restaurants around the lovely old harbour and dotted with tackle shops. Don't bother to ask about trout in these shops. You will find shrimp nets in a dozen sizes and prawning gear and any amount of metal stuff for lobbing into saltwater but nothing that a man could tell his mother about. The nearest place to talk flies and trout is 4 miles away in the village of Arques-la-Bataille.

It was 6 o'clock in the morning. Monsieur Piedefer runs a serious tackle shop in Arques-la-Bataille: he opens one hour before sunrise on Saturdays and Sundays.

There is a ritual to these things in tackle shops the world over. The visitor asks what flies to use: the locals ask to see his collection of flies. He shows them. They laugh. Locals have always laughed at visitors' flies. Charles Cotton laughed at Walton's flies. I know this. Last year on the other side of France they had laughed at my flies: not rudely exactly, but with a wondering shake of the head – they supposed that those flies might fool some sort of trout somewhere, but not their trout, not hereabouts. Their trout would not look at anything larger than an 18: their trout would sheer away in horror at a tip larger than 1½ pounds. So this year I was ready. The little box I showed Monsieur Piedefer and Michel was stuffed with tiny little flies, weeks of peering myopically at the tying vice.

They laughed.

The trout of Normandy, it seems, are trenchermen. They look for protein and lots of it. A size 20 is just so much nouvelle cuisine. Normandy is a rich land of rich food and cream and their trout want their fair share. I asked Michel what he used.

Michel Bouteloup is a renowned trout fisherman in Normandy. He lives beside the Risle, one of the finest of its rivers, just upstream of Pont Audemer. The town has given its name to the favourite trout fly of Normandy. The Pont Audemer is as near a mayfly as 'dammit' is to swearing. It has a body of pale cream ribbed with brown silk, a tail of pheasant tail fibres and a yellow hackle wound through a barred teal wing (I think). The thing is a mayfly. It is mayfly size and they use it all season if fish are seen rising – and also when they aren't. And it works. It makes you think about all this Vincent Marinaro and microflies and so on.

I got out my specially purchased spool of 1½-pound tippet.

They laughed.

They have big trout in the chalkstreams of Normandy and they have weed and to prevent one getting into the other you lean into a fish and you do it with nothing less than 3 pounds, perhaps 4 pounds.

As we bought a combined ticket and licence to the local club (there are two hereabouts, but don't bother with the *Gaule Arquoise* – get the *APPMA de Dieppe*), something – a nuance of accent, perhaps, or my request that he repeat everything very slowly – told Monsieur Piedefer that I was English. He called us back from the door and disappeared into a back room. He returned with a bottle of the local cider and two plastic beakers, pressing them on us and telling us to have a fine day. You don't get that sort of thing in Banbury tackle shops.

Three rivers converge on the village of Arques-la-Bataille to form the river Arques on its way to Dieppe. They fan south across the lush water-meadows of Normandy: La Varenne, La Béthune and L'Eaulne. We went first to look at the Varenne near the village of St Germain d'Etables.

The Varenne is an unassuming little stream, swinging with remarkable pace through the meadows, throwing itself into loops. Like many chalk-streams, it seems to ride over the fields rather than through them. The water carried a slight tinge of white – I can't think of a better way to describe it – like the Windrush after the spring. There was not a rise to be seen on that cold morning and so we set about trotting nymphs through the tasty runs on the outside of the bends. Michel's nymph was on the same scale as the Pont Audemer and all but dwarfed the small trout that took it. But it was one fish more than I hooked that morning. The wind was blowing from the north. It was, Michel said, a very bad sign. The fishing is very poor in a north wind. This must be something of a trial for the dry-fly fishermen of Normandy: all the rivers flow north and they will be casting upstream into the teeth of any favourable, southerly wind.

We moved on to the Béthune. It was hot now. The wind had dropped and the sun was like it had been all summer. I did not take to the Béthune close to Arques. It has fish, to be sure, because I saw two of them swinging from the hand of a fisherman as we parked the car. Big things. They had fallen to a Mepps spun through the deep, lifeless pools. This is sea-trout water. Not sea-trout-rattling-up-the-stony-shallows-after-dusk water: more there-are-sea-trout-down-there-somewhere sort of water and a worm or a spinner is the favourite way to get them out. Perhaps the heat was getting to me. Or the cider. I was prepared to settle for an afternoon snooze at this point but Michel wanted to try one more river: the Eaulne.

I first saw the waters of the Eaulne peering between the high nettles and rosebay willowherb of the bankside. There in the sunlit depths, suspended in the crystal water, was my first sight of a live Normandy trout. The Eaulne was different from anything we had seen. It is impossible to say why. It just looked fishy. Nothing was rising: the sun shone just as relentlessly but the water had a clarity that sparkled life and we could see fish. I was itching to collect my rod from the car. I do like to see fish.

I do not necessarily like to see fishermen. Two figures were walking down the bank towards us. Like us, they were prospecting the river through the heat of the afternoon. In a land where much of the trout are still fished with worm and spinner, there is a particular camaraderie amongst fly-fishers. These two had travelled from troutless Amiens to fish the Eaulne. They had marked down one spot where they had seen huge trout. They were waiting for the evening to fish it. Would we like them to show us the spot? Well, what do you think?

The sun was lowering a little but it was hot and humid amongst the towering vegetation as I nestled forwards to crouch beside Guy, trying to distinguish the darker shapes under the trees. You look for a pale patch on the bottom and watch until it is blotted out as something swings over it and suddenly you can see the trout. You can hang on to it as it moves back into the shadows and then it is gone again amidst the reflections. It was big. I worked my way back from the riverside and followed another track of beaten vegetation to find Eric deep in the stuff, staring upstream. I couldn't see the rise under the bush, just the result as slow waves rather than rings spread outwards. There was no hurry. It was the first rise we had seen that day and there it was again, further out and not quite breaking the surface. We watched that fish for quarter of an hour: it was feeding – a bit – but steadily. Eric worked himself gently into the water, moving less of it than the trout. We waited. The trout rose again. Eric reached slowly up the rod to pull the leader through the rings. We were watching intently for another rise and none of us saw the bloke coming across the field opposite. He was just there: a big bloke in shorts and a white sunhat, on the bank just where the fish was rising. Only now it wasn't. He didn't say anything. Nor did Eric. I was surprised. Then the bloke turned and clumped off along the bank downstream until he got to bend where Guy had been watching the huge fish under the bank. The bloke stood and looked at Guy. The fish had gone now. Michel made his way downstream and the bloke followed him on the other bank. Michel stopped. The bloke stopped. And then he stomped off across the field to a small house where the family were watching all this through binoculars. I had the feeling I had missed something. Clearly the bloke did not wish us to commit fishing. We did not know why. We gathered on the bank and it was decided to send Eric over the river to enquire. He plashed through the water and trudged across the meadow towards the house. The man left his family while we watched them through our binoculars. It was beginning to look like one of those movies set in Berlin in the 1960s with Michael Caine meeting that affable KGB bloke with the eyebrows at Checkpoint Charlie.

There was no bloodshed. Eric trudged back. The bloke had told Eric that this stretch was a *réserve de pêche* – a section set aside as a sanctuary. It would explain the huge fish. Eric agreed it *had* been a reserve but the fishing card stated that it would be opened for fishing in 1995. The bloke agreed that it would be opened in 1995 but the card hadn't said when in 1995. Eric said he thought it might have been at the beginning of the season. The bloke said he understood it was to be at the end of the season. Eric said there didn't seem much point in opening it at the end of the season. You couldn't fish then. The discussion never got much further than that. You can have a perfect right to fish but if a big bloke stands on the bank next to your cast there isn't a lot of point to it. So we left.

The sun was low as we assembled our gear where we first met beside the Eaulne. We were a band of brothers in adversity now. Had we been American we would have bonded. The heat went out of the day as we crossed the river and, for the first time on that long summer day, we began to catch fish.

Eric took the first, on a nymph fished down the deep water above a small lasher: a bright little fish that dashed down into the pool below. Then Guy found a better fish rising in a small branch of the river that swung out to enclose a meadow. The trout took a Pont Audemer like the good Norman trout it was. And then fish began to rise in odd corners the length of the river as it threaded its way through the pastures, the sun sank and we all began to take fish.

We had waited a long time for that final, finest hour. But that's how it is on a long hot day in summer.

7

Disgusted, Cropredy

Dear Sir,

What the Hell is happening to this country? Have we become a nation of namby-pamby, snot-nosed, limp-wristed milk sops – or what? I refer, of course, to the nanny-knows-best attitude of the pipe-smoking, sandal-shod, beardie-weirdie liberal do-gooders and social workers who would feed us all a diet of poached fish and brown-bread-without-the-crusts-and-never-leave-go-of-mummy's-hand-in-the-streets. Children these days are over-protected, padded and pampered and feather-bedded against the Knocks of Life. Call me old-fashioned if you like but in my day children were encouraged to injure themselves, painfully and frequently: it made men of us, real men. We wore short trousers in those days (and at a time, mind you, when, as a matter of historical record, we had proper winters with snow and icicles, skating on the frozen Thames, chestnuts roasting on an open fire, Jack Frost nipping at your toes . . . where was I?) and below these trousers we wore our knee scabs with pride. I doubt if there was a day in the early years when my knees did not bear those noble campaign medals of youth. I blame the Boy Scouts: a fine movement in many respects but latterly perniciously undermined by the introduction of long trousers and – now I come to think of it – berets. Berets! I ask you, who wears berets but convent girls and the French, a nation that gave the world the singing nun, cheek-kissing, the poodle and Jean-Pierre Rives, a flank forward with blond curls who retired to become, gawd-help-us, a sculptor. What sort of occupation is that for a marauding back-row forward? I ask you! Well?

Where was I? Jean-Pierre . . . poodles . . . berets . . . Boy Scouts . . . knee scabs . . . over-protection . . . the nanny society – that's it, that's it! Pipe cleaners.

What could be more noble, more manly, more redolent of damp tweeds and the faithful black Labrador beside a favourite wing chair than a packet of British pipe cleaners? And yet, when I popped into town to pick up a packet of pipe

cleaners in the Early Learning Centre, I was told by a charming young woman
that they no longer stocked them. Worse: they had been withdrawn from sale.
New safety regulations preclude toy shops from stocking pipe cleaners.

What has happened to this fine country?

Yours,

Disgusted, Cropredy

*   *   *

It was all very well the young woman telling me I could get pipe cleaners
from any tobacconist. That wasn't the point. And anyway I had set my heart
on a packet of the sparkly tinsel ones in silver and gold that the Early
Learning Centre used to supply for some worthy educational purpose.

Let us talk of fish anatomy: in particular, scales. Fish scales are much more
than primitive lurex. The silvery appearance is the result of light reflected from
millions of flat crystals of guanine laid down within the scale. The alignment
of the crystals in each scale differs subtly, depending where the scale is on the
fish. In scales on the fish's flank, the crystals lie parallel to the scale surface:
in scales on the fish's back, facing upwards, the crystals lie at right angles to
the surface. And those in between are – well – in between. Why? The result
is that all the reflective crystals of guanine are aligned up and down. Light
from above passes between them and is absorbed so that in crystal-clear
water with the sunlight beating down on a fish an inch or so beneath the surface there is precious little to see, certainly no blinding flash of the reflected
sun. Light from the side *is* reflected. A fish looks silver from the side, even the
bits that looked dark from above. Underwater the fish disappears, reflecting
only its surroundings – as long as it stays on an even keel. Sea trout in the
bottom of a deep pool can be well nigh impossible to spot until a fish rolls
onto its side to scoop up a morsel from a stone as sea trout are wont to do –
then the sunlight catches the flank as a brief flash of silver. I once fished for
an hour over fish winking like this in the depths until the shoal of mullet
moved on up the river. Another time I had just stocked a river with vigorous
and expensive 12-inch brown trout. These trout had dispersed and disappeared into the grey green water of early spring and there was nothing to be
seen. There was a kerfuffle in midstream and then, in the depths, the curious
sight of a 12-inch trout on its side proceeding upstream, dorsal fin first. The
trout was quite easy to see: the pike that had it held in its jaws was invisible.

This alignment of the guanine crystals within each scale works wonderfully
well provided the fish stays fit and healthy. Until, that is, the fish is wounded

and wobbles. As it tilts from the upright the sunlight catches the silver flanks, flashing a reflection to anything hungry. It does not pay to wobble underwater. Hence spoon and plug lures.

None of us look our best when we are under the weather, and a sickly or wounded fish often has scales damaged or out of alignment. As the poor wee thing limps along, these misplaced scales catch the light and twinkle in the gloom. It does not pay to twinkle underwater either. Hence my search for the silver-and-gold pipe cleaners at the Early Learning Centre. Wound round a hook shank these pipe cleaners give the best imitation of a small damaged fish I have seen.

And they had stopped selling them in toy shops because there was a risk of some small child poking them into places that should not be approached with anything sharper than a moistened flannel. It seemed a little harsh (the legislation – not the pipe cleaners). I went back into the shop and asked if they perhaps had an odd packet left in the stockroom. They hadn't: all the pipe cleaners had been withdrawn and sent back to head office. We could have been dealing with faulty ammunition. I asked for the number of head office. Back home I dialled the number. Did they have any pipe cleaners left? I could have been asking for hard drugs. Would they give me the name of their suppliers? It felt like I was asking for the man who brought the stuff in from Colombia. They wouldn't tell me. But they would give me the number of a toy-trade hotline that dealt with all such enquiries. Was I being set up? Would the call be traced? I didn't care. By now I was determined to score sparkly pipe cleaners and to hell with the consequences. That's what this stuff does to a man. The toy-trade hotline could not have been more helpful. Could not – or would not. I was beginning to suspect everyone. They had no listing under 'Pipe cleaners – sparkly' or any other sort, but they gave me the number of a large wholesaler who might stock such things. I got the impression I was down at the imported-ninja-turtles-with-eyes-that-drop-out-and-choke-small-children end of the market. I made the call. No, they didn't supply sparkly pipe cleaners. Who had told me they did? I got the idea that someone at the toy-trade hotline was in line for getting their ear stapled to the wardrobe. I didn't care.

But I was back to square one. My only positive lead had been the Early Learning Centre. They had had the stuff at one time, only now they weren't talking. I made the call to head office again. Once again I explained what I needed – the name of their supplier. Nix. I begged. I only want one packet of sparkly pipe cleaners. That's what they all say: then it'll be two, before long it's a dozen – it's a filthy business. I pleaded. Finally she cracked – they all do in the end. The name was Hewitt & Booth.

I phoned Hewitt & Booth and spoke to Sarah. She came from Huddersfield. She sang like a canary. This pipe-cleaner game is big business. The firm makes 4 million cleaners a week and half of these are taken out of the country. She said 'exported' but I knew what she meant. I asked her how many sparkly ones they made but she didn't have that sort of information. It was 'need-to-know', I guess. She asked me why I wanted the sparkly pipe cleaners. I told her. Then she said something that made my blood run cold: 'Oh yes, we made some for Lureflash.' So. They had been here before me.

I could, it seems, have popped into my local tackle shop and snapped up a packet of something similar at any time. Pish and tush. There is something deeply unsatisfactory about making all your own flies and then buying all the materials to do so in small – sometimes very small – plastic packets in the tackle shop. I know that sometimes this is unavoidable. You have to be unnaturally lucky to happen upon a roadside casualty of a jungle cock or a first quality Plymouth Rock cockerel. No jury would swallow it. And it must surely be worth a pound or so to have someone else remove a hare's mask. If you don't live in shooting country, it can be difficult getting hold of some feathers (although most butchers have cock pheasants in season and the tail feathers can be begged or filched), but however urban your environment, there is a surprising amount that can be gleaned. Immensely satisfying.

Every busted electric motor contains a lifetime supply of lacquered copper wire, perfect for nymph underbodies, weighting and ribbing. This last few weeks all the supermarkets around our way have had bottles of Rioja on special offer. The Rioja is not all that special: the bottle is. It is wrapped in a net of fine gold wire. Perfect. The lead wrapping from wine bottles is, of course, the only thing for leaded flies.

There are natural materials to be had. Have a good look at your carpets. The sort of fluff that gathers when a carpet is newish makes superb dubbing: the one in our dining room is the exact shade of lamb's-wool-stained-with-blackberry required of a Tups. If you want a bit more variety, I suggest you call into a carpet showroom and show the slightest interest in almost anything. You will have samples and swatches pressed on you in riotous abundance. Rather more muted and subtle tones can be found on the fluff screen of the tumbledrier: it is a curious thing that, no matter what clothes are washed, our fluff always comes out a sort of bruised purple. Dogs are famously good for providing dubbing, but don't overlook other animals. There is a splendid pig in the children's part of a zoo not far from us. It is, I think, a saddleback. Whatever it is, this pig provides the finest dry-fly tail whisks I have seen on any creature: springy and steeply tapering, they come in two shades, black and white, if you are quick with the wife's nail scissors.

But it is the artificial materials that are the easiest to find. You can buy small packets of polystyrene balls to make suspender nymphs and buzzers – but upstairs in the children's bedroom there is a huge beanbag containing a millennium's supply. A handful eased out through an unpicked seam will never be missed and the split seam can be blamed on careless rough play and the children sent to bed early. Much of the best stuff belongs to the children, and a thoughtful parent will ensure that their toys are chosen with due care. A Red Indian headdress is a splendid selection of dyed feathers handily displayed. Most girls enjoy making jewellery with a selection of colourful beads but, for safety's sake, it is best to let an adult pick out all the smallest gold and silver beads that could be easily swallowed. Especially by a fish.

And so we have arrived at things gold and silver, at things that go flash in the light. Christmas, you will recall, is coming and Christmas is the season of goodwill, tinsel and odd sparkly bits of gold and silver. A man with his wits about him can garner more fly-tying stuff from Christmas Eve to Boxing Day than he could use in a lifetime. Those ootsy little boxes containing three chocolates are tied with a bow of fine gold thread. Presents come wrapped in sheets of gold and silver Mylar – or, even better, in striped metallic colours. Almost everything you put on a Christmas tree sparkles. It was on the tree that I first came across the sparkly pipe cleaners. Wife and daughters were using them to twist on those glass baubles, one of the few things for which I have not yet found a practical fishing purpose. Come Twelfth Night a few of these pipe cleaners found their way into my fly-tying box. A few, but not nearly enough, because over the next few years I found they were just the thing for big predatory fish. I tried them first on the large and savage lake trout of Canada's far north. Silver pipe cleaners are not a subtle material. They might almost be described as garish, but this sort of thing is overlooked in a land where aficionados favour a 9-inch spoon in pink with black diamonds. And the pipe cleaners work wonderfully. Except that pike grab them just as readily. On another trip a pipe-cleaner fly was the preferred food of the wild rainbows of the Rockies. I have never had the nerve to use the fly in British waters – until, on a first foray into salmon fishing, I spent a fascinating, frustrating day beside a sea pool on a beach below the Giant's Causeway in Co. Antrim. One tide ago these grilse had been feasting on things that looked exactly like my pipe-cleaner fly. I searched through the box. It was not there. It had not seemed quite the thing to take.

But it does now. A packet of sparkly pipe cleaners arrived in the post from Hewitt & Booth this morning.

8 ♌

The Hunting of the Shark

I had always taken it for granted that the British had some sort of deal with nature. Nothing formal, just a gentleman's agreement: we would get a small, damp island surrounded by cold grey seas but in compensation there would be nothing there that would eat us, poison us or sting us to death. The Caribbean may be a paradise of palm trees and sun-bleached sands but they have spiders the size of your hat, small lethal snakes and hurricanes. In Australia the beaches are longer but so are the snakes and crocodiles: the spiders are smaller but much deadlier and they lurk in the lavatory. And there are sharks. Wherever a palm-fringed beach is washed by a warm sea beneath the tropical sun there are sharks: it is nature's way of keeping things fair. Your appendages may be blue with cold after a dip in British surf but you will come out with the same number you went in with. I thought that was in the contract.

Listen: the world-record porbeagle shark was caught beneath the cliffs of Dunnet Head in Caithness in 1993. It weighed 507 pounds. The porbeagle is described in an encyclopedia of fishes as '. . . very voracious with large triangular teeth'; the entry continues: '. . . occasionally attacks human beings, it may be regarded as a dangerous pest'. Its scientific name *Lamna* 'is derived from a Greek word for a horrible monster of man-eating tendencies, a creature used by ancient Greeks to terrify naughty children'. Well, it would. It terrified me.

A porbeagle shark would not get much of a taste for bathers off Dunnet Head. These forbidding cliffs form the most northerly point on the British mainland, further north than either John O'Groats or Cape Wrath, which just have better names. This is the Pentland Firth where the tides and currents of the Atlantic and the North Sea dispute the stormy strait between Scotland and the Orkney Islands. The turbulent waters are rich with the cod, ling and pollack that a world record porbeagle shark likes to get its large triangular teeth round.

The boat that had taken that record shark was the 48-foot *Karen*. She was moored behind the Seaman's Mission in Scrabster harbour waiting to take a party of anglers out into the firth to hunt for another of these monster fish. And because I write about fly-fishing for *Trout & Salmon* I had been invited along. It was a little after dawn in late November. It felt like it.

Paul Gough is the skipper of the *Karen*. I asked him whether the sharks always fed at dawn. They don't. Sharks are civilised, it seems: they would be arriving for lunch just after noon. Meanwhile we had to catch lunch. The wind was gusting Force 6 from the southwest. It had started to rain. It was cold and wet but the sea in the lee of Dunnet Head was only moderately choppy. Paul handed out rods. As we drifted beneath the cliffs we commenced fishing.

We were feathering for cod or pollack or anything else down there. A 12-ounce lead weight carries a team of six hooks to the bottom. Each hook has a chicken feather that, when agitated by a sweep of the rod, looks like something-or-other edible to a cod. That is the theory. In practice, the fish were so abundant in these shallow waters that most were simply foul-hooked in the tail or a fin as the feathered hooks were pulled up through the shoal.

That got to me after a while. I know it cannot possibly matter to a pollack by which part of its anatomy it is hauled to the surface. It only matters to the fisherman. A fish hooked through the lip is a victim of its own greed: 'Nobody forced you to put that hook in its mouth: you only have yourself to blame,' and so on. A fish foul-hooked is an innocent bystander. It should not matter but it does.

One way or another, we had fish.

I do not know what I expected of shark tackle. I did not expect a balloon. It was a small, sad semi-deflated red balloon like the day after a children's party. Beyond this was a long, flexible wire trace to counter those large triangular teeth and a hook the size greengrocers use to hang bananas. Our largest cod was impaled on the hook, the wire and its balloon clipped to the line on a powerful rod and the baited hook flung overboard. The *Karen* drifted down the wind away from the floating balloon.

Nature did not fashion me for a fisherman. I do not have faith. I need to see a trout rise or a salmon leap before I am convinced there is something down there. A dorsal fin the size of a card table slicing through the waves will do nicely. I did not see it at first but hands were pointing out towards the two balloons just visible amongst the waves. And there it was: a grey triangle slicing through the wave crests, just like in the movies. It was huge. We gathered around the two shark rods, waiting for the reel spool to turn, slowly at first and then accelerating as the shark took off with the bait. The spool clicked tantalisingly with the action of the waves. We waited.

Nothing happened. And it happened for the rest of that freezing, soaking afternoon.

You will read stories of huge fish landed and of huge fish that got away, but for each of these there should be a hundred stories of huge fish that did nothing at all: most fishing for huge fish is like that.

This has been one of those stories.

Gadgets, Gifts and Gizmos

This appeared in an April edition of *Trout & Salmon*,
traditionally the biggest of the year.

Just feel the weight of this thing. It is nearly two hundred pages long and it
weighs a ton. It is a bumper edition. There is a reason for this. It is April: it
is the time when a young man's fancy turns to trout fishing. An old man's
too, if it comes to that. And not a few ladies'.

But it is the young men I need to speak to. It may be that you are standing
in WHSmith. You have picked up this tome from the rack, attracted by its
obvious bulk and quality, swayed by the free fly-box stuck to the front. You
are not yet a committed trout fisherman but your thoughts are drifting that
way. Now listen carefully: be advised by one who is older and, if not wiser,
then sadder: *put the magazine down.* Quietly tuck the thing back in the rack
and simply walk away. Don't think about it, *do it*. Now. You don't have to
walk far, a yard or so will bring you to any number of magazines on golf,
classic cars, steam engines, yachting, gardening, amateur photography . . .
health and fitness . . . and that is probably far enough.

You are still reading the magazine. OK then, you can become a game fisherman on one condition: you must never tell anyone. And especially not a wife,
girlfriend, mother or aunt or anyone else who has a tendency to give you gifts
at Christmas or birthday or any other time. A new hobby is manna to wives,
girlfriends, mothers and aunts: a rich new seam of presents to be tunnelled,
mined and extracted. And if the hobby is fishing then they have hit the motherlode. There are more gadgets, gewgaws and gizmos attached to fishing than
any other sport in Creation. They fall into three broad categories. I am going
to describe them: if you are determined to take up trout fishing then it may
help to leave this page open in the hope than a W, G, M or A will read it.

First, there is the piece of fishing tackle you really need and want. This is
very rare. And usually expensive or you would have bought it for yourself. If
an unprompted W, G, M or A gives you one of these, you should consider
giving up fishing and devoting your days to laying fragrant garlands at her feet.

Second, there is the piece of fishing tackle you don't need or want. These are more common. Their hearts are in the right place; the aim is just a little off-target. A tool with a combined disgorger and fish descaler, say. Incidentally, I have never met anyone who has used a descaler in anger: coarse fisherman blench at the idea, no one bothers to scale a trout and salmon are too big to tackle with a thing the size of a nail file. That leaves us with members of the Grayling Society. Is that possible? Surely not.

Most fishing tackle presents comes into this second category: the present would be perfect for some fisherman but not, alas, the one who is given it. Non-fishing wives, girlfriends, mothers and aunts are well aware of this problem and, sensibly, they usually steer clear of fishing tackle unless severely primed and prompted.

So they plump for the third sort of fishing present. They are on safe ground here. Sort of. These are things that are no use in fishing and were never intended to be. Ordinary, everyday things – so why do they end up in the fisherman's stocking? Because they have a fishing *motif.*

I have a bushel of these things. Some of them I love, some of them I hate and I am not about to tell you which is which because all of them were well meant. Some are wonderful, some are ghastly and some are so ghastly that I am no longer sure whether they might not have become wonderful. All of them are in questionable taste: some of them are way past the questioning stage and are remanded in custody with no chance of bail.

I have a fly-fisherman's handkerchief. This is the same as an ordinary handkerchief but it is decorated with twenty salmon and trout flies from a Lunn's Particular (scarlet and grey) to a Durham Ranger (turquoise, yellow and orange). I know this because I see them when I iron my fly-fisherman's handkerchief; I don't care to look too closely at other times.

I also have a fishing tie. It was given to me by my big daughter for Christmas. I don't know the names for the bits of a tie but the big bit at the front is subtly printed to form the body of a fish – a pike in this case. I could see that much when I opened it on Christmas morning. Immediately above the fish was a pattern of asymmetric light and dark diagonals which made no sense until I put the thing on. The stripes are on the part of the tie that forms the knot and the knot itself forms the triangular tail fin complete with radiating spines. Rather cunning. From a distance, in a poorish light, you would swear I was wearing a dead fish on my shirtfront.

What I really need to set it off is a fisherman's waistcoat. This is not an olive-green number with a score of cunningly wrought pockets and D-rings and patches of sheepskin. I mean a real fisherman's waistcoat. I saw one once at a fishing-club dinner in Somerset. It was quite the most manifest waistcoat I have seen. It was a thing of brocade, damn near tapestry, with gold and silver thread not so much depicting as illuminating a landscape at sunset in which an angler with arched rod fought to subdue a leaping salmon. The overall effect was sudden to a degree. If anyone reading this knows where such a thing can be obtained let him keep that dangerous knowledge to himself. I already have the key ring that will dangle from the watch-chain. It was a present from my little daughter. I think it was a present. It was bought with her own money and presented with some ceremony but ever since it has resided in her treasure box. It is quite a treasure. It is a golden fish, articulated in seven pieces with eyes of real ruby – so it is probably safest in a treasure box for the time being.

I don't have a watch for the other end of the watch-chain but the other day I saw something ominous in an American mail-order catalogue – *Wireless: A Catalog for Fans and Friends of Public Radio.* Inside I came across:

> Gone Fishin' Watch. It's an idyllic day on your favourite lake: just you, your boat, your fishing pole, and all the time in the world . . . The second hand is a sunfish that circles the face once every minute – think of it as the one that got away.

I had a look at the photograph. The little fish swims round and round the watch face with no obvious means of support. How do they do that? Why do they do that? What is ominous about all this is that I saw the mail-order catalogue in my mother's kitchen.

The fly-fisherman's walking stick I have already. I once bought a rather tasteful item with a handle that could have been bone exquisitely carved by Eskimos to portray a twisting grayling. It was actually cast in plastic resin, whether or not by Eskimos I could not say, but it was off-white and mellow and rather English and I bought it as a gift for the father of my big daughter's French penfriend. We were going down to meet them in southern France. As a present it was not an unqualified success: it turned out that he was a physiotherapist and he regarded the gift of a walking stick as an oblique insult. I wished I'd never given him the thing because I rather fancied it myself. Later, I made the mistake of mentioning this to my mother-in-law. She is a sweet woman and went off in search of a replacement for my next birthday. The walking stick she found has a fish – as near as I can tell it is a cod – about to engulf an ephemerid spinner in the air above a tangle of multi-coloured reeds. It is a striking piece. More or less between the eyes.

Fish, rather than fishing, seems to be the general theme in these doodahs. Some of them are charming. A pair of brandy glasses, one engraved with a trout, the other with a salmon, is a souvenir of a hot Game Fair several years ago. This Christmas some friends gave us a set of glazed napkin rings in delicate blue and white pottery. A small fish sits on top of each ring, and the little hollow between the raised tail fin and the curved back, I am told, is designed to support a chap's chopsticks above the linen. Last year the same friends gave us a pair of char. They look like char, anyway. They have loops to hang them and each has two pairs of moveable metal fins underneath which look as though they ought to be for something-or-other but I have never discovered what. Perhaps they are just for looking at.

My favourite fish came as a raffle prize. The event had nothing to do with fishing. All the other prizes were bottles of sherry and boxes of chocolates and those presentation sets of bath salts that always end up as raffle prizes sooner or later. I have a feeling that our prize was no stranger to the raffle-prize table: indeed, it might have had a long and fruitful career as a raffle prize until the day it was won by a fisherman with no taste whatsoever. By me. It is a toilet-roll holder in the form of a leaping salmon, crafted in melamine and chrome. It is a dilly.

Jumble sales are a constant hazard to the man who admits to being a fisherman. Little daughter's school holds one every term. The politburo of elderly ladies who kindly sort through the mountains of stuff before the sale know everyone in the village and, if they find something that they feel is just up your alley, they put it to one side and nobble you after school. My alley is fishing. A few weeks ago I was nobbled. What had been put aside just for me was a Work of Art. In the centre of the scene was a largish haddock with trout colouring leaping high out of a pond. The vegetation in the foreground was real grass. The object of the haddock-trout's leap was to capture a fisherman's fly – a real fly attached to a length of nylon curving across the scene. The fly, nylon and grasses were kept in place with a plastic film that had been shrink-wrapped over the whole thing. I cannot tell you what fly had excited this haddock-trout to such a frenzy because a previous owner had torn the plastic at this point and removed the fly. I hope it worked. The old ladies smiled at me. There is nothing to do in these circumstances but to pay up. You have been done up like a kipper and you and the village ladies know it.

'How much?' you ask feebly, but you are up against professionals: they have been doing this for years.

'Oh, just give us what you like, dear.' And the only thing you will get for being stingy in our village is a reputation for being stingy. You dig deep and you are now the owner of another fishy doodah.

There are exceptions to this fish-only theme. I have a Fisherman's Mug depicting the 'Anatomy of a Fishing Expert'. This depicts the typical fisherman and points to the salient features: the baggy eyes, the bristly chin and so forth. This ponderous jocularity is what makes it a Fisherman's Mug. I understand that: but it came pre-packed with a Fisherman's Flannel and Fisherman's Soap. Is there something I am missing in all this? I have always been a rather solitary fisherman, fossicking along the wooded banks of small rivers or sharing a boat with another fisherman on a small loch. Is there a whole world of fishing I am missing? Fishing as a team sport. A gaggle of anglers walking back through the early mist that is gathering across the waterside meadows. They are mud-spattered from their exertions. They trudge back like the First XV, tired but happy. Their studded waders clatter on the pine veranda as their womenfolk, who have been preparing sandwiches for the last hour, come and clap them home. They peel off their dirty fishing togs in the changing room, grab a pint from the bar and climb into the steaming communal bath. Each has his Fisherman's Flannel and Fisherman's Soap. There is laughter as they recall the day's exploits and the minor injuries of battle are soothed away in the hot water and lather. Sooner or later one of them, always the same one, will start to sing: others join in, for they all know the words, and another Saturday evening is under way.

Does this happen? I am beginning to wonder, because there was another item that caught my eye in that catalogue in my mother's kitchen:

GOIN' FISHIN' – *The Greatest Fishing Songs Ever*

Are these bawdy ballads familiar to every fisherman but me? Do local branch meetings of the Salmon and Trout Association degenerate into a sozzled sing-song around the old Joanna as soon as that Old-Wet-Blanket Beer has shuffled his notes and left the room. Where do they come from, these Greatest Fishing Songs? I imagine a smoke-filled back room in Accrington where the members of a subcommittee of the Grayling Society are cudgelling their brains to find a rhyme for *Thymallus*,* each casting hopeful glances to the end of the table where sits, eyes screwed in concentration, the hunched figure of the Chairman, a legendary rhymester who in his prime had given the angling

---

*There was a young lady from Dallas
 Who used frozen fish as a phallus.
 Her favourite rooter
 Was a stiff *Salmo trutta*
 Or a frigid *Thymallus thymallus*.

world such classics as 'Never Fish Your Dung-fly on the Dangle, Mother' and the rousing, if unprintable

> While fishing the Taff near Caerphilly,
> I was roundly abusing my ghillie . . .

Alas, no. I read further in the catalogue description:

GOIN' FISHIN' – This light-hearted collection of musical catches includes 15 classic fishin' tunes recorded from 1951–1994. You'll hear Andy Griffith's 'The Fishin' Hole', Elvin Bishop's 'Fishin'', Tennessee Ernie Ford's 'Catfish Boogie', Taj Mahal's 'Fishin' Blues', Bing Crosby and Louis Armstrong's legendary duet, 'Gone Fishin'', and many more . . . DON'T LET THIS ONE GET AWAY.

Well, I have got a note from my mother which says I am excused anything with the word 'Fishin'' in the title. And if you still insist on being a fisherman, I suggest you do the same.

10 𝔏

The Passing of the Peugeot

It was the twentieth of September. I know that because my M.O.T. ran out on the twenty-first. We've been together a long time, this car and I, and you get a funny feeling about M.O.T.s at our stage of life: not premonitions, exactly – foreboding, perhaps. We've visited a few rivers together in our 136,000 miles and not a few of them have been in the hills of the Welsh borders and west. So, in the last few days of the trout-fishing season, we took the road west one more time.

I don't know if you remember, but it was a funny sort of time that last week or so in September: half the country was thinking, 'This can't go on, surely' – meaning the drought that had lingered past summer. The other half, the southern half, were thinking exactly the same thing – but meaning the rain which had been lashing down for the past few days. So we weren't quite sure what to expect as we went west.

The Severn usually gives us some idea: coming out of the benighted Midlands, the Severn is always the first glimpse of water that has come from the trouty country to the west. As we looked down at its low and greenish water beyond Worcester it struck me that I had crossed the Severn a hundred times but had never actually fished the thing. We would go to the Severn.

The troutier bits of the Severn are still a long way from Worcester and we polled west along the Teme, crossed the Lugg and followed the Arrow to Kington and that extraordinary bit on the A44 where England suddenly stops and Wales unmistakably begins. The car purred in that healthy, resilient and reliable way that old cats have when you are driving them to the vets for the last time. Heartbreaking.

At Rhayader we joined the Wye and followed it upstream towards the bulk of Plynlimon where the Wye and the Severn both trickle into life within a mile or so of each other.

And so to Llanidloes. I don't think I had ever chanced on Llanidloes. And you wouldn't these days because it is bypassed by the road that shoots up the Severn valley from Welshpool and the like. Long may it be bypassed, for it is a charming little town and deserved to be visited only by those who choose to do so. It has one of those ancient half-timbered market houses on stilts that forms a tricky and rather ambiguous sort of roundabout in the middle of town and it has the Llanidloes and District Angling Association – and that has an awful lot of water.

Funny sort of water it looked, though, on that day in late September. The upper Severn and its tributary, the Clywedog, meet just above the bridge in town. The Severn was low and almost still. You could wade across in gum-boots – in galoshes in some places. The Clywedog swung around a corner like something looking for trouble: big, bright and brash and full of water going like a train. You would have thought there had been a cloudburst upstream, but the Clywedog was perfectly clear with none of the murky brown of a cloudburst. The explanation lies further up the Clywedog valley – Llyn Clywedog. The lake, built in the 1960s, is a compensatory reservoir and, if I have grasped the concept of the thing, this means that water from the Clywedog basin is stored during the wet winters hereabouts – the same as any other reservoir. Come the dry weather, the water is not siphoned off directly to the good folk of Birmingham or wherever but is released into the Severn to be abstracted by the towns further downstream. As a result of all this, at the end of a long, dry summer, when the upper Severn is little more than a damp face flannel, the Severn below Llanidloes is fairly fishable and the Clywedog itself is tumbling down the valley like the first week in March.

And the water felt as cold as the first week in March. The waters of Llyn Clywedog settle during the calm days of summer: the cooler water sinks out of the reach of the sun as the upper layers warm. The result is that the water dashing down the Clywedog river is much cooler than the stuff that just falls from the sky and trickles down the rocks. How this would affect the fishing remained to be seen.

We had come to fish the Severn but the sight of this brawling mountain stream was all too tempting after a summer of limpid pools. We would start on the Clywedog.

The road to Llyn Clywedog swings left over the town bridge and starts to climb. A turning on the left a short distance from the town announces a car-avan park which is the only short stretch of the river the Angling Association does not control. We took this turning, passed the caravan park and headed down a rapidly narrowing lane beneath autumn trees. A tiny track between bramble banks led down towards the river. On another day I might have thought twice about the paintwork, but paintwork isn't part of the M.O.T. A tiny patch of meadow appeared in front of a ruined cottage and, ominously, the rusting hulk of an abandoned car. One moment you are winging down the highways, munching up the miles, and the next some bloke in an overall says there's excessive play in your offside front bottom-arm bush and you are a streamside development for enterprising robins. Makes you think.

We parked the car a decent distance from the hulk and tackled up. A rusting footbridge at the end of the meadow carries the track across the Clywedog. It is as tasty a piece of mountain river as you could wish. The water was rushing down over a bed of hard grey slate in vertical ridges across the stream. This makes for interesting wading. We stood on the bridge and looked for any movement of fish in the series of pools upstream. In vain.

Flies there were: small, pale up-winged jobs, popping off the surface to fly laboriously up into the trees that fringe the banks. But not a sign of fish. I tried a dry fly, hoping to drag something up to the surface. Nothing. There has to be trout in water like this: cool, fast and lots of it with deep pools and runs beneath overhanging trees. It is an upland trout's paradise. But they were not up near the surface. So we went down.

I am not good with a nymph at the best of times. And a rushing river under dappled sunlight is not the best of conditions for spotting the subtle sliding of a leader as a nymph is sampled below. The usual solution is some sort of indicator, a wisp of bright wool, or better still a dry fly on the dropper that stands a chance of a fish should one take it into its head to rise. I put on a nymph, a big one, to get it down quickly in the fast water, a pearl-head hare's-ear nymph that looks as businesslike as everything else made from that wonderful material. I have no feelings either way about pearl or gold or silver heads. This fly has one and from time to time it catches a fish. And sometimes it doesn't. And it seems to work just as well without any sort of head. Sometimes.

The dry-fly-and-weighted-nymph is a splendid option for this dappled, rushing water when, lord knows, a dry fly on its own is hard enough to spot in all that sparkle. You lob the thing upstream wherever there looks like some depth that might house a trout on the bottom. You watch the splosh of the heavy nymph and then search the vicinity for the dry fly. It swims down towards you and you strike on anything odd. Oddness is often the result of a difference in the surface and subsurface currents: the dry fly pauses or accelerates a little: if it disappears then you strike. Not hard or you will end up with a tangle in the dense foliage overhead: a heavy nymph and a dropper are wont to act like an American gaucho's bolas in the presence of an alder tree.

It often happens like this. You reason your way through a problem; you devise a solution and lo! the thing works. You have cracked it. 'Now,' you say, 'I will clean up.' But you rarely do. On the second or third trot down a deep-ish run the dry fly dipped, the rod lifted and a heavy fish surged off upstream, attached to the nymph. That first fish from the tumbling Clywedog was a corker. A short, deep fish with the elegant head of a mature trout. A single, tiny red spot on either flank amidst the bold black spotting on a pale-amber background. Perhaps the handsomest trout of the season and one ounce short of a pound.

And that was it. A fine fish on the third or fourth cast and then not a sniff for the next three hours. We trudged back to the car, baffled and defeated, and brewed up coffee. It was such a familiar scene, the Kelly Kettle belching steam and smoke in the afternoon sunlight, the old maroon wagon, back open and awash with tackle and sandwich wrappers. How many more river-sides would it visit? I took some photographs there in the meadow: not a premonition, exactly – more a precaution.

We had fished the Clywedog. Perhaps it was time to do what we had come to do: fish the Severn. We loaded the car and drove back down the hill to Llanidloes, mercifully oblivious of a 'nearside wiper split' and a 'hole through corrosion within 12 inches of a seat belt mount'.

The Severn below Llanidloes is a world away from the tumbling Clywedog. Here the river winds gently over an even bed of gravel through a broad valley. It is a well-behaved river under summer flow: sometimes a little deeper on that side, sometimes a little deeper on this. Nothing sudden. The sun was shining as we arrived in the afternoon but, with the upper Severn down to the knockings, all the water gliding serenely past was cool Clywedog water. There was not a rise to be seen. I still had the dry-fly-and-nymph rig on the rod and, as there was certainly nothing happening up top, I decided to stick to searching the depths. Depths are not so easy to come by on this bit of the Severn. I was working my way up a slight run beneath the bushes on the far bank. Not deeper, just moving a little faster than on my side. A couple of times the trailing nymph touched a stone and bobbed the surface fly. A week or so later in the season and a deep nymph will spend much of its time react-ing to sunken leaves, driving the angler to distraction with hopes raised and dashed, but on that quiet afternoon the odd false bob was quite welcome. The pale remnants of a fertiliser bag showed at the bottom of a deeper scour at the top of the run. The line dipped as it got to this point and I struck anyway, just in case. The leader catapulted out of the water, the tippet and nymph broken off at the dropper, firmly fixed, no doubt, in the fertiliser bag. I sat on the bank and tied on another tippet and nymph, remade the dropper and replaced the tired dry fly. I cast again above the deeper hole. This time a grey shadow surged up and fastened onto the dry fly. A fine grayling was swooping me all over the river, then hung in the depths and jerked the line like a salmon until I could get it to the surface and slide it into the net.

I unhooked the fly and laid the fish alongside the rod. I had asked the rod maker to draw an inch-scale up from the handle and the fish was a fraction over 14 inches. As I was admiring it there, I noticed a length of nylon trailing beyond the tail. I followed this back up to the fish and found, tucked under the grayling's protruding lip, the small nymph I had thought to be firmly fastened in a fertiliser bag. I had broken off in a fish: a fish which then calmly took a dry fly, five minutes later, on the next cast. They build them tough hereabouts. Or stupid.

The sun was getting low in the sky by the time we had fished up to the junction pool above the town bridge. A small island all but separates the two streams at this height of water, the thin, sluggish flow of the Severn on one side and the sweeping stream of the Clywedog on the other. There is a fine pool on the corner, Horse's Pool, and here we saw fish rising for the first time that day, grayling in the middle and tail of the pool, trout at the head where the water sweeps in from a small weir. We caught some of each in the last half-hour of light. Why they waited until then to show themselves was a mystery. I had put it down to the cold water of Llyn Clywedog but the water was every bit as cold as the sun sank and the fish rose steadily in Horse's Pool.

It was growing dark as we climbed back into the old car for the journey home. I switched on the lights ('nearside front headlamp low intensity/offside front headlamp poorly adjusted') and headed back, blissfully ignorant of 'excessive imbalance on front brakes'. It had been our last trip together.

I don't know: my own headlamps seem to be getting a bit dim these days, particularly when tying wings on a size 18 hook, and sometimes of a damp autumn morning I get a sort of twinge in my offside front bottom-arm bush. Thank God they don't have M.O.T.s for old fishermen.

An Ice-Hole in the Arctic

We still play this game with our small daughter in the car. The first person starts: 'The other day I went on holiday and in my suitcase I packed – an appetising apple.' The next person brags: 'The other day I went on holiday and in my suitcase I packed: an appetising apple and a big bishop's mitre.' The third person might boast of toting this same appetising apple, the big bishop's mitre and, say, a cadaverous canary. And so it goes on through the alphabet and the miles.

I have my own version. The other day I was on a fishing holiday. I took one look out of the window and I put on: a pair of deeply unattractive long underwear of the sort advertised in leaflets that come loose in the *Radio Times*. Also a vest of the same ilk in the same shade of grey. A padded shirt in very loud red check bought from a bloke on Banbury market. A pair of thick moleskin trousers. A pair of thick woolly socks. A thick fleece jacket. Another thick fleece jacket on top of the first thick fleece jacket. Thick was more or less the theme for my wardrobe that morning. I took another look out of the window and added a pair of breathable waterproof overtrousers.

The thick woolly socks had become impossibly itchy by now, but, what with the two fleeces and the padded shirt, the vest and the two pairs of trousers, the region of my waist had become somewhat congested so I couldn't get down there to do anything about them without taking all the other stuff off. I did this. I took off the thick woolly socks and put on some comfy cotton ones and put the thick ones on top. I replaced everything else.

So then I was ready to put on my outdoors gear. This was a windproof all-in-one suit in a startling shade of red. It was quilt-lined. Entrance was effected by means of a lot of zips and Velcro but not without first removing the fleece, pullover, etc. in order to bend down and get my feet into the legholes. I could see the way things were going so I put on the padded moon boots at the same time, tucking them up inside the legs of the scarlet babygro. Then it was just a case of rebuilding the upper storeys, squirming into the top half of the babygro and zipping the whole thing shut. I stepped outside.

Nearly done. I pulled on the thin balaclava which my wife had once tried to iron. It is made of something synthetic and it had melted leaving a shiny smear as if someone – presumably me – had blown their nose into the thing. A wolfskin cap, fur-side in, went on top of this, the two furry flaps tied down over my ears. Finally, I slipped into the rabbit's-fur mittens. Only eyes and a nose peered out of this mountain of clothing.

Then my nose started to run.

It was around this time that I remembered my handkerchief was in the pocket of the thick moleskin trousers, somewhere in the Lower Cretaceous layers of my person. I started to sniff.

It was 8 in the morning: the temperature was –27°C: it was the first week in April in the mountains of Swedish Lapland, a few miles below the Arctic Circle. It was the beginning of the best time I have ever spent in pursuit of a fish.

We stood beside Mikael and Vanja's wooden cabin overlooking the upper reaches of the Juktån. Giant icicles hung from the eaves, reaching almost to the drifts which surrounded the sturdy cabin. The smoke from the chimney rose vertically into the still air and the sun shone blindingly on the frozen lake below us. Cocooned inside my layers of clothing I was approaching meltdown.

But not for long. In front of the cabin were two snowmobiles. Look: *skidoo*-ing is simply the best fun there is to be had with clothes on. This is not an opinion: this is fact. It might also be the best fun there is with clothes off but it is not something I would care to try. A snowmobile is more or less Easy-Rider on skis. Wearing sunglasses against the glint of the snow and with only my nose peeping out of the layers of stuff, I bore an uncanny resemblance to Peter Fonda when the sunlight caught me in a certain way. Or it seemed that way to me.

In the normal run of things I am a pretty green sort of a chap: pretty much against pollution and pretty much for the breathless tranquillity of nature. But a snowmobile between your legs can blow all that away in a moment: sod all that breathless tranquillity, let's burn some fossil fuel. We started the motors, slithered down through the trees and roared off across the frozen lake.

Mikael Linder was born in this valley. His father, Staffan, was the postman in the days when it would take fifteen hours of walking and rowing to deliver a letter to the farms at the end of the valley. The family farm a short distance up the lake was bulging with generations of Linders who had arrived to celebrate the Easter holidays. These were the first sunny days in a long northern winter and everybody was in the mood to go fishing. Soon enough we had gathered a skein of snowmobiles skimming across the snow. The smaller children and dogs travel in *pulkas*, snowmobile trailers that range from a simple sled for carrying wood to a fully sprung carriage-on-skis with folding hood and a luxurious bed of reindeer skins. One intrepid Linder chose to ski, towed behind a snowmobile.

At the far end of the ribbon of lake the trail began to twist extravagantly through the forest, dipping and swooping up and round trees and boulders. It would have been hard work in summer but in the snow it just adds to the fun. As we wound up through the woods Mikael stopped to point out the tracks of wolverine and lynx in that arctic wilderness just a few hours' flight north of the humdrum streets of Stockholm.

We had arrived. It was not at all obvious to me where the lake began and the forest ended but people were climbing off their steeds and throwing back their fur hats. Strange implements of torture were retrieved from beneath the piles of reindeer skins in the *pulkas*. An ice drill is little more than a 5-foot-long, two-handed corkscrew. Tommy Stenlund demonstrated how the thing worked, cranking both arms to drive the screw through first the snow and then the ice of the lake. Four feet down the screw broke through into water. The hole is about 4 inches across and satisfyingly neat but full of floating ice shavings, which are scooped out with a small wooden cup carried on the belt for the scooping of ice and the drinking of coffee.

It is hard to take ice-fishing tackle seriously. So they don't, not in these high mountain lakes where the fish are small and nobody is counting. The rod is vestigial. Mine was 16 inches of luminous plastic with a single ring in the end. I thought someone was having me on. The reel was a simple spool of nylon that free-wheeled when I pushed a plastic flap and locked when I didn't. It was not a tool designed for subduing big fish.

So it was all the more surprising when I saw what went on at the business end. The spoon I was handed would have daunted a fair-sized pike. It turned out the thing was not a spoon: it was a *blänke* – a flasher.

I hesitate to tell you this. The whole thing undermines the much-loved mystique of the Cunning Fisherman fooling the Wily Trout with his Painstaking Imitation of the Natural World. This is how it works. The *blänke* dangles on the line like a shiny saucepan lid. Six inches below that is a size 10, long-shank hook. Impaled on the hook is a maggot. I don't know what it is the maggot of but I would love to find out because there is a fortune to be made in a British winter: the things were still wriggling like the dickens after a night in the fridge and a snowmobile ride at –20°C.

The kit is lowered through the hole in the ice, which by this time has fingers of new ice growing across its surface. It is lowered until it touches the bottom. Then the whole thing is set dancing by the upward flicks of the rod. Given that one is fishing through a 4-inch hole, an upward flick is about all you can do to the thing – and so, of course, the exact style and rhythm of this flicking is deemed crucial to success (in much the same way that the exact shade of dubbing, width of ribbing or length of hackle is deemed crucial to the success of a fly).

Before long, the family Linder were dotted about the ice, the girls with hats off, facing the precious warmth of the sun and chatting, the boys and men taking the whole thing more seriously, lying full length on the ice and peering into the depths through the 4-inch hole.

There is much serenity in lying on the snow of a frozen mountain lake, staring intently down one's own ice-hole. By shading the hole in the crook of an arm, movement begins to emerge in the darkness below. At first there is just a dim blink of light as the *blänke* flutters down after each flick. With the right rhythm it can be made to dance in a circle or trotted across the narrow field of view. Then the dim disc of reflected light is eclipsed by a dark shape or a pale line flickering alongside. It is a fish – which is, after all, why you are lying here in the first place. It seems an unlooked-for bonus. And then the little rod jerks in the hand and there is the indescribable but unmistakable presence of life on the other end.

I leapt to my feet. That's what it felt like beneath the layers of Damart, shirt, fleeces, quilt and waterproof. It may have looked different. I cranked on the tiny plastic handle of the spool and the line crept out of the ice. Later, I copied the local method, winding the line over my outstretched arms as my mother would use me to wind wool. After some furious cranking there was a modest commotion in my ice-hole and into the bright light of that day popped the handsomest little fish that swims – an arctic char.

I had caught my first arctic char on Lake Coniston using the 16-foot bamboo poles of the traditional char fishermen of those parts. The fish we had pulled from those 100-foot depths had captivated me then, exquisite, ruby-bellied gems sheathed in tiny scales like the finest embroidery. I had come across them again, fresh from the tide, in an Icelandic river. This was our third and finest encounter. I sat happily on the snow and looked at this ludicrously gaudy little creature of the north. You have to drink in this beauty while you can: within a very few minutes the little fish was stiff as a board, misted in frost and looking like something left in the freezer too long.

Across the ice, Mikael was preparing lunch. The people of these parts are great firelighters. Any break in the day is an excuse for a fire and a brew of coffee. Considering that there is snow here for longer than there isn't, this is a happy feature of life. The makings of a fire are always carried in the space beneath the saddle of the snowmobile and more logs were stored in the *pulka*. I was curious to see what would happen to a fire on the ice of the lake but the whole thing did nothing more than sink into the snow a few inches. The meal of potatoes, onion, bacon and reindeer meat was fried on a steel hotplate held over the flame on three legs. The char were baked in the ashes in foil and the coffee boiled in a kettle that looked, like all Lapland kettles, as if it had done more than its fair share of boiling on an open fire. Mikael and his brother-in-law carved us a long seat in a snow bank and we settled to steam gently in the sun.

That afternoon we pushed on higher into the mountains until the trees petered out into low stunted scrub. We fished on the high tarns, taking more of these startling little fish between welcome cups of hot coffee until the shadows of the surrounding mountains stretched across the ice and the day grew chilly. The journey back across the windswept and barren tops was the most exhilarating ride of my life. In the forest lower down the mountain we startled a pair of reindeer and followed them as they plashed their silly way through the soft snow of a small lake.

I don't often get to do that on my way back from fishing.

12 𝒮

Some Like It Hot

There is something rather noble about fishing in January and February. I will paint you the picture. A low sun on a bright morning illuminates the mist rising from the river, drifting through the stooped, dead stems of last year's willow herb and sedge. The light catches the frost-rimed branches of a sparse hawthorn, its limbs twisted in the cold. In the distance, half-shrouded in the mist, a hare limps trembling through the frozen grass. Not mine, that last bit – Keats's 'The Eve of St Agnes' – I'm a bit hazy when St Agnes's Day is but it sounds like grayling weather to me. In a few minutes the low sun rises into a bank of grey cloud that is spread across the top of the scene like the sky in a child's painting. The chill damp closes round you as the brightness fades. And suddenly, in a blinding moment of divine revelation, you know: you know with an intense certainty that belies hope and experience; you don't know how you know, you just know – you know that you are going to catch Sweet Felicity Arkwright today.

And sometimes you are right. Fishing in the dead of winter can be futile. And yet you carry on fishing through the short winter day. There is a sort of nobility in that.

But there is no need to be a martyr about this. There is a streak of dour Calvinism within most fishermen, a vague unspoken conviction that discomfort and suffering itself will be rewarded. Well, let me tell you, it won't. 'No pain, no gain' does not apply to fishing.

It was, I think, Dame Edna Everage who once remarked to Joan Bakewell, 'You look like you could do with something hot inside you.' How right she was. You are going to need a fire. This is not to be a neat little affair contained in a circle of rocks that one sees on a summer evening. This is a real fire. If you've ever forgotten to mow your lawn in October, you will know that the thing does not dry until next April. And the same applies to any wood lying amongst it. Wet wood will burn but it needs a body of heat to do it. Collect a lot of wood. This is not the time to worry about the world's resources: besides, the stuff will only burn if it is dead anyway. Start with any obviously dead branches *still on the tree*. If it is not actually raining, these will probably be bone dry. How do you tell a dead branch when all the leaves are gone? Look for any branches with few (or none) of the tiny twigs of last season. Then, if a thin branch snaps easily it is probably dead. Touch the snapped end against your upper lip: you will feel any residual sap. Get a big pile, the twiggier the better. A small bow-saw will make the work infinitely easier: an axe is next to useless. It is probably useless my suggesting this is done before you start fishing: no fisherman has that strength of character. But look around as you fish and gather this big heap at the first break in fishing. The excuse and reward for this break will be a warming dram of sloe gin, the best and brightest thing for a chill morning – unless you have some damson gin.

Sloe or Damson Gin

Pick 12 ounces of ripe sloes. They are the purple-black (sometimes shiny) fruit of the blackthorn, a common hedgerow tree. They are ripe in autumn and traditionally are picked after the first frost. You will see why in a minute. Wash them and pick off the stalks. Put them in a big jar. Add 6 ounces of sugar and then 1 pint of gin. Screw the lid tight and swirl them up. That's it. Give it a swirl every day or so until the sugar dissolves. Soon a pink hue suffuses into the gin. This is *slightly* hastened by softening the tough skins in the frost. Or you can pop the sloes in the freezer for a day. Or not bother. Some folk add an ounce of flaked almonds to give a smoother taste. I decant mine through a coffee filter paper when it is ready to bottle on Christmas Eve. It tastes wonderful the next day and even better if any survives until next Christmas. Use damsons in exactly the same way. I think the flavour is slightly subtler.

*   *   *

Back to the riverside. Light the thing: the fire, not the gin. Keep it going by piling masses of thin twigs over the column of flame. Damp ones can go on now and larger logs: keep moving the unburnt ends onto the top. Once you have built a glowing heart anything will burn. There will be lots of smoke. Pile on some big stuff, leave it and fish some more. It will be a relief to get back to the cool of the river.

You will be looking forward to that fire again by lunchtime. Unless it is lashing with rain it will have mellowed into a smokeless heart of red-hot ashes. It is ready for anything.

The most important cooking utensil is a piece of strong weld mesh. Plonk this over the ashes, supported on anything you like. Almost as important is a pair of heavy leather work gloves. Almost everything that goes near this fire is going to get hot and the gloves will let you hold handles or pick potatoes out of the fire. You will also need a good wooden chopping board for preparing ingredients and, if you get lucky, filleting fish.

The meal you cooked the first time you were allowed to spend a night in a tent was sausages, beans and jacket potatoes. No surprises there: when Moses led the children of Israel out of slavery in Egypt, across the Red Sea and into the desert, that first night they spent under canvas the children of Israel had sausages, beans and jacket potatoes. It can still be a great combination, particularly if you have forgotten to pack any cooking utensils. The sausages are spread on the weld mesh grill, the potatoes are buried in the ashes (wrapped in cooking foil if you want to eat the skin, which is the best bit) and the tin of beans is opened and sat on the grill to heat through. Nothing wrong with that except that the sausages are cooked approximately one hour before the potatoes and it is difficult to eat the meal with one hand. Next time try cassoulet.

Riverside Cassoulet

I have called this Riverside Cassoulet to distinguish it from the original cassoulet, the regional dish of the northern slopes of the Pyrénées. Both are based on sausage and beans but one of them takes three or four hours to prepare and the other takes ten minutes.

Do not take the quantities too seriously. Chop up a small onion and two or three stalks of celery. A rasher or two of bacon, chopped, would also be nice but not essential. Fry them gently all together in a saucepan. By 'gently' I mean that the onion should not go brown. After six or seven minutes stir in a tin of baked beans. The sausage is a 'smoked pork sausage'. These are sold in most supermarkets in the form of a U-shaped ring of 8 ounces. They are sealed in shrink-wrapped plastic and will keep for months unopened: being pre-cooked they can be eaten cold and there is no risk of undercooking at the riverside. Several frankfurters will serve almost as well. Slice the half-pound sausage into half-inch slices and add to the beans and stuff, season generously with black pepper and a good glug of Worcester sauce if you have it in your food box. Move the saucepan or the grill so that the cassoulet barely bubbles. This amount will feed two fishermen. It can be eaten as soon as it is heated through but it will be even better if it is kept just below simmering for another 15–20 minutes, or as long as it takes to prepare the mulled wine.

Mulled Wine

This is wonderfully warming on a chill, damp day. The preparation is best done at home, when several 'sacks' can be made at once and stored in a sealed tin or jar until needed. At the riverside you do little more than dunk.

The basic mix: 3 cloves, a 2-inch cinnamon stick, a pinch of dried ginger (if you like ginger), a pinch of nutmeg or a blade of mace. Tie all these up in a square of muslin or some other clean cloth.

At the riverside you will need an orange or a lemon, 2–4 ounces of sugar (3–6 level tablespoons), about half a pint of water and a bottle of red wine.

Put the water, sugar, thinly sliced orange or lemon and the little sack of spices into a pan and heat until the sugar has dissolved. Bring to the boil and keep it around simmering for 10 minutes – it doesn't matter if it goes off the boil. Add the wine and heat through, taking care not to let it boil. And it's done. Pour into glasses, or mugs to show you don't care, and eat with the cassoulet.

Less well known but more interesting is Mulled Ale. The method is similar, but use half the amount of water and sugar and add 1½ pints of beer or brown ale.

I'm not sure that cassoulet is quite the thing with mulled ale. Mulled ale seems to me the stuff of baronial halls and trestle tables and Brian Blessed tearing at a leg of venison while quaffing a pewter pot of the stuff. And you can do that at the riverside. Nearly.

Grilled Shoulder of Lamb

This is a spectacular item to produce at the riverside but cooking it is simplicity itself. The trick is to keep it cooking without burning and the secret of that is a big fire, a winter fire. A small fire will burn a joint when it is still blazing, but the small pile of ashes cools rapidly. The ashes of a big fire retain their heat for several hours. The lamb can be cooked straight from the butcher or prepared at home by marinating in various unguents or 'spiked' with flavouring on the riverbank. A quick method is to stab the meatier parts of the joint with the point of a knife and then push a slice of garlic or a couple of rosemary leaves into the puncture. Do this all over the joint: as it cooks, the flavours will seep into the meat immediately around each incision.

The fire has reduced to a large heap of ashes beneath the weld mesh grill; place the joint on the grill above the ashes. Keep an eye on the joint for the first 5 or 10 minutes to check it is not burning. It should show signs of cooking. Turn it over as it browns and do the other side. Keep turning every ten minutes or so. As long as there is a large pile of hot ash it is always better to go slowly. You can test when the joint is cooked by pushing the sharp knife into the meatiest portion. If it is cooked, the juices that flow out will be clear. If they are still bloody then the joint needs to cook a little longer. Usually this happens when the shoulder has been cooked too quickly: the outside is succulent, brown and done: the inside is still pink – and the outside shows every sign of burning before the inside is edible. What to do? No problem: you have just reinvented the doner kebab. Carve slices of cooked meat from either side of the joint of lamb and pop it back onto the grill to finish the job.

The lamb is delicious in a bun with mustard. If you are feeling adventurous, you can usually find wild watercress growing along the margin of most streams and rivers. The older green leaves have a tangy, peppery taste that suits the lamb perfectly. But beware: watercress from stagnant water and water flowing through pastureland can house the eggs of the liver fluke, a nasty little number.

*   *   *

Puddings were always a problem until the year my mother made jars of apricots and prunes in brandy to give as Christmas presents to friends in the village. I count as a friend in the village and got one as well. The pudding problem was solved.

Jean's Apricots and Prunes in Brandy

For enough to fill about four 1-pound jars.
1½ pounds dried apricots
½ pound pitted prunes
1 pound granulated sugar
20 cloves
6–8 fluid ounces brandy.

Put the apricots in a bowl and cover with plenty of water. Leave them to soak overnight. Drain the apricots and reserve a pint of the liquor.

Pour the pint of apricot liquor into a pan with the sugar and the cloves. Add the apricots, heat to dissolve the sugar and then bring to the boil. Boil gently (a bit more than a simmer – a sort of 'plopping' boil) for 30 minutes, uncovered, adding the prunes after 15 minutes. Remove from the heat. Add the brandy. Ladle into clean, warm jars with screw-top lids, making sure that the prunes are evenly distributed. Screw on the lids and store for at least three weeks before using. If you get one of these for Christmas it will be perfect for an expedition in January or February.

Open the jar and spoon out the fruit. Do not omit to drink the juice.

I popped round to ask her just now about the cloves. Could you take them out just before the brandy is added? You can, apparently, but Mum thinks the flavour is better if you leave them in and work round them while you eat. There you have it.

Bon appétit.

13

The Lone Ranger Turns Fifty

I have no idea whether Ladbrokes run a book on the outcome of court cases. But, on the off-chance that they do and you fancy a little flutter, allow me to mark your card. There is a very nice little civil action coming up in South Wales.

The runners are a coal-mining outfit, Celtic Energy, and the local anglers on the small River Kenfig. On the face of it you might expect long odds against the fishermen. They will be claiming that their fishing rights have been disrupted by a discharge of suspended solids – silt – from a treatment lagoon into a small brook, the Nant Iowerth Goch. No fish died when the stuff was washed into the river but the bed was covered with up to half an inch of silt from the mine. Any good lawyer, you might think, could talk Celtic Energy out from under half an inch of non-toxic silt and a few disgruntled local anglers.

Listen: take any odds you can get and put your pension on the Kenfig anglers. And you might put a hefty side bet on Celtic Energy settling out of court: Kenfig anglers are being represented by the A.C.A.

Remember the Lone Ranger? He used to go round the West in an immaculate shirt righting wrongs, defending the weak and good against the strong and bad. You would have thought that word would have got around about a hero-type with silver guns and bullets and a big white horse. Not to mention the mask. But after each wrong was righted the grateful rancher would always have to ask his neighbour, 'Who was that masked man?'

And so it is with the A.C.A. Few folk, even fishing folk, have heard of them. As long as the wrongs get righted, it seems, we are not too fussed who does the deed until it is our longhorns getting rustled or our river receiving half an inch of black goo. But as long as you are going to take my tip and put the family jewels on the A.C.A. righting this particular wrong, you might wish to know a little more about them.

The A.C.A. – The Anglers' Conservation Association – takes people to court. It is not a glamorous business, but if many of our waters are healthier and fishier than they were fifty years ago then that is due, in no small part, to the A.C.A. quietly going about its business of suing the living daylights out of those industries and individuals who have poisoned and polluted those waters in the past.

Litigation is a chancy business. The people who suffer when a river is polluted are individual anglers and fishing clubs, neither of whom are about to go into the ring against one of the water companies or a giant of the chemical industry. River pollution can be difficult to pin down. Something horrid spills into the river, fish die and the corpses leave the scene of the crime on the current. By the time they are spotted, retrieved and analysed, the stuff that did the deed has been diluted and washed away, leaving that stretch barren of fish. Just as deadly, and harder to detect, is the pollution that wipes out the water's insect life and leaves the fish to starve. The cost of preparing such tricky litigation, and the fair risk of losing it, would deter most clubs and individuals from going to court.

And that was the starting point, fifty years ago this month, for the A.C.A.

Originally the Anglers' *Co-operative* Association, its annual subscription was used to prepare and fight court actions against the polluters. Nowadays they can act on behalf of any member whose fishing interests have been damaged. This may be a riparian owner, a club or syndicate member or just a ticket holder.

I can't afford *not* to be a member: pollution seems to follow me like a pestilent stray dog. No sooner do I come across some idyllic new spot to fish than some dangerous clown spills liquid fertiliser or washes his sheep dip into it. Or the local inhabitants get a virulent and simultaneous bout of the trots and the sewage treatment plant fails. Or the sludge pump from a coal mine's settlement lagoon is left to run unsupervised and deposits half-an-inch of gunge over the river bed.

Which brings me back to our little wager. The case of the River Kenfig anglers versus Celtic Energy is unremarkable, a typical example of the misery that can visit a river. In the fifty years since its birth the A.C.A. has handled around 5,000 actions like this on behalf of the folk who have thought to fork out the £8 annual subscription (it rockets to £10 in September).

You get good at something after fifty years: of those 5,000 actions, the A.C.A. has lost just three. Place your bets.

14 ♌

Bubblegum and the Boardmaster

I was once a psychologist, so I know about these things.

There are four basic drives, instinctive urges, which shape all human behaviour. They are Hunger, Thirst, Sex and the Compulsion-to-Buy-Unsuitable-Gifts-for-the-Rest-of-the-Family-on-the-First-Day-of-the-Holiday.

It was this last one which drove me at the age of twelve to buy my parents a huge but delicate ornamental brandy glass on the first day of a cycling tour of the Thames Valley. It was the same urge that made us buy enormous earthenware garden pots for the folks back home on the first day of a family motoring holiday to Italy. We had just arrived in Ventimiglia, three of us with a tent and an inflatable dinghy, in a Citroën 2CV.

The last time was a couple of months ago. I was on a short fishing holiday to Scourie, near the northwest tip of Scotland. I had caught the Caledonian Sleeper train from Euston at 9.30 the night before and had woken up in the Pass of Drumochter, the stunning gateway to the Highlands, with the boring bits of Britain behind me and the best bits trundling past the window as I grazed through breakfast. We reached Inverness at twenty to nine. The train north would leave from the next platform at eleven. I had two hours in Inverness.

I have done this before and I fancy I have the kit for a Highland fishing trip nailed all round. In my backpack I carry a change of clothes, lightweight waterproof jacket and overtrousers, and lightweight plimsolls for the evening: I wear the walking boots when travelling – they weigh more. The plimsolls can also be worn with the pair of featherweight stocking-foot chest waders if it looks like a filthy day in a boat or if I have to wade the shore of a loch. A book and a washing kit, a camera, minimal fishing tackle in a bag, a small ditty-bag with compass, lighter, penknife and other Boy-Scouty bits and a lot of big socks. Two rods – a four-piece 9-foot loch rod and a tele-scopic dapping rod – are strapped to the side of the backpack. Everything has its job: everything has earned its place in the pack. The thing you don't need on such a trip is a life-sized hollow plastic head-and-shoulders bust of Buzz Lightyear.

It was in a sweet shop in Inverness. The thing wasn't even for sale. It was a dispenser: it stood on the counter, half full of bubble gum, and I knew I had to have it. Smallest daughter would just love it and a life-size bust of Buzz Lightyear would irritate the bejazus out of her new brother-in-law who is a big Buzz Lightyear fan. I went into the shop and opened negotiations: I don't suppose Lord Elgin gave much thought to how he was going to get his Marbles home. An hour later I caught the train north with the cumbersome, fragile thing in a plastic bag swinging from the fishing rods. Also a lot of bubble gum.

Ninety minutes later the train pulled in to the tiny station of Lairg. The post-buses that deliver the mail and passengers and anything else that needs delivering to points north and west were waiting for the train. Within a minute we were off to Scourie.

It was late in an afternoon of light drizzle interspersed with heavy drizzle. With occasional rain. I had been a long time getting to Scourie – and so have you – so I will do now what I did then. Go fishing.

It was a delight to find Rob at the hotel. We had fished together years ago and he would be at Scourie ghillieing for a couple of days. We shoved stuff into his car and set off into the gloom. Loch á Mhinidh is an unexceptional little loch, just one of 250 or so controlled by the Scourie Hotel. Its chief recommendation that afternoon was that it sits beside the road: we could be fishing in minutes. There is something magical about the first casts of a Highland hols. It sets the tone. I *know* there are trout in these lochs and I *know* they can be caught by pulling some flies past their noses. But it is always nice to check these things.

And then there are the flies. Fishing on a southern river, I choose a fly like a stage director casting the juvenile lead: *this one* is perfect for the part, with *that one* as understudy. On a Highland loch I am a canny old football manager, looking for strength in the midfield with width up front and a solid back four. My first team is usually a small dark number on the point, a slim gold or silver item playing number two and something bright and bushy on the top dropper. I might kick off with the dream team of Bibio, Cinnamon and Gold, and Golden Olive Bumble, but the Bibio has been having a run of bad form of late: I might pull it off after thirty minutes and bung on a Dunkeld, hoping to sneak a quick fish before half-time and then adjust the balance of the team during the interval, perhaps bringing the Golden Olive

Bumble into the midfield and playing a Coachman at number 3. In the event, it was a Black Pennel playing up front in place of the Bibio – who had failed to turn up despite a frantic search through the box – who did the business within a few minutes of the kick-off. Funny old game, fishing.

We knocked off at six and squelched back to the warmth and welcome of the hotel. The Scourie Hotel has been a blissful haven for damp fishermen for generations and each generation of fishermen has worn away at the edges and corners until the place fits a fisherman like a favourite armchair. First, of course, there is the fishing. The hotel has fishing on over 250 lochs (no one is quite sure) amongst the wild and remote confusion of heather and granite of the northwest tip of Scotland. There are salmon and sea trout on loch and river beats and there are brown trout. A lot of very big brown trout hang on the walls of the bar and lounge of the hotel. There are the usual monsters from the 1930s and 1940s, but many of the best have been caught in the 1990s, including a beast of 4 pounds 2 ounces taken on a tiny dry cul-de-canard last year.

The Scourie Hotel does not have everything: it does not have a television in the bar or lounge. It does not have a juke box or an electronic games machine. What it has is the *Boardmaster*.

The Boardmaster is a Scourie institution. The Boardmaster is a hotel guest who has a good knowledge of all the hotel fishing. This sounds a tall order with 250 lochs, but many Scourie fishermen have been coming for many years, often several times a year. The Boardmaster controls the Board. The name of each guest who wants to fish is written on the Board in the order of their arrival. After dinner the guests gather round the Board to choose their beats for the next day. The person at the top of the Board has the choice of all 38 hotel beats – a beat may be a remote cluster of lochs, a roadside loch, a stretch of river or all of these. The Boardmaster can advise newcomers on the sort of fishing to be found at each beat, how to get there and the walking involved. The next person down on the Board then has the choice of all the remaining beats, and so on. Each day the name at the top goes to the bottom and everybody moves up one place. It is transparently fair, it is run by the fishermen for the fishermen and saves the hotelier getting his ear bent by folk after favourite beats. And it works.

I had been a long time in the train. I fancied a bit of walk to my fishing. I mentioned this to Rod Bueler, Boardmaster for the week: he put me down for Stalker's Loch.

It wasn't exactly raining the next morning but then it wasn't exactly not raining either. The track that leads to Stalker's Loch begins where the Laxford river flows out of Loch Stack and fresh-run salmon flow in. We climbed out of Rob's car and looked at the track threading up across the heather towards the grey bulk of Arkle to the north. There were three of us off to Stalker's that morning: Rob, me and Pat. Pat was carrying an oar. The last guests to fish at the loch had broken one of the oars and, seeing that Rob and I were fishing there, Pat thought he had better come along with us to replace the oar. We said we could take the oar for him if he wanted, but Pat said he would rather do it himself: apparently replacing an oar is the tricky sort of job that a hotel owner has to do himself despite the inconvenience of leaving the hotel for the day. Apparently running a fishing hotel is full of these little chores. I noticed he was carrying his fishing rod as well, though.

Stalker's Loch is one of the more remote of Scourie's beats, a pattern of hill lochs lying in the cleft between the forbidding masses of Arkle and Foinaven. The track from Loch Stack leads around the flank of Arkle. The gradients are not steep and the track is easy to follow, but it is an hour-and-three-quarter slog whichever way you slice it. We were all feeling pretty manly by the time we looked down the spongy slopes of Loch an Tigh Shelg – the Stalker's Loch.

It was quite a sight. They come and go, these hill lochs. From one spot you might see nothing but undulating heather and rock, a few paces further and a glint in the folds reveals a lochan, and then another above and beyond, and then a whole pattern. The path takes you into a shallow dip and they are gone again. Our path led towards a broad burn sweeping in extravagant meanders from another loch hidden behind the bulk of Arkle. We squelched down across the slope towards the loch. A feeble sun broke through the clouds to reveal a bottom of pale sand with a stain of weed where the burn entered the loch. A small green boat was stranded on a sandy beach. We had arrived.

We went fishing. I am never hopeful fishing over sand: I can't quite picture what the fish would be doing there. I like rocks. I like to cast around them and then to stand on them and cast along the shore, gradually fanning out the cast over deeper water before getting back to shore and working around to the next rocky outcrop. It is the still-water equivalent of fishing a tasty little trout stream where each bend leads to the sight of another pool which looks just that little bit tastier than the one you are fishing and so you fish up to that pool – and on to the next, and the next and the next – until you look up to find you have run out of river or daylight or wives. The huge advantage of a loch is that you end up where you started.

I look for trees too, but there are not many trees on the lochs of the north-west. A loch with a single holly tree is apt to get called Holly Loch. People will tell you that the northwest coast is a mild place, practically subtropical, coddled in the breath of the Gulf Stream and tosh like that. Do not believe these people. Ask them why there aren't any trees. A stunted rowan clings to the shore of the loch. It is child's play to convince me that this makes a good lie for a loch trout, so I always cast carefully around such places. Pat caught a trout under that tree and so did I later that day. Of course, it could be that there are trout everywhere in these lochs and you catch them in the places you cast carefully.

We were having lunch by the boat on the sandy beach, well pleased with half a dozen fine 12-inch trout – good fish for a hill loch – when something better rose in the weeds off the mouth of the burn. We had been given instructions for finding the other oar. 'Turn your back to the loch and look for a rock on top of another rock.' That had sounded quite sensible at the hotel. Facing a soggy hillside of rocks on other rocks (how big is a rock?), it sounded absurd. We eventually found the oar by tracing the faint, plashy footmarks of the previous fisherman. Rob and Pat, being the ones wearing wellies, as they explained, pushed the boat off the beach and rowed towards the rises.

It was 5 o'clock when they returned with three trout, all over 12 ounces and one above the pound. Summer nights are long in the north but all fishing on Scourie lochs stops at 6 o'clock. There are reasons for this. A Scourie fisherman can be an hour-and-three-quarters of rough country away from the nearest car and another fifteen minutes from a drink and dry socks. So if a fisherman doesn't turn up for dinner he probably needs help.

Actually, a fisherman who doesn't turn up for dinner at the Scourie Hotel these days probably needs his head examining.

Since Pat and Judy bought the hotel this spring they have been careful to change none of the traits and traditions evolved over the generations of visiting anglers. But they have changed two things: they changed the beer in the bar to a real ale – a rare blessing in the Highlands – and they changed the menu. That night, an hour and a hot bath after stumbling out of the wind and rain, I sat down to a banquet of fresh lobster and langoustine served on a bed of asparagus tips.

You don't move around a lot after something like that. I staggered out to consult the Board, genuflecting before the Boardmaster, whose majesty was only slightly tarnished by a pair of socks in a violent shade of coral – which is not what a chap needs to see after indulging in lobster and langoustine. I looked at the Board. The next day I would be fishing for the salmon of Loch Stack.

You know how it is with fishing hotels: I think it is something they put in the coffee. You start the evening talking pretty sensibly about the next day's fishing, asking about lies and flies and so on and suddenly it is one in the morning and you are involved in a head-to-head needle-match trivia quiz with Rodney the Boardmaster on the subject of *The Archers*.

I thought I knew a thing or two about the Archers but I was up against Rodney, a man who confessed to owning a compilation cassette of *Archers* highlights: his favourite is the moment in 1955 when Grace Archer died in the stable fire at Grey Gables.

Suddenly, backpacking around the Highlands with a life-sized hollow plastic bust of Buzz Lightyear seemed quite normal.

Principia Piscatoria

Being the complete principles of fly-fishing for river
trout in 2,660 words

In 1670 the English philosopher John Locke had a group of the lads round at
his house, including his friend Robert Boyle, the eminent chemist and founder
member of the Royal Society. They were discussing, as chaps will when they
get together, the nature of knowledge emerging from the rapidly burgeoning
new experimental sciences. (What other angling book gives you this sort of
erudition?) Things were getting sticky. They found themselves in a dilemma,
unable to distinguish what they knew, what they *could* know but didn't, and
what they couldn't possibly know even if they thought they did. They thought
they ought to get this nailed down first. It didn't seem a hard task, and John
Locke offered to sort the thing out before the next meeting. He finished it *(An
Essay Concerning Human Understanding)* twenty years later. And even then
he was wrong.

I know just how he felt. Here goes.

All fishing is dead simple. It consists of getting something containing a hook
in front of a fish: that fish being inclined to eat it. And then, when the something is in the fish's mouth, pulling the hook into the fish. That's fairly
obvious. But how about the reverse? If you are not catching fish then one (or
more) of those elements must be awry. On each cast – that's quite a thought.

Consider the elements in order:

1. You can have a Wosname's Irresistible on the end of your line and the
trout as keen as mustard to grab it, but if you don't put it where the trout are,
nothing happens. Getting the something in front of the fish can be broken
down into two parts: (a) finding where the fish are, and (b) putting the fly
there. The first bit, (a), is dead easy when the fish are feeding on the surface:
you can see where they are. Even the second bit is fairly simple because you
can see where your fly lands and floats. People will tell you that dry fly-fishing
is difficult. Do not believe these people.

If the fish are not feeding on the surface then (a) becomes a little trickier. You can look for the trout, peering into the water with polaroid specs: possible, but not recommended, as you will see later. You can simply ignore (a) and move right along to (b), putting a fly into as much of the water as possible on the off-chance that there is a fish there. This is not a bad approach, particularly if the river is big and featureless. It is important to vary the depth of the search as well as the area. Sooner or later you should arrive at (a). Better still, if only because it saves time and energy, is to work out (a). This is 'reading the water' and is not the slightest bit mysterious. Experience helps. Experience of that water with rising fish giving away their positions; experience of similar waters and similar features. But mostly it is the appreciation that trout have the same problems as the rest of us: how to get the most of what they want while expending the least effort. They have to avoid being eaten as well, which makes life more interesting for them. This balance between effort, food and fear is the key to where the trout are to be found. So much for (a), finding where the fish are.

Now for (b), getting the fly in front of them. This is straightforward if the fish are feeding at the surface. As long as you land the fly upstream of the trout, the fly will pass the trout's nose by and by. The trout may be in no mood to take the fly by then, but that is another consideration (2b, down the page a bit: we are going for systematic organisation here. John Locke would have been proud of us). If the trout are feeding well below the surface then you are going to have to get the fly down to them.

Next: the fly. Once it has broken through the surface (and the fluffier the fly, the more likely it is to get trapped there), the fly sinks. Left to its own devices, how fast the fly sinks depends on its drag and its density; a light fluffy fly sinks a lot slower than a slim heavy fly (and much the same applies to the leader and line). But the fly is not left to its own devices. It is joined to an angler and, as his rod is usually above the water, any pull on the line will result in the fly rising – or at least not sinking as fast, if at all. This is the still-water fisherman's 'sink and draw': the fly sinks when the line is let slack and rises as the line is drawn back. But in a river current the line will always be drawing back when the fly is downstream of the angler. It will always be sinking when it is upstream of him. More or less.

The speed of the current is crucial in determining the depth of the fly. When the fly is upstream it just sinks. That just takes time, sometimes a surprising amount of time. The faster the current, the further upstream the fly must enter the water to have time to sink to the trout's level. If the water is clear enough to let you see the fly, it really is worth counting how long it takes to sink to somewhere near the bottom, and then you can aim your cast accordingly.

When the fly is downstream, the pull of even a modest current keeps it surprisingly high in the water, often just inches below the surface. In any reasonable current it takes an indecent amount of metal, distributed between the fly and its line, to get the fly to any great depth. This is called salmon fishing. Sometimes it catches some very fine trout who live deep in the water.

There is one more point to consider when the fly travels downstream of the fisherman. The pull on the line causes the fly to swing back across the current. You will have to cast the fly upstream and *beyond* the spot where the trout lurks, allowing it to swing in front of his nose. It may be travelling like a train and scare him spitless when it does – but that is the next item on the list.

2.   The fly has arrived in front of the fish. But is the fish inclined to eat it?

I have an aunt in Wales. When I was a small boy I would spend holidays with this aunt. She would drive from Wales, my parents would drive from Hemel Hempstead and halfway between the two I was handed over. It was a long journey, even halfway, and warm – for the summers were warmer then – and we always had an ice-cream at the handover. It was my very first encounter with trout. They hung in the current beneath the stone bridge over the River Coln at Bibury, oblivious to the visitors watching them. If you dropped a blob of ice-cream onto the water it would drift over a trout, which would glide up and take it and instantly the ice-cream would billow out of its gills. It must have been rather frustrating. These trout had no fear and they would sample almost anything that came their way. Trout are like that.

When something small drifts before the trout's nose, it may grab or it may not. At that moment there is a balance between the stimuli that say 'grab' and those that say 'don't grab'. I can find no reference to fly-fishing in the biographies of the great lyricist Johnny Mercer. This is strange, for in one of his songs he clearly states the secret of getting a trout to take a fly in front of its nose. He says: '(You've got to) ac-cen-tuate the positive, e-lim-inate the negative'.

Let's take a look at these two strategies.

a) Ac-cen-tuate the positive

This is the stuff of fly-fishing magazines. All those flies that do the trick, that save the day, that solve the problem. The materials that add that bit of sparkle, that bit of life, that translucence, that subtle shading. All of these things create a better fly, a more enticing fly. *Hmmmm*. It is implied that without that sparkle, that translucence, that wing-case, the trout would ignore the fly. I'm not asserting that all flies are equally attractive, any more than all sandwich fillings are equally attractive: they aren't. I prefer bacon-and-lettuce to ham-and-cheese. But I'll eat ham-and-cheese if I want to eat and that's what is offered to me. Ac-cen-tuating the positive isn't going to make that much difference. As long as it is some sort of sandwich it will do. If I don't eat the sandwich, it is probably because there is something terribly wrong with it. And so it is with trout.

It is fun tying new patterns and changing flies and matching hindwings and so forth. But if the chips were down and I had to catch fish, I would be happier with a nondescript brownish thing on a size 16 and concentrate on why the trout does not take this every time.

b) E-lim-inate the negative

Fear is a major turn-off. This does not have to be head-for-the-hills panic: the fish may stay exactly where it is, its feeding hardly faltering, uneasy rather than frightened, but just a little more cautious: the balance is tipped slightly from 'grab' towards 'don't grab'. People will tell you of the fastidious discrimination of chalkstream trout. Do not believe these people. The crystal water and unruffled surface of a chalkstream make the trout easy to see. They also make the fisherman easy to see and the chalkstream's low banks outline any movement against the sky. All trout become fastidious when they are scared; it is just easier to scare them in a chalkstream. Scare it a little more and the trout sinks to the bottom. Now you can bounce nymphs off its nose and the chances are it will ignore them. I used to do this years ago, and then I'd change the nymph – and then change it again, searching for the pattern that the trout was waiting for. The trout was waiting for me to go away.

There are other good ways to put a trout off. An unruffled, confident trout will grab any small, nondescript fly: it could be food. But not if the food starts doing unnatural and bizarre things. One of the unnatural and bizarre things it can do is to skate across the surface of the water. Food does not do this. Unfortunately the morsel you are laying in front of the trout has to be attached to a line and, unless that line is slack and floating along with the current, it will pull the fly across the surface, slowly at first, but soon the fly will skate. This is drag. Some time ago I asserted that dry fly-fishing is easy. Drag is what makes it difficult.

If the fly is under the surface, a little bit of drag is no problem. A lot of food moves about underwater, often to avoid becoming food. Trout are used to that. And if a trout is feeding on the surface in a spot where a dry fly will drag instantly, you should switch to a suitable nymph and carry on as before. The trout will usually not mind the food being half an inch below the surface and moving. You should do this, but you won't. You will do what I do. You will try the dry fly first because that is what you have on the end of your line. You will alarm the trout, just a bit, with drag, and then you will give up the dry fly and switch to the nymph. And then you will wonder what on earth they can be feeding on when they will not take nymph or dry fly – if only you could find the right pattern, you will think. We are ac-cen-tuating the positive when we should be e-lim-inating the negative.

Trout don't mind their underwater food moving a bit, but they do not want it flashing past their noses. Food doesn't do that. In anything above a very modest current all food will be drifting downstream at nearly the speed of the current. So if your wet fly is swinging across a lively stream it may well pass the nose of a trout, it may well be cunningly wrought from the finest materials, it may be indistinguishable from a hatching caddis pupa, but at the very best it will appear to the trout as a jet-propelled caddis pupa. Of course, the trout may grab the speeding fly as it zips past anyway. They sometimes do. And that is the point: you don't need to persuade a trout to eat a fly. The trick is to avoid putting it off.

A small, nondescript, brownish artificial fly is drifting down the current. It is slowly sinking until it arrives on the doorstep of a trout. The trout is feeding steadily and takes the small brownish thing on board. It could be food. It isn't. The trout spits it out. The fly drifts on.

3.   Hooking the fish

You would think it was enough, getting a fly into the trout's mouth. Sometimes it is. Sometimes, when you are fishing with a wet fly or nymph, the first thing you know is that there is a fish firmly fixed on the end of the line. The trouble is that there is usually no way of knowing how many times fish have taken the fly without getting hooked. If only for the sake of symmetry, I will divide the hooking into two parts: a) detecting that the trout has taken the fly, and b) doing something about it.

Part (a) is the hard bit. It is easy if you can see the fly, particularly if it disappears with a satisfying plop and a vigorous swirl. Even if the fly is just under the surface, the commotion is just as unmistakable. It is another matter when the fish and the fly are deep. In clear water with an even flow and the light just right you can see the fish and any movement: an opening mouth, a sideways twist catching the light, is evidence of a take. All too often, particularly in rain-fed rivers, there is too much disturbance to see anything much under the surface. A trout can sample the fly and spit it out without the fisherman being any the wiser. Unless the fly moves. Even then nothing will show up top if there is slack line between the fly and the surface.

This poses a problem for the man fishing deep. The line must be slack for the fly to sink to any depth (1b, remember?) – but if the line is slack he will miss the take. The trick, then, is to draw in any slack as the fly reaches the fish – or where you think the fish might be. The fly rises, the fish grabs and the twitch on the line is seen up on the surface. You may even feel it. No one pretends this is easy.

There are ways to make it easier. You can use a float. This allows the fly to sink to the right depth and hang there with no slack. It also detects the twitch of the take. It is perfectly OK as long as you call it an indicator.

Part (b): You have found a trout, delivered a fly to its vicinity and you know that this trout has taken the thing in its mouth.

If you don't know what to do now, Lord help you. I can't.

Back-End Blues

I went grayling fishing last week. It was on the River Kennet.

That is not strictly true: the water I was fishing had been in the River Kennet shortly before and would be part of the River Kennet soon after. Also the River Kennet was nearby. So I was very nearly fishing on the River Kennet. I was on a Kennet carrier.

There are no carriers on the sort of rivers I usually fish, but I have read about carriers for years. They crop up in angling literature all the time, but the people who fish on rivers that do have carriers are too sensitive to the feelings of other folk to patronise them by spelling out what a carrier is. So I had formed a sort of impression of what a carrier is without ever having seen one.

I knew, for example, that it was not the Main River. A Test carrier is not the same as the River Test. Carriers are a minor branch of the family; they don't live in the big house; they are in trade; they may get invited for weddings and funerals but they don't sit at the top table.

Carriers, in short, are the grayling of chalkstream waters. The thing is, I don't sit at the top table myself and I rather like it down amongst the carriers and the grayling.

There is something delightfully dilapidated about fishing for autumn grayling. It is something about the tatty brown grasses and drunken old teasels on the riverbank, the raft of leaves in the eddies, the straggly branches and brambles that are left hanging over the water. It is something to do with the flies.

My fly-boxes have limped to the end of another trout season. Trout tighten up after the easy days of May and June: by late August and September the fishing is getting tougher, the changes of fly becoming ever wilder between patterns of dry flies, heavy nymphs, wet flies, light nymphs and aberrations that do not fit easily into any of these. The boxes that started the season neatly sorted have become hopelessly muddled. Flies that began as gloriously hackled as a Roman centurion have been snipped and trimmed when something stubbier looked like it might be more to taste. Favourite flies have long gone. Where once there were neat rows of essential patterns in several sizes, there are now scatterings of odd flies, singletons of unlikely dimensions. From a model army drawn up on the parade ground and prepared for a set-piece battle it has become the raggle-taggle remnants in the disorder of full retreat. Guerrilla tactics and hand-to-mouth improvisation are all this lot are capable of from now on. I rather like it that way.

Everything about grayling fishing has this melancholic mood to it. It is autumn and everything is dying, the nights have been drawing in since June but I never really notice it until it is suddenly getting dark at six and then on a day in late October there is the shock of the clocks going back. From now on any fishing is snatched rather than planned and is all the sweeter for being unexpected.

I was charmed by my first chalkstream carrier. At Denford, a mile or so below Hungerford on the old A4, we pulled off the road through a gate and crunched down a steep little track, over a miniature bridge to park in a small corral strewn with newly fallen leaves. A bright little stream beetled out from under the brick arch we had just crossed. When I was a little lad, we were taken on a school trip to Beckonscot, a miniature landscape of model towns and villages in an unlikely suburban street in Beaconsfield. You will see it signposted on the M40. I returned many times and so have my children. England in the 1930s is frozen in the streets of Beckonscot. You walk between the rooftops along little streets, wind through fields and harbours, towards a funfair and village greens and zoos and the like that you can see across the miniature countryside way before the winding path brings you past them. The fishing at Lower Denford is just like that. From the miniature car park a pattern of six neatly mown paths lead off through the bushes and tall grasses of the old water-meadows. A small, green gingerbread fishing hut with a dinky little verandah overlooks the stream beside the car. Follow any of these paths and you will soon come upon a bright little stream going in one direction or another. You can follow that stream until it joins another or itself divides, each branch hurrying out of sight around a bend in the greenery. There are little bridges and miniature hatchpools and mysterious little culverts where water slips out and round and under. You think I am exaggerating? I'm not. At one rather puzzling point one small stream is carried over another in a bantam aqueduct. I never quite got to grips with how this was done – or why – but it happens.

On the River Tees the other day, I was ruminating on how one could get a handle on the fishing of such a large and rumbustious water by considering it as a woven plait of smaller, simpler streams. The good folk who created the Kennet carriers at Denford had done this for me, taken a large river and teased it apart into a skein of charming 7-foot-rod-sized streams, each with its own banks and borders and bends. It is most convenient.

There were grayling everywhere. It was the Winter Palace the morning after the revolution: the lower orders had taken over the state rooms, they were lounging around the banqueting hall, they were wiping their proletarian boots on the tapestries and peeing in the bidets. You got the feeling they shouldn't be there.

They shouldn't. Denford Fisheries is a trout fishery. It is a rainbow-trout fishery and may well be a very fine rainbow-trout fishery but, what with it being the end of a successful trout-fishing season, there were precious few of the gentry left. The place was left to the poor relations.

We commenced fishing. There were grayling everywhere – did I mention that? That, in a way, was the problem. The little carriers of the Kennet were slow and clear after another dry summer and the pale-grey shapes of the grayling could easily be seen scattered across the bottom. And they, of course, could see us just as easily. As we walked down the path mown neatly alongside the Road Stream that led away from the car park, the shapes were already sliding across the bottom, ghosting into the slightly deeper water under the bank. I was crouching behind the straggled brown grasses of the bank and looking at a bevy of fish that had spirited into that channel. It is a deceptive sight. It appears that the grayling are congregating in one spot for the convenience of the fisherman, saving him the trouble of all that tedious casting to individual fish scattered hither and yon across the river. How much more efficient to have the grayling gather together and make your sales pitch to a crowd? Alas, it does not work that way. The grayling that had gathered in the deeper channel were not buying anything I had to sell. The grayling on that bright day were devilish difficult to approach on the shallow flats.

So I looked for something to hide behind. A little story: my daughter's hamster escaped the week before last. We emptied out cupboards and lifted floorboards but there was no trace. We had left the cage, open, on the floor in the hope that it might wander back and, miracle of miracles, it did. The problem was that it wandered back in the middle of the night and then wandered out again. We found a trail of food. So the next night Alice slept in our room while I planned to spend the night in hers and catch this hamster in the act. At 2.30 a.m. I was woken by the sounds of the drinking bottle rattling. I had the torch in my hands and swung it round onto the cage. With a single heroic, but chilly, bound I was there, ready to slam the door shut before the wily hamster scuttled off. I need not have bothered. A startled hamster does not budge. It freezes. So do most animals unless flight is absolutely necessary. Evolution discovered long ago that it is movement, not colour or shape, that is most likely to get you spotted. You can wear a camouflage jacket, you can stick leaves in your hat as you fish: it is movement that will give you away and, what with casting and so on, movement is inevitable with fly-fishing. The trick is to hide behind something moving. That is why loch fishermen look for a wave. And chalkstream fishermen look for a hatch pool. The inevitable movements of the fishermen are lost in the twisting, fracturing surface of the water below a hatch.

There are several small weirs along the carriers beside the Kennet where the crystal waters plunge into a pool scoured in the bright bottom. The bubbles from all this activity hide the angler as effectively as the splintered surface and invigorate the slow waters of a dry season. It was just a shame there were no grayling in the pools to enjoy all this. They should have been there. I was fishing a pool just such as this the week before. In one small corner of the pool, in the eddy at one edge of the plunge, hard against the weir, I had hooked and released a dozen grayling one after the other. But not here on the Kennet. I have been pondering the difference since then. The pools on the Kennet carriers are smaller. Also, the waters of the Denford Fisheries carry some fair old rainbows during the season: almost a thousand rainbow trout were taken from these small waters and not a few were over 2 pounds, some over 4 pounds. It may just be that the grayling had been evicted by these large and aggressive rainbows during the trout season and had not yet slipped back into the prime pools as the numbers of rainbows thinned.

If they had thinned. My leader, which had been serenely sinking as it was carried on the current down Pansy Pool, suddenly lurched to the left. I lurched to the right. There was something solid on the end. It was one of those rainbows. It was a fine, heavy fish and it was quite ridiculous to feel a little tinge of disappointment as soon as I glimpsed the silver and magenta sheen in the depths of Pansy Pool. But something akin to disappointment happens hooking grayling when you are after trout: it happens hooking trout when you are after grayling. I have no idea why.

The grayling were to be found on the broader reaches. I could not find them in the deeper pools: I could not get near them in the shallow runs. The solution, if that is the word, was to fish the broader, shallower reaches from a long way off. Few of the hundreds of grayling we had spotted were rising but we dared not creep close enough to look for fish. Once the options had been narrowed to these, I could settle into the rhythm of a long sidecast under the trees, searching my way upstream with a small nymph or something-in-the-surface. I could not pretend to be stalking a fish. I was not even fishing over a likely spot. If I got close enough to see if it was likely, it wasn't likely any more. So I fished on up the water, and in this curiously unsatisfactory manner I began to catch grayling. One or two at first and then another one or two.

I am sounding ungrateful. I am not. I had come to catch grayling. I caught grayling and I was delighted to catch them. It was a wonderful, warm day at a time of year when wonderful warm days are a rare blessing. I was fishing amidst the charming and charmed waters of an English chalkstream. And in those magical waters there were more grayling than you could chuck a stick at. The trouble was that I felt a little like I was just chucking a stick at them. Some of them fetched it, most of them didn't and I felt it was more their choice than mine.

Sometimes grayling fishing just has a melancholic mood.

Anatomy of the Perfect Fly

There are times, dark times, when even the sincerest believer has Doubts.

There are hundreds, perhaps thousands, of books on fly patterns. There have been thousands of articles in hundreds of magazines extolling the fish-catching qualities of this pattern or that pattern. There is no doubt that the choice of pattern is terribly, terribly important.

But I have grave doubts as to whether it is terribly, terribly important to the trout.

What's this? Has he finally toppled over the edge? Half the lore and literature of fly-fishing is absorbed in this business of choosing the right fly for the conditions. Approaches to this selection may vary, of course. In one approach the choice could be an emerging female of the Pale Evening Dun, 'dressed to imitate a stillborn dun with one wing trapped in the nymphal shuck'. In another approach it could equally be 'what all the locals use – a Blue Lieutenant – rabbit-fur body with blue Andalusian hackle that does very well upstream of the town weir'. I do not deny that the Blue Lieutenant does do very well upstream of the town weir. Similarly, no doubt, the stillborn Pale Evening Dun really does do wonderfully well in a hatch of Pale Evening Duns, stillborn or otherwise. And yet both these flies are doing the same job equally well: both are catching trout, probably from the same species, possibly from the same hatchery. Why is it that such disparate approaches to fly selection produce much the same results?

The answer, I suspect, is that the choice of fly matters very little to the trout. But it makes an enormous difference to the fisherman. If he believes that the trout are selecting crippled Pale Evening Duns then that pattern will be successful, not least because it is the one he is using, but mainly because he has faith in his fly. And if all the locals swear by a Blue Lieutenant above the town weir, it is small wonder that most of the trout caught there are victims of the Blue Lieutenant – and hence their faith in this fly is quite justified. Faith in fishing flies is self-fulfilling. And, unfortunately, so is lack of faith.

The first trout I ever caught on a fly lived in the icy waters flowing off the Cairngorms. Before the small river joins Loch Morlich it runs crystal-clear, deep in places, over a bottom of pale sand. The fly was home-made. It was a simple dry fly with a body of dubbed natural wool from a barbed-wire fence and something like a badger hackle. I had lost the six flies that I had originally bought: they had caught nothing and I cannot remember what they were. This home-made effort represented all I could make with the only cape I owned. The fly was rocking gently down the centre of a deepish pool when a small dark shadow, previously unnoticed, detached itself from the bottom of the pool and rose vertically to intercept this unlikely offering as it proceeded serenely on its way. The surface shattered in the sunlight and the small fish started on its way down again. The miracle had happened.

I was immensely impressed. Clearly with a fly like this the thing was easy: you just trundled it over fish and they grabbed it. What could be simpler. I really couldn't see what all the fuss was about.

Two things happened that evening. First, I caught another five trout where the evening before I had caught nothing. Second, my legs and everything else below the waist went blue. I had no waders at the time. To work my way to all the likely looking places I waded in bare feet and jeans, first to my knees and subsequently to my waist, oblivious of the numbing cold of water a mile away from melting snow. I would never have put up with such pain and discomfort the evening before (and, to be frank, I won't again). Such is the effect of faith – and the results were in my bag.

For a time I used only that fly. It was, after all, responsible for every trout I had ever caught. But all flies fail sometimes; another succeeds and the first one has lost some of its magic. From then on the fly-fisherman is looking for some reason to believe that the fly he is tying on is, in some way, the 'right fly' for the occasion.

Fred J. Taylor recounts the tale of one 'superfly' he introduced to British waters from Minnesota. The black-and-white Integration was an 'incredibly effective streamer' which Fred used for two seasons, hardly ever bothering to tie on another fly, and keeping the pattern and appearance a strict secret. Eventually the secret got out and Integrations were in use all around the reservoir: they became just another lure – 'it still catches fish, but it is not the fly it once was'.

The same story has been repeated time and again with other secret superflies. Why do they lose their super powers once they are in general use – even

'It is a privilege to be there when a man catches his first trout' (*Educating Douglas*)

Dougal – 'our Highland pack pony in a three-mint mood' (*Just a Closer Walk With Three*)

'I bore an uncanny resemblance to Peter Fonda when the sunlight caught me in a certain way'
(*An Ice Hole in the Arctic*)

'A stunted rowan clung to the shore of the loch... Pat caught a trout under that tree'
(*Bubblegum and the Boardmaster*)

People will tell you that grayling do not jump: do not believe these people
(*Rocky Mountain Breakdown*)

Hot to trot on the River Irfon: 'Paul... fancied a go at the grayling on the day after Boxing Day'
(*A Winter's Tale*)

Above: *Fishing with Father*

Right: Alice has struck a deal with the devil: huge fish in return for one soul to be delivered at some inconvenient time in the future (*Fishing with Alice*)

on waters that have never seen them before? It isn't the trout that travel from water to water. It is the fishermen. The magic of a 'superfly' works on the angler, not on the trout.

I'm overdoing this. Of course there are attributes of a fly other than simple appearance. The shape and materials will affect, to some extent, how the thing rides in, on or under the water's surface, how it moves under the opposing forces of current and leader. These properties, and the size, translucency and outline, may have some effect on the trout – but not nearly as much as some sages would have us believe. The overriding difference between a superfly and just another fly is the fisherman's faith in it.

Now, this is all fine and dandy: But how does a fly acquire such charisma? Is it possible to describe (or, better still, create) the characteristics of a superfly that can inspire such faith? In the past (June 1990) I have looked at the *physical* characteristics that are common to many of the great all-purpose dry flies. They could be summarised as 'mixed hackle, grizzle and (usually) red, with a dowdy fur body of hare's ear, rabbit or similar'. Heron herl looks much the same and is another contender. The result is a subdued, rather nondescript concoction. At least it won't frighten the fish. Neither will it catch them – yet. As yet it lacks a reason to believe. It lacks charisma.

There are several routes to this charisma, to the vital conviction that this fly is the very thing to do the trick.

One is the entomological approach described at the beginning. It has an impeccable logic: the trout are feeding on something; if you can offer them something indistinguishable from that something then they will take your offering in the normal course of events and lo! the fish is yours. Even the most sceptical could believe in this.

There would seem to be two drawbacks: it can be very difficult to identify what trout are eating, and creating an exact imitation can be even harder. No matter. It is enough that the angler *thinks* he has identified the food. The March Brown is a very effective early-season fly – despite the fact that the natural fly is very localised and completely absent from most waters. Flies simply named after an insect have built-in entomological promise – provided, of course, that the insect is one the angler has heard of. One excellent general-purpose fly (with its mixed-grizzle hackle and heron-herl body) is named 'Dusky Yellowstreak' after a rather uncommon ephemerid. It would catch a lot more fish if its creator had thought to call it the 'something-or-other Olive'. Everyone has heard of olives. And sedges.

We had taken nothing on a large Irish lough. The occasional fish was rising but we had seen no obvious hatch of fly. Just then a small sedge, borne on the gentle breeze, fluttered into the boat and settled on the thwart. We looked at each other and then more closely at the water surface. Other sedges could be seen dancing close by. Aha! Feverishly we switched to sedge imitations, small and dark like the insects arriving on the wind. The first fish came minutes later, not large but holding the promise of more to come. And they did; not in droves but enough for supper. And as we cleaned them that evening we could examine the last meals of those logical fish. Not a single sedge. So why did our switch to sedges do the trick? Perhaps because we believed it would and fished accordingly.

Nothing succeeds like success. The most effective way for a fly to gain fish-catching charisma is to catch fish. Even the most hardened entomological angler, after a fruitless hour, finds it difficult to resist asking of a brother angler seen netting a fish, 'Er ... what have you got on?' And if the answer is 'Coachman', it takes nerves of entomological steel to persist with a Hatching Blue-Winged Olive. Four more fruitless casts and the BWO is guiltily snipped off and a Coachman tied on.

The Coachman is a fine all-purpose fly with an impeccable fish-catching track record. But then it has had 150 years for word to get about. The Greenwell's has a similar pedigree and the added advantage of the epithet 'Glory' (provided by an admirer), which is bound to inspire confidence. The would-be inventor of a superfly is often reluctant to wait this long. He would be well advised to choose a name that implies its sterling qualities without un-English boasting. The 'Imperial' invented by Oliver Kite refers to the purple-tying-silk underbody; the 'Indispensable' of the Tup's refers to the anatomical origin of the wispy wool used for the thorax – but 'purple silk' does not have the inspiring ring of 'Imperial' and 'Tup's Scrotum' is, frankly, a non-starter. John Goddard's 'Super Grizzly' teeters on the edge of brag-gadocio. But it is a highly regarded (and hence highly effective) general-purpose fly, although differing from the poor old 'Dusky Yellowstreak' only in the colour of the secondary hackle. The West Country fly calling itself 'Infallible' is, frankly, carrying this tactic too far: it is asking for trouble under the Trade Descriptions Act.

Kite's Imperial and Goddard's Super Grizzly are fine examples of another means by which a fly can acquire lustre – by being linked to a respected angling personage. Sawyer's Killer Bug leaves you in no doubt as to the effi-cacy of the thing or its provenance. Its effect on fishermen must have astounded the unassuming maestro of the Hampshire Avon. Three layers of beige darning wool wound around a hook shank is undoubtedly, in the hands of such a maestro, a deadly fly. But such was the faith and reverence it evoked that, now that the exact shade of darning wool has been discontinued, small cards of this original wool change hands for £20 or £30. Nearly indistinguishable shades do not, it seems, have the same magic. Can it matter to the trout? Any species that fussy about the shade of its food could surely never have survived the hurly-burly of evolution.

In fact, the use of the genuine Chadwicks 477 Darning Wool *is* vital – for the fisherman. The history of great flies is littered with ingredients that are so potent in their taking of fish that they became closely guarded secrets, passed on in whispers at the deathbed of the fly dresser. If the secret ingredient became common knowledge, why, the rivers would be cleared of fish in a weekend.

But these dressings are not kept secret because they are so potent. Think of Fred Taylor's 'Integration': *they are kept potent because they are so secret*. Take away that secrecy and the fly becomes just another fly.

Using such secret weapons feels (and so, of course, *is*) almost like an unfair advantage. I would strongly recommend any inventor of a superfly to get the use of his fly banned on at least one water. Nothing so enhances a fly's reputation as prohibiting its use. (Fishing on dry-fly-only water, I am always convinced that I would take any number of fish easily if only I was allowed to drift something downstream under the water.) The final seal on the reputation of any fly is to be banned: the implication is that it makes the whole thing too easy – like shooting the fish in a barrel. The Gold Ribbed Hare's Ear was once banned on some waters: Oliver Kite thought it was like using 'worms, maggots and minnows'. The Alexandra was once banned on the grounds that it was too effective. It rapidly became a firm favourite, although it is less potent in these tolerant times. I have always thought that there was more than a suggestion of the illicit in the name 'Dog-nobbler'.

Curiously enough, my own standby (which has become something of a legend amongst the small coterie of responsible anglers who were entrusted with its arcane recipe of dubbings and dyes) is Dick Walker's 'Fatal Attraction', a fabulous fly whose dressing is, unfortunately, still the subject of a court injunction brought in by the Environment Agency and the Salmon and Trout Association. Let's face it, with a pedigree like that, the dressing is immaterial.

18

Once Upon a Time in the West

I don't know how many of you have experienced the thrill, the downright joy, of reading the works of Franz Kafka.

I haven't.

I know I should. People who read Kafka are always telling me I should, but I have my doubts. So this morning I looked him up in *The Reader's Encyclopaedia* to see if Kafka and I would have much in common. I was stunned. In Kafka's works, it said, 'a world of absurdity and paradox, of aimlessness and futility, and sometimes of faint hope, is revealed' – which is uncanny because that has always seemed to me to be the very essence of trout fishing.

But there was more: in his writings '. . . Kafka explores, mainly through symbolism and allegory, the problems of . . . the psychological ambivalence of family relationships, especially between father and son'. Which, once again, is spooky because much the same happened to me and dad last month on a fishing trip to Cornwall.

It did not start well. The forecast said it would rain a bit in the morning and they were dead right. It was lashing down on the M5 between Gloucester and Stroud when the engine of the camper van backfired twice and then died. We coasted to a spot equidistant between emergency telephones so I was good and soggy by the time I had walked through the spray along the hard shoulder. The emergency phone didn't work. Bits of it worked: I could just about hear the bloke in the control centre but he couldn't hear me at all. I shouted into the mouthpiece; I hit it; I dismantled it and rebuilt it. Not a thing. Then I remembered a toy phone I had had as a child and I shouted into the *earpiece*. A faint squawk told me that the bloke on the other end had heard something, but I couldn't hear what he said with the earpiece in front of my mouth and by the time I had got the thing to my ear he had finished saying whatever it was and was waiting for an answer to the question I hadn't heard and which I couldn't give without taking the earpiece from my ear and shouting into it for him to repeat the question, which he did but I couldn't hear what he said because the earpiece was . . . and so on. Kafka would have enjoyed that phone.

Eventually we were rescued, recovered and repaired in a nearby garage, and so it was some eight hours behind schedule when we finally got to the Cornish border. It had rained throughout that eight hours and the Tamar, glimpsed from the A30 through steamy windows, was looking big and dirty which is all very well for a salmon river and perfectly splendid for a snog at the office Christmas party but not what one looks for in a trout stream. We were a bit gloomy as we drove on past Launceston and on into Cornwall.

The purpose of the new, improved A30 is to get people from England to Penzance, relieve them of their spending money and then get them the hell out again as quickly as possible. One is not encouraged to potter. The planners of the new, improved A30 did not envisage anyone visiting Treguddick, which once lay in a network of small lanes between the villages of South Petherwin and Lewannick. But not now. Now Treguddick is a dead end, a tiny turning off a four-lane motorway. One minute we were at 70-plus miles per hour, swept along in the stampede of holidaymakers sensing the western beaches like thirsty longhorns scenting a waterhole. I caught sight of the turning for Treguddick and father wrenched the wheel over: a second later he was standing on the brakes, hedges brushing both sides of the camper and the road petering out into a narrow track in front of us. We had arrived at the Inny.

It was still raining. A damp figure approached us in the dripping gloom. Roger Lane is a member of the Launceston Anglers' Association, who fish the Inny hereabouts. He was going to show us the river. We described the state of the Tamar we had just crossed: fishing would be futile. I took it for a strange but touching local pride when he assured us that the Inny remains fishable in anything short of exceptional rain. Where I come from, eight hours of solid rain *is* exceptional. But not, it seems, down here. The Tamar, it seems, is a creature of lush Devon farmland whose rich red soils we had just seen swirling down to the sea. The Inny, just a dozen miles to the west, comes from the moor. For a westward cloud, Bodmin Moor is the first high ground since the Blue Ridge Mountains of Virginia: it catches anything the Atlantic cares to send this way. Anything easily washable has been washed away long since.

That is the theory but it was hard to believe. A few yards down the track the Inny was bouncing along in fine style. It was tinged with colour, certainly, but we could still see a clean gravel in the shallows. It was full but far from bursting. It was fishable.

So we fished.

I do not, as a rule, hand out many practical details like 'how to fish the rolled nymph' or 'inducing the take with a sunken emerger', things of that sort. But I will tell you how to fish a small, wooded, swollen stream in the pouring rain. It is very simple. You do the best you can. Roger began with a nymph cast across the current, looking for the lightning flash of a fish as the fly swept past. How he could see anything in that bouncing, pock-marked surface was a mystery to me, but before long there was a splash and a small fish was on, and then off again.

Father thought it might be easier to see the rise to a dry fly and was muttering as each fresh salvo of raindrops dowsed his fly into the surface. And so he switched to a wet fly. I started with a team of wet flies and didn't get a touch as we worked our way through the first field downstream. Perhaps I wasn't getting down to the fish, so I switched to a weighted nymph. And so on.

Beyond the first fields the valley narrows and steepens. Here, we waded the swollen stream and climbed up through the dripping ferns into a meadow hidden between the wooded river bank and a steep wooded hillside. It is an enchanting spot, forgotten by the outside world beyond the woods. And that, strangely, has been the problem.

Nature, left to itself, is not necessarily in the business of producing trout. In times past, the densely wooded banks of the Inny had been coppiced to produce a steady supply of high-quality alder charcoal for smelting. The demand for charcoal collapsed, the coppicing gradually ceased and the alders of the Inny were forgotten. The once-coppiced alders lived on, divided into many trunks at the base and now, twenty or thirty years on, formed a dense canopy across the river. Light is the power source of a river. Without light, the Inny's riverside weeds and grasses died back leaving the soil between the alder roots open to erosion. Without light, the micro-organisms of the Inny's gravels and riffles, the start of a trout's food chain, cannot flourish as they might.

Until now. This hidden meadow on the Inny is just one of many spots along the Tamar and its tributaries that is benefiting from the Tamar 2000 SUPPORT (SUstainable Practices Project On the River Tamar) Project. The project's aim is to work with farmers, landowners and local clubs to restore and conserve the habitat of the whole river for man, beast, bird, plant – and fish. This is quite a project. Its £1.6 million is being used to provide practical advice and training in the best management of riverside lands, and some initial cash to push the thing along. For the Launceston Anglers on the Inny this has meant an awful lot of blood, sweat and sawdust.

On the Inny, the problem had been overshading from the alders. Here, the river swings down in a series of riffles and pools. Fallen trees had been pulled from the river and the ancient coppices cut back along the riffles, bringing light and life back to the most productive bits of river bed. The green stuff had not been slow to take advantage. Within weeks of the lights being switched on, ferns and grasses had rocketed to waist height and beyond between the thinned trees. All this is just dandy for billions of bugs and the trout that feed on the flyers and fallers: it is a pain in the butt for the wet fishermen pushing through the drenching stuff to get to the newly opened riffle. It was raining harder now, with huge drops hammering into the surface. Roger and father had each had fish somehow or other but I was getting desperate. That is the only excuse I can think of for putting on a size 12 Klinkhåmen Special, which is splendid for 2-pound grayling on the Kaitum but really has no business on a small West Country stream. What makes it good on the wide, wild waters of the Kaitum is that it floats and floats, come what may. Also you can see its white wing like a beacon through a maelstrom. And, by golly, I needed both those qualities in this lot. A small West Country trout has no business taking a size 12 Klinkhåmen. But it did. In fact, they did.

The Inny was rising and thickening as we retreated in the face of all this wet to the Archers' Arms in Lewannick. I can remember a superb beef and Stilton pie and a spotted dick and custard, some Dartmoor Best and not much more than that. It was not raining the next morning but by this time even the Inny was unfishable. It looked to me as if it would stay that way, but Roger had assured us last night that if the rain held off it would be back in condition by lunchtime. So we had a morning to look at a little miracle on the other side of Bodmin Moor.

I had heard of the De Lank river: I had never seen it. The rivers of the southwest all hold brown trout, but they are famous for their salmon and sea trout. Except for one: the De Lank. The De Lank had migratory fish once but it also had high-grade building granite along its course. In time the accumulation of spoil from the quarries at the edge of the moor gradually blocked the little river to migratory fish. The De Lank, isolated in the heart of Bodmin Moor, was forgotten by fishermen. It has been rediscovered by the biologists. The De Lank is now recognised as a rare and precious example of a pristine habitat, one of just a handful remaining in Europe where the hand of man has had little impact on the indigenous plants and wildlife. It is now designated a Site of Special Scientific Interest and is rapidly being viewed as one of the most important SSSIs of its type. It is the traditional pastime of fishermen to bemoan the state of rivers and to dream of fishing in a golden age before man ruined everything. Well, on the De Lank you can do something like that.

We drove down to the river at the hamlet of Bradford. Here the miniature river spills out below a low bridge before swinging down across the moor. After all that rain the water was miraculously clear, not crystal but a mixture of whisky and soda. A swallow dipped and plucked something from the surface and then, as we watched, a trout did the same at the tail of the current. We were in business.

It is an extraordinary place. Below the broad pool the river divides into channels that wander off across the moor to rejoin and divide in a bewildering network. There are deep, dark pools and foamy runs beneath undercut peat banks. There is streamy weed as bright and lush as in any chalkstream. There are waterfalls and sandy-bottomed glides. It is a wonderful place to fish and it looks about as trouty as water gets. And there are trout. Look: this is a moorland trout stream as nature intended. The richness of plant life and water weed is astonishing; the water is clean and unpolluted. It is a pristine habitat: that's official. Up here, where there is no competition from salmon parr, where no sea trout are carting the biomass down to the briny, the trout are plentiful and beautiful.

And they are tiny. In a pristine habitat a 6-inch moorland trout is a biggy.

The wind had torn the clouds to shreds and a fitful sun was breaking through. It was time to head back over the moor to resume battle with the 10-inch monsters of the Inny.

Are you wondering what had happened to 'the psychological ambivalence of family relationships, especially between father and son'?

It was 3 a.m. the following morning. I lay awake on a disused bridge on the A30. The *old* A30 – not the new, four-lane-superhighway A30 which swung past us somewhere close by and which was why I was awake at 3 in the morning. Through the din, I could hear father sleeping in the berth below. I was struck by a coincidence. You muse on things at 3 in the morning: they fester. Thirty years ago, almost to the day, I had spent another sleepless night in Cornwall, parked, as now, on a bridge on the old A30 on the edge of Bodmin Moor.

From time to time one sees an Austin Maestro containing four elderly parties drinking tea from a thermos, parked beside a junction on a busy road. Chances are they are part of a traffic census. In the summer of '68 they were a common sight along the A30 in Devon and Cornwall. I was eighteen. I had spent most of the summer in Cornwall, doing whatever eighteen-year-olds did in the 1960s and living in the back of my Morris 1000 van. The traffic census was recruiting people to take over from the elderly tea-drinkers for the hours of darkness. Two watchers would be enough for the sparser night-time traffic. The Cornish ratepayers, it seemed, would pay me to spend the nights with the companion of my choice on the mattress in the back of my van. It was a dirty job but someone had to do it. The mother of the Companion of My Choice did not see it that way and I spent the first night of my new employment alone in the van by the bridge on the old A30. The next morning I went round for breakfast with the COMC and her parents. I was using their address for any mail anyone cared to send: a letter had arrived for me. It was from my father, reminding me to return home in time for my sister's wedding at the end of the month. It was the first letter he had ever sent me. And he had spelt my name wrong.

Stuff like that leaves scars.

19

Ode to Melancholy

I was taught English Literature by Mr J.A. Davison, whom we christened, without a speck of imagination, JAD. He was a tall, bony and much-feared teacher. It says much about his ability to inspire fear that I can remember what JAD said about any piece of literature far better than I can remember the stuff itself.

Take Keats. Keats used to put a fair amount of spin on the ball, as I recall. It was written in English, right enough – I recognised the words – but, put together, the meaning of it all eluded me. Totally impenetrable. But not to JAD. A couple of sentences and he would have the whole thing summed up, just what Keats was getting at. Apparently, being a poet and being about to die of consumption, Keats had this terrific insight into the human condition. I have just looked this bit up:

> Ay, in the very temple of delight
> Veiled Melancholy has her sovran shrine,
> Though seen of none save him whose strenuous tongue
> Can burst Joy's grape against his palate fine;
>
> From 'Ode to Melancholy'

I don't know about you, but I hardly laid a glove on that. But what it means, according to JAD, is that you can only experience great joy if you have also experienced great sorrow. Something like that. Or else the other way about.

I don't know if Keats was a fisherman; frankly, I doubt it. But he is right: the pleasure of fishing, the joy of catching fish, is inextricably entwined with the melancholy of not catching fish. Anyone who fly-fishes for trout in these islands, and anywhere else for that matter, will have experienced a fair amount of this brand of melancholy; anyone who fishes for salmon almost anywhere will have had nothing but melancholy for most of the time. It goes with the territory. It is what makes a trout a fine thing to catch and a salmon even finer.

I mention this because I have been looking back through past years of *Trout & Salmon* and I cannot help feeling that there has been a bias towards the rosy. Even if it starts out hard and dour, it All Comes Right in the End. Fish occur. Persistence is rewarded. Changing the fly or the depth or the presentation or the approach or the tippet size or the drift or the floatant or, Lord help us, the underwear rubbed on the line does the trick and a fish is caught. This is all very encouraging.

And sometimes it happens that way. But sometimes it doesn't and then you will rarely read about it because there is not much of a story in no fish. And not many photographs either. And who wants a fact file on a place where you caught nothing? And thus we end up with tales of great days and brilliant fishing.

It is time to redress the balance. Let us talk of one or two disasters.

Some years ago, in March, I got a phone call from a publisher. It was one of those things that Grow, Week By Week, Into An Encyclopaedia Of Angling Knowledge. I was to be a very small part of Week 49. The thing was, they needed to get something in March. I used to quite fancy March in those days – new season, raring to go, trout blissfully unaware of the angler – all that. Completely doused in flattery, I spoke vauntingly of the March Brown hatch on the Usk and of the certainty of my taking trout by the basketful. I arranged to meet the reporter and the photographer at the riverside the next week. Just as a precaution, I went down to the Usk a day early to get my hand in.

The Usk is magnificent at Talybont, a broad sweep over gravel and pebbles and everything a trout river should be. By midday the March Brown were bursting out of the surface and drifting downstream. Totally unmolested. Obviously the trout were preoccupied, gorging on the rising nymphs, so I concentrated on the wet fly just below the surface. Obviously the nymphs were so numerous they were being intercepted before they had risen to mid-water, so I put on a fast-sinking leader. Obviously the trout were taking the nymphs as they struggled from between the stones, so I put on a leaded nymph and cast upstream to bounce the thing along the bottom. Obviously by this time they were so gorged they were not feeding at all. I would get them tomorrow. Perhaps it was just as well I had not caught any. All the more for the next day when the reporter and the photographer would be there.

But I didn't catch a trout the next day. Or the day after, come to that. By this time we were not a jolly crew on the banks of the Usk. The reporter, it

turned out, had no deep interest in fishing: he had been working on a magazine about steam engines, his first love, when that closed and he was shifted
onto this angling encyclopaedia. He really preferred steam engines. You could
see his point. I had no interest in steam engines but, after three fishless days
on the river, steam engines held a certain attraction: they were there when
you wanted to find them.

The photographer was the gloomiest of all. He was, and is, a fine fisherman
but he did not touch a rod for those three days. Except for once. I had just
bought a new rod, a sweet 6-foot slip of a thing in split cane. In the cold
March waters of the Usk it would be as little use as a toothpick, but I had
taken it down to the water to show to the photographer, an old friend. As I
was wasting my time down in the river, he took off his cameras and picked
up the new rod, giving it an appreciative waggle. And at that moment a
bailiff strode from behind a tree and asked to see his licence. This was in the
days before the national licence, and the photographer, because he was not
fishing, had no licence for Wales. It was an unfair cop. And so there we sat:
the steam fanatic, the failed fisherman and the felon. And still we had no fish.

*   *   *

Three days is not the longest, and Wales is not the furthest, I have been for
no fish. Last September we went to Sweden. Sweden has the largest land-
locked salmon in the world: a race of magnificent beasts, some over 20
pounds, inhabits the waters of Lake Vänern, the vast inland sea in southern
Sweden. Here they can be taken by trolling, sometimes on the surface, usually deep below, using spinners and plugs and something called a fly. But, in
due season, these beasts ascend the rivers to spawn. In the normal way of
things it is illegal to catch one of these salmon in running water but there is
a place, one magical spot where it can be done. And that was where Paul and
I were heading.

The ferry from Harwich takes twenty-four hours to reach Göteborg. All the
seats for *Four Weddings and a Funeral* in the ship's cinema were sold out, so
we converted our cabin into a fly-tying factory and spent the time in delicious
anticipation tying tiny shrimp patterns on doubles and trebles. We had boxes
of them by the time we hit the road to Karlstad at the northern end of Lake
Vänern.

The Magical Spot lies 10 miles or so north of Karlstad at the village of
Forshaga. Here the splendid River Klarälven is interrupted by a weir where
the ascending salmon are stymied in their efforts to get upstream. The

Forshaga fishery is run by the local club, which has been given a special dispensation to catch the salmon 'for scientific purposes' – much as the Japanese catch whales. This was only granted because they have shown great restraint in fishing this magical spot where an unscrupulous man could clean up. Just how much restraint we learnt when we arrived at the river.

The prime time for taking a Klarälven salmon is June to August and from 20 May until the last day of September the fishing is fly-only. Fine, we had plenty of flies. Also the rule is single-fly-only. Oh dear. Well, we could remove some of the hooks from our collection. There is another restriction. You can only use floating lines and leaders. This was more of a problem. It had been raining on and off throughout the journey and now it was coming down harder. So was the river. The locals have adapted to these conditions by using huge salmon irons, the sort that our grandfathers would whorl around the heavens a century ago. Forshaga may be the last refuge of such beasts.

There are three beats at Forshaga. Two of these are only fishable from boats, the third can be waded – *must* be waded – when the water is below an orange line on the big rock. The level lapped just below the lower edge of the line: we were wading. It was all rather unnerving. You borrow a boat, an extremely elegant wooden boat, from the small bay below the car park. You row across the fierce main current to the middle of the river and step out of the boat. Here there is a ridge of gravel, just below the surface at this water height, marked by two piles of driftwood. This narrow ridge of gravel becomes steadily narrower and deeper as you wade upstream. When the water is almost, but not quite, deep enough to sweep you off your feet in the strong current, you begin to fish down the main current beside you. When you have edged a few paces downstream, another angler will leave his seat on the pile of driftwood, wade gingerly past you and wait until you are a cast-length downstream before he begins to fish. This precarious underwater ridge is known hereabouts as 'The Monkey Walk'. There is just enough room on the Monkey Walk for five anglers and that is the number of fishermen allowed on beat 2.

We did the Monkey Walk for two days. Paul had a fish on for a few seconds on the first day. I think I might have had a touch. That was about it. The water rose another inch. Towards the end of the second day the local expert was watching from the fishing hut by the car park. 'When the water is this height,' he said, in his humiliatingly perfect English, 'the fish lie out of the main current but you cannot cover them from the monkey walk . . .'

Listen: someday, somewhere, you are going to be fishing in some river and not catching very much. Someone is going to come up to you and tell you that you are not covering the fish. Then he is going to ask: 'Are you a good wader?'

I will give you a piece of advice. The answer to this question is 'No'. You may think you are a good wader, a corking little wader, nevertheless the correct answer to this question is still 'No'.

Looking at him, tall and reassuringly balding, one would say that Paul is as free from sin as anyone could be, but even Paul is prey to a certain amount of Pride. He is as good a wader as the next man. He clambered into the boat and rowed back to the shore. From the middle of the river I watched the two of them, Paul and the local expert, scramble down to the bank where a large rock jutted out into the current. Deep underwater a series of lesser rocks leads upstream. The trick was to edge into position by stepping from one of these unseen stepping stones to another. Even on the stepping stones Paul was lapping the top of his chesties. And I noticed that the L.E. was 2 inches taller than Paul.

It was undramatic when it happened. For those of us watching, anyway. A turn of the foot, an extra ounce of water pressure and the other foot floats off its precarious rock and 'gloop'. The L.E. put out a hand instinctively and there was another 'gloop' as the current swept both of them towards the rock and the main stream. They were lucky. The current took them round the rock and into the eddy behind, where they could scramble into shallower water and get a foothold. Spectators from the fishing hut were there to drag them out.

We were the victims of ignorance. A month or so earlier and these rare fish are a lot easier to come by, fresh from the lake: easier to get down to in the lower flows of summer. The visitor is never going to be embarrassed by catching too many fish at Forshaga: after catching one fish you must stop fishing for the day and you can catch only five fish in a season. But that wasn't going to be our problem at the end of September.

We had come for a land-locked salmon and, by jiminy, we were going to get one. The surest way to catch a Vänern salmon is to troll for one on the lake. It felt like an admission of defeat. In our case, it was. I expect the editor will delete this next bit: I rather like trolling. I used to be terribly disparaging about it. Before I did it, that is. Then I went out on Coniston with some traditional char fishermen. There is something arcane and Heath Robinson about char trolling tackle which appeals to me. There is nothing Heath Robinson about trolling on Vänern. The boat we clambered into the following day is owned by the regional tourist-fishing board. Its control panel would not be out of place on a medium-size aircraft: nor would its engines. It has a navigational system that can record the position of a fish strike to a metre or so and plot a course to take you back through the same spot in case the foolish fish wishes a second bite at the Rappala.

What it doesn't have are stabilisers. As we came out from the lee of the peninsula, heading for the deeper, salmony water, a roll of cloud the size and colour of Orson Welles came rumbling over the horizon. We heard later that the storm that had chased us back into the harbour had injured twenty-three passengers on a passenger ferry in the North Sea. That was of particular interest to us as we were catching the ferry the next day.

The seats for *Four Weddings and a Funeral* were sold out again on the way back.

*   *   *

Disastrous fishing trips do not need to take a long time. My shortest one ended exactly three minutes after reaching the river. We were in the camper van, father and I. We had just driven 225 miles to a wooden bridge over a small river in Cumbria. It had been a longish drive. First, we would have a cup of tea. I boiled the kettle, filled the teapot and then spilled the whole thing down father's leg. And then, after a painful interlude at a casualty department in Carlisle, we drove 225 miles back.

*   *   *

It still happens. The latest one happened five days ago. Do you remember that lovely spell we had, the third week in March – just before it snowed again on the Tuesday? It was all shirtsleeves and dark glasses that Thursday. The daffodils were sitting up on all the roundabouts in Wales with not a hint that they would all be flattened by frost within a week. We turned off the M4 at Junction 36 and headed down into Bridgend. I had remembered the River Ogmore from a visit twenty-five years before with my sister and her husband. Then we had crossed a bright stream on the way to Merthyrmawr and its staggering sand-dunes.

It is not enough just to fail to catch fish. Anyone can fail to catch fish, any time. Melancholia parks herself in her sovran shrine most stolidly just at the very moment when the fisherman had banked on bursting Joy's grape against his palate fine. I would have put money on bursting Joy's grape last Thursday. Everything was perfect: the first warm spell of the season. Little wind, just a hint of a breeze to stir the flies that appeared on the surface in the afternoon. They had even stocked 4,000 fish a few weeks before. Two weeks ago they were taking fish, a few on the fly, in a bitter northwesterly. But on that balmy Thursday there was not a fish, not a rise, not a touch for the half-dozen of us up and down the river. But even that was not the root of the melancholy that started this off: it was the state of the river I had remembered as a sparkling little stream.

The Ogmore River is a short Welsh stream with a run of sea trout that compares, square foot for square foot, with any water in Wales, and that is saying something. The water is not the problem. The problem is the rubbish. There is hardly a bramble, branch or boulder that does not have a skein of ragged plastic rattling in the breeze. This is not the odd fertiliser bag, although those are there as well, but bin liners, carrier bags and every form of plastic known to man. And not just plastic: there are rags and remnants and every sort of rubbish, a cornucopia of urban detritus. All inhuman life is there.

I apologise now to the Ogmore Angling Association for these remarks. They could have a lovely river. It has gentle runs and good holding pools and dramatic rocky bends and – I don't doubt – fine fishing in its season. It is better, they assure me, when there is leaf on the tree. Better still, I am sure, when the sea trout rattle over the shallows below the Sheep Dip Bridge. You hardly notice the rubbish then, they say. Especially if you are night fishing.

But this article began as an antidote to the rosy bias that is inherent, perhaps inevitable, in fishing tales. It would not be right to ignore the rubbish on the Ogmore and other rivers of South Wales. I don't know who is to blame and I don't know what can be done. But someone is and something should.

20 ℞

A Winter's Tale

I thought I had learned this particular lesson some time ago.

In 1969, two Saturdays before Christmas, I had come back from college for the holidays and had dipped in to the local rugby club in the evening for a drink with old mates. You must understand that they do something in rugby clubs with damp shirts and cut grass and stale beer and carbolic soap and mud and cigarette smoke and a faint hint of embrocation. It is heady, intoxicating stuff. It induces a flood of comradeship, a warming of the human spirit and a belief in the essential nobility of your fellow man. Particularly if, like me, you have not been on a rugby pitch with fifteen of your fellow men trying to knock six bells out of you. So there I was with the milk of human kindness and several pints of beer swishing through my veins when this bloke comes up and says, 'What about a game on Boxing Day?' The vision came to me so clearly. A crisp morning, stretching the limbs dulled by Christmas Day indoors. The cold air clearing the head, the springy turf beneath our feet. That sort of thing. 'OK, I'll have some of that,' I said and he wrote my name down.

I will not dwell on that Boxing Day rugby game. It was the last time I ever played rugby and, for what it is worth, I am now eligible to wear a Camelot Club tie reserved exclusively for those who have been sick on a rugby field.

At the back end of last year Paul phoned up, a week before Christmas. His son Stuart was back from his first term away at college and said he fancied going fishing with his father. Bonding, I suppose. So Paul was phoning to see if father and I fancied a go at the grayling on the day after Boxing Day.

Not many of you will have seen 5 o'clock on the twenty-seventh of December. You missed nothing. It was dark and very, very cold. Radio Five reported on the blizzards raging in Shetland and Scarborough was cut off for a time. Wales, they said, was covered in a 6-inch blanket of snow. Do not go to Wales, they said, unless your journey is really necessary. Sound advice. We were heading for Mid Wales, for Llangammarch Wells, west of Builth and the River Irfon. We decided to press on until we met the first drift.

I had last fished on the Irfon in July. You will remember last July. It was very hot and very bright and the fishing everywhere had been very hard for a month or so. And yet on the Irfon that day there were fish rising steadily. They were grayling, good grayling, up to 1½ pounds. I had my best catch of the season through that blazing afternoon, so I knew there were grayling there. That's a good start for a winter grayling trip.

We met by the side of the river, four Michelin men in jumpers and padded shirts and several socks. Father and I had come from the east; Paul and Stuart from the north. Not a flake of snow had fallen on either of us on the journey. I think it was too cold for snow that day in Wales. But not, I suppose, in the studios of Radio Five.

It was the first time I had been fishing that much below zero. Two weeks ago we had been worried that the river would be flooded; the Wye had been high and dirty and there had been snow and rain since then. But a long, low frost can have a magical effect on a river: by freezing the flood water in the fields and locking up the smaller rivulets in frozen waterfalls, the Irfon had dropped to just a little over its summer level and was running clear over the grey rock and gravels. We started above the lower railway bridge. Here in summer there had been fish lying the length of an inviting run below the tumbling falls. With another 6 inches of depth and a foot firmly on the throttle it still looked inviting.

We were going to experiment. Paul was going to trot for the fish with bait: I was going to fish with fly. These roles were ironic. Paul learnt to fish with a fly when he was eleven and spent much of the years at school trying to lead me towards the light and away from worms and such like. I came later to the fly, only when persuaded that it might be more effective than bait. I stayed because I discovered it was more fun and simpler. To this day I cannot comprehend why anyone should regard fly-fishing as purer, nobler or worthier. Paul got to trot that day because he was the only one who had taken care of his coarse tackle during the intervening quarter of a century.

Paul stood at the head of the run and swung the float out across the current. The worm was 5 feet below the float, a foot or so more than the depth of the run. As the float trotted away down the current the centre-pin reel turned freely, checked by a finger to hold back the float a little, allowing the worm to swing up a little, clearing the bottom and arriving hopefully in front of a grayling's nose. Not bad: the art of trotting for grayling in a single sentence. Just to clear up one point though, in case you were puzzled, it is the angler who is hopeful – not the worm.

Nothing happened. The float trotted to the end of the run and hung in the slackening current and didn't do anything. Paul tried again. That first run was to be the easiest of the day: now the rings and the line were wet, each cast and trot was apt to get a little jerky as the line froze in the rings. The trick is to keep things moving. Soon each ring is a ball of ice with a small hole in the middle where the monofil line threads through. And so, after a dozen or so trots, I tried with the fly.

Two days before, on Christmas Day, I had been given a little pot of bright-orange Float-Do wrapped in Christmas paper by my daughter. I had been dying to use it. You rub a ball the size of one of those cranberries that have been in every supermarket all Christmas. This is squeezed around the line at the depth you want the leaded fly to fish. As soon as it hits the water it cools hard and sticks firmly to the line. If you are embarrassed about such things you can call it an 'indicator'. It is a float. On more refined waters a dry fly on a dropper will do the same job if the nymph is not too heavy, but at 5 degrees below it will also freeze to a little ball of ice every cast or so. Once you have mastered the wide loopy cast that a ball of dough 5 feet up the leader calls for, it is easy enough to use. I worked my way up the run, casting upstream to let the nymph sink as quickly as possible. The ball of orange Float-Do bobbled past and I checked it to get the nymph to swim up in the prescribed manner. Let's face it, I was trotting a nymph. Where was the difference? Both rods had centre-pin reels and used floats to swim a hook bouncing the bottom down a run. If my fly didn't look as natural as the worm, it was not through lack of effort on my part. I had done my best to tie something that looked natural. But it still didn't work.

That is the trouble with fishing a place you know well. I *knew* where the grayling lay – in summer. They do not lie there in the depths of winter. First find your grayling. So we set off to explore. Paul and Stuart went off upstream, we went downstream.

A river in deep freeze is a miraculous place. Every grass stem and twig hanging low over the water had collected an icicle. Not one of those long stilettos that hang from the gutters in children's comics; the icicles on the Irfon were perfect teardrops of crystal clustered above the water like swollen grapes. The rivulets of water from the banks had piled cowpats of ice beneath them before they too had frozen in mid-dribble. The smooth rocks on the banks of the Irfon are slippery at any time of year but now even the miniature beaches of sand and mud between them had set like a polished screed. The place was lethal. The wading, contrariwise, without the algae of midsummer, was mercifully ice-free and the water must have been several degrees warmer than the rest of Wales. But still not that cosy.

Two figures were approaching through the trees from upstream. I assumed they were Paul and Stuart, but, incredibly, two other fishermen had thought this was just the sort of weather for a day on the river and had come over from Swansea. One of them wore the vest-badge of the Welsh Fly-fishing Team, so he probably knew whereof he spoke in these matters. He had had several grayling that morning, all from one spot above the upper railway bridge. I knew just where he meant.

A fast channel of water races down the far bank and runs into a grand pool above the buttresses of the bridge. In summer there are grayling in this pool and trout higher up in the run itself. The fast channel is bounded in the middle of the river by a gravel bank. On the our side of this gravel bank is a rocky basin, dead water in summer, still and clear with a colony of pond skaters on the surface and fry that flitter away as you wade past. The channel was rocketing beyond the gravel bank now and the extra 6 inches or so in the river was spilling water over the gravel and down between the rocks at its head, filling the basin to the brim and forming a deep, slow pool.

With my summer eye I still fancied that splendid channel and the pool below, but a blank morning had shown there was nothing in these swifter runs. The Welsh Fly-fisher had been using a team of three with a weighted point *fished deep and downstream*. The only spot hereabouts you could fish both deep and downstream was in this slow basin that I would have dismissed any other time. And so it was. I stood on the gravel bar and let the weighted nymph swim gently down the basin. First at the head where the water spilled in, then by the rivulets over the gravel and eventually in the deep sink under the near bank. And eventually that little orange ball dipped from sight and there was the slow draw of a cold, cold grayling on the other end.

Paul, meanwhile, had come to the same conclusions by himself. Below the bridge is a deep and slow pool fringed with trees, undercut on our bank. In the summer you can look down into the water between the trees and see a shoal of chub lazily turning in the dappled shade, and you pass on to livelier stuff upstream. Paul had been feeling his way down this slower reach, trotting a long line to explore the deeper holes beneath the tree roots under our bank. He had found the grayling halfway down the run and by the time I called to him from above the bridge he had taken three from that same spot. He had also run out of worms.

Consider the maggot. It has a very bad press. Amongst game fishermen, that is: amongst coarse fishermen it is still far and away the most popular bait. This is unlikely to be just a matter of sentiment. The maggot must have something going for it. It does: it works. British game fishermen have always had an endearingly ambivalent approach to catching fish. They are nervous about anything that might work too well. Several flies have been banned because they were thought to be too effective. Various baits are banned on certain salmon waters for the same reason. It is as though we know we are weak and greedy creatures whose base bloodlust would lead us to wholesale slaughter without outside restraint. Perhaps it might. There is something to be said for playing left-handed to give the children a chance. And fish are not very bright. What I do find odd is our elevation of these practical measures of self-restraint into the realms of morality and ethics.

I know I am right about this because, in his time, Paul has been a school prefect, a member of the Scripture Union, something-or-other in the Parochial Church Council, a barrister and a stipendiary magistrate. He is practically a saint. And as he walked towards me that afternoon Paul was pulling a tub of maggots from his fishing bag. And with those maggots we caught another five grayling from the little basin above the bridge. We also caught a very funny look from the Welsh International Fly-fisher. The section of river above the first bridge is normally fly-only but we had been given permission to trot bait by the owner of the water at the Cammarch Arms Hotel.

We had really got the hang of the thing by now. The short day was dimming as we walked downstream. I had often walked straight past a big slow bend some way below the first bridge. Now we headed for it with anticipation. The fishing in the last pool had come alive when a few maggots had been trickled into the current to be swept down to the cold fish lying in the bottom of the basin. Groundbait. But if groundbait works for the trotted maggot it should also work for the artificial nymph: the grayling doesn't know it is artificial and what is Sawyer's Killer Bug if it is not an imitation maggot? Having transgressed every code of civilised conduct, it seemed worth a go.

We started as we had begun that day. I stood beside the deep bend and cast up and across, allowing the nymph to sink deep. Nothing happened. I am not saying it wouldn't have if I had persisted. But for several casts nothing happened. Then Paul, standing in midstream above the bend, trickled a few maggots into the current and set his float trotting downstream. It is not a delicate thing, Paul's grayling float. You know when something is interested. Within a few trots things were beginning to happen. The float disappeared near the end of the run and a good grayling was on. The old split-cane roach rod dipped as the fish struggled deep and was pulled upstream. As Paul was unhooking that first fish I cast the nymph along the same course. The orange ball bobbed down the current and past me. I thought it had dipped under with the pull of the current downstream but as I broke the grip of the iced rings and drew in the line I could feel the solid resistance of a fish.

I lost that fish. Perhaps in the cold I had mistaken its size: a frozen fish does not fight as hard as it might earlier in the year. Perhaps I had struck too soon. After a brief fight it came off. Meanwhile, Paul was back in business and there was no mistake with his second fish. Or his third. Whilst he was unhooking I tried the nymph again. Again it was taken and again I lost the fish after a brief struggle. They were keen enough now. Paul had handed the rod to Stuart. The fish were moving up towards them, the better to investigate the source of these goodies. This time the float dipped within a few yards of the cast. It was almost dark as the fourth grayling came to the net. I had climbed out of the water as Stuart sent the float for a final trot. It had barely plunked into the water when it disappeared. This was the best fish of that short day. Just over 1½ pounds.

So what of all this maggot business? None of us had touched a single trout or salmon parr. There was sport to be had on the fly, to be sure, but in the frozen depths of winter the bait was more effective. Particularly with a trickle of maggot as groundbait. And that little trickle of groundbait had also improved the interest in the fly – and presumably would have done so even if had we been fishing only with flies on the end of the line.

Is that still fly-fishing? Is it legal?

I don't know.

21 &

A Lot of Learning is a Dangerous Thing

Fishermen are always nodding sagely and admitting – with candid modesty – that they are still learning something new every time they go fishing. Well, pish and tush! I know more than is good for me about fishing already; I just wish I could unlearn some of it.

I have a passion for prawning. I do not mean catching salmon on a prawn bait. I mean catching prawns. Prawning has everything: it has the hunt, the capture, the count and a large dish of fresh-cooked prawns into the bargain. A splendid little field sport. Received wisdom has it that prawning is best during the biggest spring tides of summer, around days of the full moon and new moon. And so each year we scour the tide tables for a part of Devon I have no intention of naming, looking for the lowest tides and the best possible prawning days. This year we completely mistimed the holiday: we were in Devon for a poorish neap tide but we were on holiday and so went down to the rocks with the nets anyway. Guess what: we caught more prawns than I have ever seen, so many that we stopped well before low tide with more prawns than I ever wish to peel again. Which makes me wonder just what prawning I have missed all these years by only waiting for the 'best' tides.

And so it is with fly-fishing. Once I just went fishing whenever I could. Then gradually I learnt about hatches and temperatures and percentages-of-dissolved-oxygen and so forth, and, lo! I became more discerning. Gradually I began to settle on the best time to visit this stretch of river or that sort of lake: the biggest run of salmon here, the most productive hatch of fly there. In short, the 'best' time to fish. And now I am wondering if learning all this might not be a big mistake.

It wasn't just the prawns that got me wondering. After Devon we had a week in Perthshire. The River Lyon is a stunning tributary of the Tay. I was not there to fish, you understand: it was a family holiday. But still, there was no harm in calling at the teashop at Bridge of Balgie (all there is at Bridge of Balgie) where one can buy a ticket to fish for trout. They have a new system this year. The ticket costs £5 but £2 is refunded when you hand in your fishing return with the number of fish caught. For the first time they have a record of what is caught and when. I would have wagered quite a sum on the best months being May and June, the worst being August (which is why I had not come to fish). And perhaps sometimes it is thus. But the returns show that the most and the biggest trout were caught in early August. Hmmm.

July can be a difficult time on a trout stream. Last year July was hot and dry; I had spent a week fishing several fine rivers to little or no purpose and frankly I had had enough. July can be like that. Then, for some reason, I needed to get out of the house and so father and I drove to Wales for the day. It was hot and dry in Builth Wells and the River Irfon at Llangammarch Wells was as shrunken and warm and hopeless as everywhere else. We walked down to the river: we had nothing else to do. Amazingly, the odd fish was rising and so we fetched our rods from the car. We each caught a grayling and thought ourselves blessed. Then we each caught another. Then another and another and so it went on: large grayling were fighting for the privilege of engulfing our flies. Trout as well. We finished up having the best day's river fishing in years. I have no idea why.

One more scary example: in France I have been assured by several first-class fishermen that trout fishing, on rivers miles from the sea, is pointless around the time of greatest lunar influence, the days around the full moon and the new moon. Everyone knows that, they say. The trout, apparently, know it too and do not rise. Lunar tables of these unpropitious days are published for the benefit of anglers and many French fly-fishers simply do not bother to fish around those days each month because it just isn't worth it. This is, of course, completely loopy.

It isn't remotely similar to my reluctance to fish the River Lyon in August, the River Irfon in a hot and dry July or to go prawning on a neap tide in Devon. Or is it?

I don't know. I just suspect that if I could unlearn some of the guff I have acquired about best times and favourable conditions, I might fish more and expect less.

Rocky Mountain Breakdown

You know the bit where the bloke has just said something like, 'But you are a scientist, Dr Maynard. Surely you don't believe in giant mutant ants?' (Sometimes it is giant dinosaurs awakened by nuclear testing. Or sea monsters.) Anyway, soon after the poor sceptical dupe has delivered this line, he goes to put out the empty milk bottles or to find the cat that has been missing all night – as if that weren't suspicious enough. There he is with his back to the camera as *it* stalks him through the bushes. It moves in: we are right up close. He turns round and looks up at something the size of Durham Cathedral. He screams as the camera moves down onto an upturned face registering terror. All that is left for Dr Maynard to find next morning is a few mangled scraps and a shoe.

What I could never believe was that something the size of a largish pantechnicon can creep up to within mangling distance unseen and unsuspected. You would think a man looking for a cat might spot a lizard the size of a barn in his vicinity.

Well, the Rocky Mountains are a bit like that. They are big, but you just don't see them coming.

We were driving the fabled Alaska Highway. This is a staggering piece of roadway. It runs for 1,645 miles from the prairies to the east of the Rockies, through the mountains themselves, north and west and on into the Yukon and Alaska beyond; a hairline of gravel and tarmac through a vast and inaccessible mountain wilderness. The whole thing was built in 1942. It took nine months. NINE MONTHS: slightly less than it has taken to widen 7 miles of the M25 between Junctions 15 and 16: slightly longer than it took to put in a roundabout in Banbury.

The Alaska Highway plays footsie with the Rockies for the first 300 miles from Dawson Creek: at Fort Nelson it swings west into the mountains themselves. We just didn't see them coming. They materialised around us, higher and rockier as we drove on between the forest walls. We crossed rivers. Clear water with a touch of milkiness as tiny particles of eroded quartz scattered the sunlight: the rivers we were crossing come barrelling down between the broad beds of shingle spread by the melting snows of June. The rivers grew steeper and the trees thinned as we climbed up towards Summit Lake. A small herd of mountain caribou melted across the road as we approached. Further on, a family of stone sheep picked their way out of the forest shadows. And there was Muncho Lake.

*   *   *

The next morning: a small float plane was creaming across the lake at full throttle. Urs, the pilot, tweaks the stick a fraction: the left wing lifts and the left float is released from the suction of the water: then the right, like a man pulling his wellingtons from the mud. The plane is climbing out of the amphitheatre of mountains around Muncho. The waves of the Rockies roll on towards the horizon in all directions. A collapsible boat is strapped to the struts of the float: we will be fishing wherever the cloud cover allows the Beaver to thread between the peaks and drop onto some hidden lake. A circuit of the water, looking for reefs, inlets and outfalls, and then we drop down to furrow the surface.

*   *   *

We found Obo Lake on a windless morning when the snow-capped mountains were perfectly mirrored in its surface. The crystal-clear waters of the lake feed a young river that roars down a boulder-strewn channel and into a deep run. This is the exhilarating habitat of the wild rainbow trout of the Rockies.

There were no obvious rises but I ran a buoyant dry fly down the run, hoping to pull a fish up to the surface. No good. I did this for a bit and then changed to a wet fly, a Butcher with a bit of flash, mending the line in the best wet-fly fashion to swim the fly slowly across the current. Something or other hit the fly but failed to hang on.

Now, rainbow trout are notoriously unsubtle. This was a bit of luck, for if there is one quality my flies excel in it is being unsubtle. And these trout had never seen a fisherman, let alone a fly. I rummaged in my bag for something unsubtle. It was an unchristened fly that I had tied for lake trout. I will give you the dressing in case you ever happen to be in these parts. Use a large hook. Those hooks that butchers use to hang legs of lamb in the window are too large – but only just. Body: the Early Learning Centre sells packets of coloured tinsel pipe cleaners for some good educational reason. Tie one in at the eye, wind it down the body and back. That's about it. I had given mine a hot orange hackle and a black wing, but I cannot believe that a trout would notice these beside the dazzling glitz of the body. You need sunglasses to use this fly.

I cast it into the slower water beyond the fast run and let the current whip it around. Three large shadows shot out of the blue depths: they were positively fighting over the thing. One fish won, the surface exploded, shattered in the sunlight. A wild rainbow in a fast mountain river is an unforgettable experience. Time and again they leap or tail-walk across the surface before they can be fought to the net.

The wild rainbows of these unfished waters are naive: they are not stupid. They learn fast. The first trot down the pool brought half a dozen fish up to 20 inches for that monstrous fly: a second run took just one more. From then on it was ignored. A change of fly and they would hit again.

Martin was experimenting with weight, trundling a leaded nymph along the bottom of the run. The nymph stopped and he struck into a fish, not a rainbow this time but a Rocky Mountain Whitefish, a silvery member of the trout family peculiar to these mountains. They are not the only fish in these waters. Another salmonid, the gaudy Dolly Varden, a large and predatory char, haunts the deeper pools where they hunt the big rainbows, but that morning we had neither the time nor the tackle.

And so we worked our way downstream, each bend opening up another virgin run, another pristine pool, on and on through the limitless forest and mountains before we turned, late in the afternoon, and fished our way back to Obo Lake and the float plane back to the lodge.

Let's get all this flying-off-to-some-lake-to-fish stuff into proportion. I have a map of that small section of the northern Rockies around Muncho Lake in front of me. It covers an area slightly bigger than England. It has one surfaced road on it: the Alaska Highway. There is another gravel road: the Liard Highway. This makes one road junction. The only town, Fort Nelson, has a population of 3,729 (for some reason, places in Canada seem to tell you the number of people who live there at every opportunity). Imagine the Lake District with mountains several times higher stretching from the Firth of Forth to the Channel with the B4100 running through it, another very long farm drive, and one large village somewhere near Stonehenge. And nothing else but scenery. Lots and lots of scenery. And rivers and lakes.

The only way to get to these rivers and lakes is to fly. There are just two floatplanes in the area around Muncho: both belong to the Highland Glen

Lodge. One can carry three passengers, the other can carry five with their fishing tackle. So the rivers hereabouts are not overfished.

*   *   *

Another day, another lake. Smoke was rising from the forest as the Beaver circled and dropped down onto South Gataga lake, the first sign of humanity in the 70 miles of mountains from Muncho Lake. A few yards from the shore a couple of freshly shaved pine trunks stood amidst a pile of shavings and the skeleton of a log cabin. Where the only way in is a tiny floatplane, everything must be built from the forest. And everything is used: further back in the forest the small tops of the logs had been constructed into an exquisite gem of forest chic – a log cabin loo. In ten minutes the collapsible boat was more or less shipshape and we were chugging off around a rocky point.

The streams that drain the melting snows from the frost-shattered heights dump the eroded gravels into the deep lakes, building small deltas that plunge down into the glacial depths a few feet from the shoreline. In summer these torrents shrink to icy trickles. Fish cruise the steep drop-offs, feeding on the larvae and pupae carried down the streams. That was the theory. We pulled the boat onto the gravel shore and put up our fly rods. At first there was nothing. Then, a little way from shore, at the furthest influence of the tiny stream, the surface buckled a bit. I always call it 'twiddling' but I don't suppose this will convey much. It is just subsurface and looks like a minnow feeding at the surface of a canal. I don't suppose that conveys much either. At all events, something was doing it out there and more were joining it, moving up current towards the shore as competition grew. An occasional fish broke the surface. We put on small sedges and stood in the shallows beside the current, trotting the small flies out into the lake. The fly disappeared in a small twiddle. It was not a minnow. It was an exquisite Arctic grayling of 18 inches. We caught fifteen more in the next two hours: that first one was the smallest.

They were not all at the surface; in fact, the rises there came in sporadic bursts. The motherlode was down deep. During a lull, Martin, who likes something with a bit of lead in it, put on a Montana, a great beast of a no. 10. It sank down into the drop-off until it must have been resting on the steep grey shingle. He was pulling it back up the slope when something gently inhaled it in and attempted to take it elsewhere. And that is just how you do it.

After a shore lunch of grayling deep-fried over an open fire we headed up the lake to the shallow outflow which connects it to another lake a hundred yards beyond. We were after the lake trout, the huge predatory char which

prey on the grayling. We cut the outboard to drift through the shallow channel between the reed beds. As the lake opened up there was a movement
behind the fringe of reeds and a huge head appeared, trailing dripping weed.
We had disturbed a moose browsing in the shallow weedbed. The moose
stared at us, ears swivelling. We stared at the moose. A gentle breeze was carrying us out of the channel. The moose stared on – and then her jaw began
to work on the trailing weed as we drifted by just yards away. We were of no
consequence: she dipped her head back beneath the water for another mouth-
ful. We reached carefully for cameras: the lake trout were forgotten in this
magical encounter. We paddled cautiously past, freezing each time she raised
her head to watch us. And so it went on. After half an hour we were having
to whistle to get her to raise her head for the photographs. Just how close we
could have got I don't know: an adult moose at 30 yards is plenty big enough.

After an hour we left her browsing contentedly in her untrammelled wilderness. Reluctantly we returned to the floatplane.

*   *   *

Another day, another lake. At the far end of Doll Lake the water shallows and
narrows, imperceptibly accelerating between steep banks of lodgepole pine
into a swift outflow. Arctic grayling were rising steadily along the length of
this smooth glide and for a while we could take a fish every other cast. Small
fish, less than a pound, but there were larger shapes wafting across the
bottom of that clear stream.

I tried a larger dry fly, a size 12 Irresistible with a body of bulky deer hair,
too big for the smaller fish although some of them refused to believe it. And
still the large fish stayed put. Until a longer cast, drifting downstream below
me, began to drag, skittering round across the surface, creating a broad wake.
A large shape detached itself from the bottom, rose and slashed at the fly and
the little rod buckled into a better grayling. There is much satisfaction in solv-
ing such a puzzle. I sent the fly skidding across another deep run and another
large fish shot up to launch itself at the thing. And then another. I was enjoy-
ing this: I was trying a smug sort of smile on for size. It fitted rather well. And
then, in the stillness of the northern woods, there was a noise. It was the
noise of something large pushing through the thick forest close behind me.
Martin, fishing on the far side of the river, said it sounded like a moose. Quite
possibly, from the far side of the river, it did. From my side of the water it
sounded like a bear. I did not stay in that spot long enough to find out: for all
I knew it could have been a giant mutant ant.

A River Runs Through It

It is not always obvious when a story starts.

On a day in 1936 two men came to the soft country of the Usk valley to fish the river around the town of Crickhowell. They had planned to get a room in the Bear in the middle of the town, but the pub was full that night. The landlord had heard of a place a little further up the valley, a country house that was to be opened as a hotel. The two men motored on towards Brecon and took a small lane to the left, which wound up the steep shoulder of the hill. They found themselves looking at a beautiful – if bizarre – Italian villa, complete with campaniles, perched above the wooded gorge of the Usk. There was a party going on. By chance they had arrived on the opening day of the hotel. Dennis Brabner became the first paying guest of Gliffaes Hotel.

In that same year, a little downstream, in the town of Usk, a man went into a barber's to have his hair cut. The man was a salesman, travelling for a Redditch tackle firm. In the back of the shop he noticed the table where the barber tied fishing flies between serving customers. Ted Rudge was a good salesman. He persuaded the barber, Harry Powell, to take a selection of fishing tackle to display and sell from a corner of his barber's shop. A second institution of the Usk and its fishing had been born.

The following year, the local newspaper in Usk was reporting the triumph of another local man who had just won the British Amateur Salmon Casting Championships. The newspaper reporter, Mr Salter, had other reasons for remembering this particular fisherman: many years before, this same Lionel Sweet had come courting his young daughter, Molly. Mr Salter did not approve of fishermen. One way and another, Mr Salter was doomed to disappointment with fishermen. The tackle shop in the back of Harry Powell's barber's shop was doing well but Harry was getting on a bit. After another three years he decided to give up the barbering business and concentrate on the flies and fishing tackle in the little shop he had bought round the corner in Porthycarne Street. Hair-dos will be a recurring theme in this story: Molly Salter, the reporter's daughter, was having her hair done in another emporium when she heard that Mr Powell was looking for an assistant to tie flies and help in the new shop. She went along to try her hand at fly-tying and stayed. Molly's father, of course, did not approve of this either.

Elsewhere a world war had broken out. Remember the first guest at the Gliffaes? After his fishing break on the river Usk, Dennis Brabner had returned home to Cheshire to celebrate the wedding of his brother, Sam. All the Brabner boys were sportsmen but Sam was like something out of a boys' adventure comic, playing county cricket for Cheshire and rugby for the Barbarians. At the outbreak of war Sam and Jane Brabner had been married for just three years: their son, Nick, was a year old when Sam joined the Royal Horse Artillery and he was not much older when his father went off to war in the Middle East – which is where we shall leave him for the time being, many miles from the nearest trout stream, uncomfortably immured in the siege of Tobruk.

Back in Usk, Harry Powell died in 1944, leaving the tackle shop to Molly Salter. It had been something of a shock to Lionel Sweet when he had first walked into the little shop in Porthycarne Street to find the girl he had courted all those years before had become a renowned fly-dresser. Of course, this is not an unpleasant shock for a fisherman – particularly in the war years when luxuries such as fly-hooks are hard to find. Now she was also the owner of a tackle shop. Old Harry Powell had grown very fond of Molly in the years they had been tying flies on the table in the back of the shop. In his last illness he had asked his friend Lionel to look after Molly when he was gone. And Lionel did. In 1946 Lionel Sweet, champion fly-caster, and Molly Salter, fly-dresser and tackle dealer, were married. Mr Salter approved of this even less.

And in the same year, in Jubilee Villas in Usk, Mrs Lewis gave birth to a daughter, Jean – whom we will not meet again for another seventeen years.

*   *   *

Sam Brabner had stayed in the Middle East at the end of the war. He had joined the Palestine police for the tortured and bloody years that led up to the birth of Israel in May 1948, when the British Mandate expired and Sam found himself back in Britain and out of a job. It is the dream of every returning British serviceman, after every war, weary of being misunderstood in unpleasant climates and troublesome languages, to run a cosy pub in the heart of the country. So anyone coming back home three years after a largish world war would find cosy country pubs pretty thin on the ground. They did not find the

cosy country pub they were looking for; what they found was Gliffaes, the
hotel where Sam's brother had stayed and fished in those golden days before
the war.

What Sam Brabner found was a river that rushed and tumbled through the
steep wooded gorge, where the great March Brown hatches of the Usk burst
from the riffles after a spring frost and where the salmon and trout had
thrived while the world was busy doing other things.

What Jane Brabner found was a house that had suffered from the wartime
years of scarcity, a house that was 'too big and too cold'. A barn of twelve
bedrooms and two bathrooms each with a vast bathtub. And a lot of
linoleum. There was no real contest. They bought Gliffaes.

Starting in the hotel business is a bit like getting married: lots of people try
it and a few succeed and the first dozen years are the worst. For the Brabners
at Gliffaes these first dozen years were the 1950s, when the Brits, never the
jolliest race of lotus-eaters at the best of times, were at their unjolliest, living
in the grey landscape of post-war rationing, surrounded by the steaming
terry-towelling of a baby boom with no disposable nappies and only the
most rudimentary washing machines. It doesn't bear thinking about. Which
is, I suppose, what fishing hotels are for. We will leave Sam and Jane to build
up the business while the country recovers and the line of pillboxes, constructed along the length of the Usk to thwart a Nazi war machine bent on
invading Brecon, softens and settles back into the lush riverside like an old
fisherman sinking into a fireside chair.

By 1963 Harry Powell's old barber's shop in Bridge Street had been closed
for a quarter of a century. For many years now it had been Midgeleys, a
sweetshop and tobacconist around the corner from the tackle shop where
Molly Sweet tied her flies. By the sort of coincidence with which my story
abounds, it was in this tobacconist, while buying some cigarettes, that Molly
mentioned to Nellie Watkins, a conductress on the local bus, that she was
looking for someone to tie flies and help in the shop. Nellie's brother had a
daughter who was about to leave school. Jean Lewis was determined to be a
hairdresser when she left school, but she went along to see Molly for a
Saturday job tying flies in the tackle shop. That Saturday morning, in the
jumble of the back room, she was given her first grown-up cup of coffee and
Molly showed Jean how to tie her first trout fly. It was a March Brown. And
another era of fishing on the Usk had begun.

When Jean Lewis left school she went to work full-time in the shop with
Molly and Lionel Sweet. She even got to do some hairdressing. One of fly-
fishing's great all-purpose trout flies, the Dogsbody, had been created forty

years before by Harry Powell using camel-coloured hair from a customer's dog. The shop was famous for these flies and Jean had to find and clip suitable donors to keep up with the demand. And not just dog hairdressing: when Dick Walker first created the Sweeney Todd, a local fisherman came into the shop to order some for a trip to Blagdon. Molly didn't have any black squirrel tail for the wing: the first batch of Sweeney Todds were tied with wings of Jean Lewis's jet-black hair.

The story of the Usk is graced by some remarkable women and another is about to enter, stage right (which is from the south, looking downstream). Peta Wilkie was a young Irishwoman from the banks of the River Bandon in County Cork. She was returning home from Sherborne School in Dorset, where she had been the games mistress for several years. She broke the journey home along the A40 at Gliffaes and there she met Sam's son, Nick. The Brabners, you may recall, were a pretty sporty family and sporty families can be a bit daunting for chaps like me, but girls who have played international lacrosse for Ireland do not daunt easily. Nick and Peta were married the next year. By 1972 they, and their young family, had joined Sam and Jane at Gliffaes, helping to run an expanding hotel.

By this time Gliffaes had established its reputation as a great traditional sporting hotel and Lionel Sweet, the Usk builder and casting champion, was a frequent visitor to the hotel waters. By 1972 Lionel was getting on a bit – it was thirty-five years since his first British Casting Championship – but he was still a familiar and popular figure at the game fairs with his casting clinics and demonstrations. When the Gliffaes hotel decided to enter a team in the BFSS's field-sports triathlon, Lionel undertook to teach Peta to cast a fly. He must have taught her pretty well: in the years to come the Gliffaes team and Peta Brabner's fly-casting would win the national event.

Molly Sweet, Lionel's childhood girlfriend and wife, had been tying the flies of the Usk for thirty-five years. She died in the second week of the 1974 salmon season.

Lionel Sweet was still catching salmon in the Usk. He had a quiet custom which will come as no surprise to anyone who knew the man. Each season he would take his first Usk salmon round to the house of someone in the town who was ill and would benefit from a fish fresh from the sea. In 1975 the vicar's wife, Pamela Davies, was recovering from an operation and Lionel's salmon was duly delivered to her bedside. In gratitude she agreed to come along to the shop when she was fully recovered and try her hand at fly-dressing. She did just that. And twenty-three years later she is still there. In my village vicars seem to come and go. They move on to wherever vicars move on to and another one arrives. They don't do that in Usk. If the vicar goes in Usk, the supply of flies would drop by half: the fishing fraternity wouldn't stand for that. So the vicar has to stay.

Pamela Davies was one of the last to receive a salmon on Lionel Sweet's unique prescription. This remarkable fisherman died during the low water of summer in 1978. Echoing the wisdom of Harry Powell before him, he left the tackle business in Porthycarne Street to Jean Williams, the woman who had come to tie up a few flies on a Saturday and who had shared the fly-dressing table in the back room for fifteen years.

*   *   *

It is twenty years on. The end of September last year. The Usk is not famous for its back-end fishing. It is usually the first flurries of the March Brown that bring me here in the frosty days of spring. I rarely get to see the splendour of the trees in full leaf with some just starting to turn. Little has changed since I first came here. The intimate walk down to the river along the tight paths and walls of the garden set out by Jane Brabner's father after the war and the stone steps down through the trees to the fishing hut above the salmon pool. My favourite stretch lies upstream where the river makes a great bend around the meadow and rattles down in a broad riffle. There are smooth runs here and there amongst the stones and trout can lie anywhere. And they do. In the short sharp days of spring the trout rise for an hour or so around midday, later if there has been any sort of frost. It is over by 5 o'clock and the fisherman can pack up with a clear conscience and climb back up through the trees to the hotel with its splendid creeper-clad portico. At the far end of the lounge a table is loaded with a legendary Gliffaes tea: a spread of sandwiches, scones and cream and cakes and a huge teapot. It is tea as tea was understood when Sam and Jane Brabner first came to Gliffaes. It is tea as it ever shall be. This February, fifty years on, their granddaughter, Susie, returned, with husband James and their two girls, to help Nick and Peta in the running of Gliffaes.

The little corner shop in Porthycarne Street, too, is miraculously unchanged. The sign beside the door is the one painted by Lionel Sweet a quarter of a century ago. By the look of it the lightbulb over the counter dates from around the same period. Wonderful fading photos of ancient fishers and fishing feats hang higgledy-piggledy between the crowded shelves. You will not find a fax or e-mail in Sweets – or even a push-button phone, come to that. But you will find the welcome the same as ever, with a cup of tea if you look like you need it and the very best of fishing advice and news of the Usk if you want it. Fishermen still bring their catch to be weighed in the back kitchen and keep their salmon cool in the old bath on a hot day. And the Usk flies are still tied by Mrs Davies, the vicar's wife, and by Jean Williams. And next spring, like last spring, Jean will give me a ring to say that the shad are running. And I will go down to Usk and buy a ticket and, like as not, I will not catch a thing. The same as last season. Then I came to fish the Usk with Douglas. On the drive down I told him some of this story of the river, the hotel and the shop. Thirty-five years ago, it turns out, his wife Anne was taught lacrosse at school by Miss Wilkie. And so it goes on.

It is not always obvious where a story ends.

A Better Mousetrap

The case for the defence, m'lud, is quite simple: *it seemed like a good idea at the time.*

Twenty years ago I came within a toucher of angling immortality with the invention of the Poach-resistant, Rising-enhanced Trout Stocking System. It was a brilliantly simple concept, destined, you would have thought, to bring its young creator the grateful thanks of the nation's fishermen and more folding money than you could shake a stick at.

The nub of the thing was a small device that produced a mild but unpleasant electric shock for anything swimming in the vicinity. The device was connected by a thin line to a cunningly fashioned imitation earthworm. A passing trout sees the earthworm and thinks, 'That'll do me.' It grabs the earthworm, pulls the line and triggers the electric shock. Now, a trout is not bright. It does not put two and two together. It does not need to: after a tug or so at the worm, a dose or so of volts, the trout will start to avoid worms. Worms will be off the menu.

The scheme was so tasty you could pour chocolate over it and call it a profiterole. Half a dozen of these things in a tank of young fish and you would produce a generation of trout that would not look at a worm. Poaching with a lobworm on a night line would be a thing of the past. If the fashion amongst the local ne'er-do-wells favoured cheese then it would be just as simple to produce cheese-protected trout from the hatchery. What thoughtful fishery owner would buy ordinary trout when he could get bait-protected fish? Every hatchery that wanted to stay in business would have to get tooled up with the system. And every fishery would want to have its own devices sown about the waters to remind the trout that worms and such like are not nice. But that is not all: by placing the electrified baits on the bottom of the pond or lake the trout would show a marked preference for food near the surface: they were being trained to rise freely.

The Poach-Resistant, Rising-Enhanced Trout Stocking System was ahead of its time. I think that must have been the problem.

My next assault on the bastions of the tackle trade was a more modest affair. I had, by this time, become obsessed with travelling light. I would get rid of any tackle I could possibly do without. A rod was seen as something of a necessary evil: if I could have lobbed the fly at the fish I would have done so. The other day I read an account of a two-man expedition by bicycle from Bangladesh to Tibet. The riders were so obsessed with cutting down weight that they cut off all straps beyond the buckle and drilled holes along the handle of the plastic spoon they carried. I was a bit like that.

I turned my attention to the spool of tippet nylon I carried. Was it really necessary? I might change the 3 feet of tippet four or five times a day and yet I was lugging around this great 50-metre spool of the stuff. I tried using a dinky little 10-metre spool: the nylon came off coiled like a bedspring and I had to carry another gizmo to straighten it out again. My Intra-rod Tippet Tampon solved these problems at a stroke. The ITT consisted of a small cylindrical foam-rubber plug, a little larger in diameter than the thin end of the butt section of a two-piece rod. The plug had several small slits down its length. The fisherman cuts a tippet-length of nylon from his spool and slips one end into a slit in the plug. He does the same to each slit. Now he pulls the stopper from the end of his reel fitting and feeds the ITT with its trailing tippets down the shaft of the rod. It jams after a bit. The fisherman now takes the SCH (Straightened Coat Hanger – supplied with the ITT) and pushes the tampon down the rod until just the ends of the tippets dangle from the reel fitting. He replaces the stopper, trapping the tippet ends, *et voila*! The tippets are stored without spools or coils. When he needs a new tippet, the fisherman removes the stopper and tugs a length of nylon from its slot in the plug.

An excellent system with but a single drawback: no one in their right mind could be bothered to do all this.

*   *   *

Fly-fishing is a real bugger for us entrepreneurs. It needs so little stuff. A rod, a line with something to hold it on one end and a fly on the other. That's about it.

There are two possible approaches. The first is to point out to the fisherman that he needs a lot of other stuff. The possibilities are limitless for the really imaginative entrepreneur – with the added bonus that the fisherman can then be sold something to carry all the stuff. As in so many things, the Americans have shown us what can be done.

Take, for example, the field of fisherman's hand-care – not the most fertile furrow to plough, you might think. You would be quite wrong. 'If you are looking for an alternative to lotions to protect your hands, UV SUN CHECKERS gloves are the answer. The flesh-tone nylon/Lycra blend construction give you the feel of a second skin' – and makes you look like a bit of a girl. Far and away more manly is the BUG CATCHER'S MITT ($7.50) 'Perfect for scooping dry flies and emergers from the water's surface.' This is a bag to put your hand in. 'Elastic wristband and stitched finger slots make it easy to use.' Brilliant. Who would have thought that the best way to pick up something would be to put your hand in a bag? Or your thumb, come to that. The QUICK RELEASE THUMB ($17.50) 'A handy protective leather thumb cover that . . . eliminates the lacerations usually inflicted by those fish who have fine sharp teeth lining their jaws . . . such as trout.' Well, no one likes getting lacerated, do they? If you are haunted by this inevitable mutilation involved in handling trout, you could go for the BOGA-GRIP ($99.95). I have no idea how this works but I have seen a photograph of the thing. It has articulated steel pinchers to grip fish of up to 30 pounds. It is 'designed to promote "Catch and Release" fishing' because it is 'less likely to injure fish'. Less likely than what? A gaff?

If you do not put your hands in the water, of course, you will not know how cold it is. So you need a thermometer. I have no idea why you need a thermometer. You just do. But I do know why you need this particular thermometer: the MINI-THERM ($27.95) has a long lead which 'lets you drop the probe into the water while standing'. It is not clear whether standing is obligatory in taking the water temperature, but it is certainly an option should the need arise. I think that is important.

I have one more. It is not a piece of tackle but I spotted it in an American tackle catalogue and it is one of my favourites. They are TROUT EAR SPEARS ($15.00). 'The 3-D fish really looks as though it is swimming through the ear.'

*   *   *

Well, that was heaps of fun, wasn't it? Laughing at other people's fishing tackle has a long and rich tradition amongst the British fly-fishermen. Charles Cotton is supposed to have hung a London-made fly of Walton's in his window to amuse his fishing friends. And laughing at foreigners, of course, has always been good sport. Not laughing, exactly: more an indulgent chuckle, a disbelieving shake of the head and a 'What will they come up with next?' – safe in the knowledge that the old ways are still the best. Often enough they are. But not always.

Consider the fly reel. It does three things for us. It holds the line in a convenient fashion. It lets the line out when we need more, either to make a longer cast or if a fish is too strong to subdue and wishes to be elsewhere. It brings the line back in when we need less, for a shorter cast or to bring the fish near enough to be grabbed.

It does a fourth thing that we wish it wouldn't. It sits on the end of the rod and acts as a pendulum, increasing the effort needed to get the rod moving in the cast and then to get it to stop again.

The first reels were simple winches. And so are 90 per cent of the fly reels we use in Britain today, which is odd because the design is far from perfect. It is, at best, an uneasy compromise, a compromise between the weight of the reel and the speed of its line retrieval.

Everyone knows that a heavy reel is a bad thing. It makes casting more tiring and more difficult to control. There is not much point in getting a delicate 3-ounce rod and slapping a 12-ounce reel on the handle. Unfortunately, the speed with which you can wind in the line when a large fish rushes in your direction or takes the fly when you are festooned in loose line, depends on the diameter of the spool: the bigger (and thus heavier) the spool, the faster the wind. And then it is never fast enough. You know how fast a big fish can strip line off a reel as it runs away: well, it can run back again the other way even faster. A partial solution is the geared fly reel, which turns the spool twice as fast – but is, of course, heavier. Such multiplying reels account for the other 10 per cent of British fly reels.

Both the simple action and multiplying reels suffer from another major drawback. Either needs two hands to work it, one to hold the rod, the other to wind. Well, that's all right: most fishermen have two hands. They also have a landing net. And they sometimes have a wading staff, usually because, at those times, they need it. I'm sure you know the problem: you have been there. There have been several attempts to get round this by having a reel that retrieves line at a push of a button (or the pull of a lever) from the rod-hand. These were the 'automatic' reels.

The problem with such automatic reels is that a fair amount of energy is required to wind in a hundred foot or so of line at any sort of speed. Electric reels were tried but electric motors are heavy and their batteries are even heavier.

A more promising type of energy storage came with clockwork reels. These are wound up a little to begin with but most of the energy is stored as the line is pulled off the reel by the fish or the fisherman, tensioning a spring within the reel. The spool is prevented from whirling back again by a ratchet like any other clockwork gizmo. The ratchet is released by a lever under the rod hand and the line whizzes back onto the spool. Even the best clockwork reels were heavy. I have a Martin 'Mohawk' which whizzes line in like the dickens but weighs 12 ounces. There was another little snag. If a big fish took all the line and backing the reel could be overwound. The spool slipped at this point to prevent a breakage but, come the time for retrieve, it didn't have sufficient energy to wind all the line (and the fish) back to the fisherman. Despite all this there was a time when automatics were seen as the coming thing. They weren't. They went.

Other, more radical systems were tried along the way. The whole business of weight is only a problem if the reel is strapped to the rod. At least one French design had the thing fixed to the angler's belt. That too fell by the wayside while we had an indulgent chuckle, shook our heads in disbelief and went back to the comfortable tradition of the simple winch with its snail-pace retrieve and we fumbled our landing nets and wading staffs as our fathers (and their fathers' fathers) had done before us.

I first fished in France nearly ten tears ago. It was on the River Moselle in the mountains of the Vosges. By mid-morning I had had several fine grayling, which was embarrassing because the grayling season did not open for another six weeks. I met a Belgian fisherman. The grayling, he said, were all in midstream – where I had been fishing. I would find the trout tucked hard into the banks, he said, and he proceeded to winkle one as a demonstration. It was the first little Moselle trout I had seen and I asked if I might take a photograph. He laid the trout on a rock beside his rod. I recognised his reel as some sort of automatic. It had the little lever under the rod handle and no winding handle. It looked just like a Mitchell or my equally hefty Martin. I picked it up to rearrange the photograph. This was no spring-loaded automatic. It was lighter than my own dinky little rod and reel. It was an Italian Vivarelli.

The Vivarelli is a lever-wind reel. It does not store energy. The power to wind the spool comes from the fisherman's rod hand as he squeezes the lever. It is very fast. I can retrieve a 53-foot line in under four seconds: I have just tried it. Why only 53 feet? Because with that speed of retrieve I don't need to fill the spool to the brim. I cut my lines down and have plenty of backing. This also saves weight. Not that it matters. The reel is very light: at 3½ ounces it is one of the lightest reels available. And this reel is single-handed.

So why aren't we all using it and the others like it? There are several reasons. First, we are – that is, *they* are. I have fished in France often since then and most of the fishermen I meet use these lever-wind reels. So do I now. It is the British and Americans who have yet to discover them. Why? Because the manufacturers of the Vivarelli describe the reel as a *semi-automatic*. Anyone who has ever tried one of the Mitchell or Martin automatic reels will shy like a nervous horse at the mention of that word once the hernias have healed. The uncanny similarity in appearance of the single lever and the handleless spool does nothing to dispel the confusion. But just try a lever-wind and see what you think.

Look: every angler with an ounce of imagination tinkers with tackle. Most of these brainchildren, however dear to their parents, are – like most children – best avoided by the rest of us. Think of the Intra-rod Tippet Tampon. Think of the Poach-resistant, Rising-Enhanced Trout Stocking System (both, incidentally, absolutely true). But just occasionally, perhaps very, very rarely, something comes along that really is better than what went before. It would be a shame to miss it when it happens.

So perhaps I shouldn't chuckle too much until I have actually *tried* the TROUT EAR SPEARS. Perhaps I have overlooked the benefits of a couple of 3-D fish that really look as if they are swimming through my ears.

Fishing in the Forest

They are widening the carriageway on the M6 just north of Junction 31, the Preston turn-off, so there can be delays getting past this spot; usually it's not too bad. From there it is simple enough. Straight on for about 15 miles until you get to the first junction after the roadworks: turn left. Now just keep straight on. There's a fair-sized turning on the left after 7 or 8 miles: ignore it. Keep straight on. Four miles later you are there, at Whitewell.

Those directions are for a sea trout coming up the River Ribble from the Irish Sea. For the fisherman, it is a whole lot more complicated. The hamlet of Whitewell lies in the heart of the Forest of Bowland. I am always rather disappointed with these British 'forests'. The New Forest, Sherwood Forest, any number of Scottish forests and so on. It's not that they're not beautiful: they are, some stunningly so. It's just that I always expect forests to be deep, dark places with views over limitless trees. Like in my old *Rupert* annuals. Rupert Bear was always looking out from strange castle turrets over carpets of forest. Perhaps they were just easier to draw. At any event, with the exception of bits of the Forest of Dean there always seems to be precious few limitless tracts of timber in our forests – you can usually see the fields on the other side through the trees. Some have no trees at all.

Few people who don't live around those parts of Lancashire can place the Forest of Bowland. But they've heard of it. Vaguely. So had I. I had learnt all about it in class 2L when our infant teacher, Miss Langley, read us, afternoon by afternoon, a story, *The Forest of Bowland Light Railway*. I remembered only the name. A few weeks ago, knowing I was to be visiting the place, I found the book in the library. Turns out to be written by 'B.B.': a good sign. 'B.B.' was the pen name of Denys Watkins-Pitchford (and small wonder he chose something a bit snappier to write under). He was a great angler, he wrote for *Shooting Times* and others on country sports and edited a splendid collection of angling stories, *The Fisherman's Bedside Book*. He should know his stuff about the fishing in the Forest of Bowland. Admittedly I had misremembered the title: his forest was entitled 'Boland'. Also, it turns out that the forest is full of pixies and bunnikins and gnomes called Sneezewort and Cloudberry and so forth.

In point of fact, the Forest of Bowland is a beautiful area of stark upland fells sinking into pastures and tight wooded valleys. It lies a healthy distance north of Preston and Blackburn, between the valleys of the Lune and Ribble. There are no longer any pixies and gnomes. There are plenty of bunnikins but they no longer engage you in conversation. And through it all runs the River Hodder.

The River Hodder hereabouts is, as near as makes no difference, perfect. Perfect for me, that is. I suppose everyone has a size and type of river they feel most comfortable with. I like upland, stony rivers. The sort of thing I can wade across to get to the other bank. In a perfect world, one bank will be overgrown with trees so that large trout can lurk in the shadows whilst the other bank runs gently down to a shingle margin. I would have sheep on this bank to nibble away anything that might embarrass a droopy backcast, and the whole shooting match should switch from side to side with stony riffles and gravel banks and still pools and streamy glides liberally distributed up and down the length. I should just be able to cast from wader-deep to the deeper run under the far bank.

Many rivers have all this.

A deep wooded gorge is nice. When the summer sun beats down on the shrunken, clear waters out amongst the hills, there is always a chance of feeding fish in a shady gorge. And when the wind is shrieking down from the fells there are always calm spots deep in a gorge.

Other rivers have wooded gorges.

A real river should have a good working population of brown trout. That is an irreducible minimum. Grayling are a bonus and, since we're dreaming here, a run of sea trout just so that in the summer you never know. We might as well go the whole hog and have salmon.

Some rivers have all four species.

And in the middle of all this should be a pub, a cosy pub that will put you up and feed you and let you in after night fishing for the sea trout and serve you kippers in the morning. In short, a proper, double-stitched and riveted fishing pub.

How I came to have missed the River Hodder and the Inn at Whitewell all these years is a mystery to me, for it has all those things.

I found it first this June, just for a few hours on a morning of driving drizzle gusting down from the high tops to the north. Perhaps this is the best way to come to a new river: I was expecting nothing. I had arrived at the Inn late the night before, had got up late and lingered over breakfast in the dining room that hangs over the river with the pale fells for a backdrop. It was just a break in a journey and I would have to be on my way again by noon. It hardly seemed worthwhile getting soaked and steaming up the car for the rest of the day. But I did. I took a small rod and a pair of waders and pulled my hat down. It was not a fishing expedition, you understand, just a short morning walk with a rod in my hand. The Bridge Pool lies just above the Inn. There is no bridge: it fell down back in some year I forgot after reading about it in a newspaper clipping at the Inn. The Bridge Pool is a deep, slow sweep beneath a steep bank of beech trees. A month later its stillness can be suddenly shattered by a sea trout crashing back into the water like a 4-pound bag of sugar in the inexplicable way that sea trout have. But that was a month later. On this June morning it was disturbed only by the dripping trees. Above the Bridge Pool the Hodder swings the other way in a series of swift and rocky pools, and between two large rocks at the tail of a pool a fish was rising. I wasn't really fishing, you remember, but seeing as it was rising I thought to bung a fly at it. And, not on the first cast or the second but soon after, the trout grabbed the fly and the usual stuff ensued and pretty soon a brown trout of around 12 ounces was back in the water wondering what the hell that had all been about.

If I had been fishing, I would have kept the dry fly on and looked for rises on the three pools that lead up to the stone bridge at the top of the water. But I wasn't fishing; I was just relaxing and nothing immediately rose, so I snipped off the fly and tied on a small wet fly and swung it across the rough water at the head of the pool below where I was standing. On the third step and swing of the line through the bouncing water there was a tug and a grayling was edging across the current below me. It is that sort of river on that sort of day. It was still raining.

I waded the river above the bridge pool and passed the Inn perching high on the opposite bank. Here the river swings a corner and plunges over a gravel bank into a promising pool beneath Fairy Hole Wood. The name may be an allusion to the days when pixies and gnomes undertook major projects of railway engineering in these parts. Or it may be an allusion to something else. I don't know. Good fish were rising from the depths along the edge of the fast water where it plunged over the gravel. The rises had a sort of 'crunching' quality: you heard them before you saw them in the rough water. You can mimic the sound by throwing a small, flat stone high in the air. If it enters the water on its edge it makes very little splash, just a pleasing 'crunch' and a lot of bubbles.

Rises like this usually mean a trout after something about to escape. They can be reckless rises with precious little careful study and consideration. There is always hope with such rises: the trout has to grab or forego. In the pool below Fairy Hole Wood that wet morning four good trout to around a pound grabbed. And so it went on through that memorable wet and windy morning.

The River Hodder around these parts is part of the duchy of Lancaster and belongs to the Queen, but she lends it, for a consideration, to the fortunate fellows of the Whitewell Fishing Association, and if they ever forgive me for writing about their water and are short of a member for the North Oxfordshire chapter, I wish it to be known that I am available. Till then I will rub along at the Inn and I suggest you do likewise. It too belongs to HMQ but, again, she does not run it herself. The Inn is leased to Richard Bowman, who once played cricket for Lancashire amongst many other things, all of which you can read in the framed newspaper clippings which fill every inch of wall space in the gents' lavatory. She has a fair head on her shoulders, has Her Majesty, because the river lease entails four rods to be provided for residents of the Inn at Whitewell: contrariwise the lease of the Inn stipulates that a club-room shall be provided for the Whitewell Fishermen. Everyone benefits, particularly the visiting angler who can fish this splendid water for salmon, brown trout or grayling on every day of the year. But the cream of the fishing begins in mid-July when the Hodder sea trout make their way up past the M6 roadworks on the Ribble from the sea. And so, in July, did I.

I am no sort of a hand at migratory fish. I can catch them, from time to time, but there always seems to me to be more than a whiff of haphazard chance about it. I need faith to fish. I need to feel that I am using the right fly – or at least as good a fly as any other – in the right way and so on. This faith is not too hard to come by with brown trout. They are feeding on something and I try to make the fly look and behave like that something. It is a reasoned faith. You can come by the necessary faith in other ways: using a pattern and method that worked yesterday and the day before and for season after season produces faith. But I have never fished for salmon and sea trout long enough and often enough to acquire this sort of faith. There is a third way. I ask Paul.

Paul is taller than I am and his hair is thinning in a reliable sort of way and he smokes a reliable sort of pipe. He was a prefect twenty-five years ago when I was in the fifth form. Paul has faith enough for the two of us.

'What fly should I use?'

'That one.' Without hesitation Paul points to a small double with a gold body and orange hackle laying neatly amongst dozens of others that appear to be almost – but not quite – identical.

'What strength tippet should I use?'

'Six-pound.'

'I've got some 5-pound.'

He considers. 'Too light.'

'Seven-pound?'

'A bit too heavy.'

You know where you are with Paul.

Below the gorge a small hidden pasture nestles between the river and the steeply wooded valley sides. There is something remarkable at the far end of this pasture. It is a bridge. It is a huge bridge. It is a huge, three-arched bridge rendered in two tones of pale pastel and it leads from one small field to another, slightly smaller, across the river. It carries pipes – and the very occasional fisherman. Rarely can three pipes and a fisherman cross a river in such elaborate and extravagant style. I suppose it, too, belongs to HMQ. It serves one other vital function. When darkness falls on a moonless night the small pastures along the Hodder valley disappear into the blackness of the surrounding trees. Then the pale monstrosity of the pipe bridge guides the night fisherman across the field with its rotting barbed-wire fence to the riverside. If for no other reason, this makes Gelcar, the pool beneath the bridge, a favoured spot for sea trouting after dark.

It was not dark when we got to Gelcar, but it was raining so steadily that the river was rising and colouring as we watched and we decided to start fishing right away. Actually, Paul decided and I agreed. Paul would fish the long run above the bridge. He suggested I should cross the bridge and fish the tail of the deep pool below. So I did.

It is reassuring to be doing things right. I waded cautiously into the slacker water at the inside of the bend.

I had on that gold and orange double tied to that 6-pound tippet beneath a sinking braided leader as instructed. I cast across into the current beneath the bank and let the fly work round into the tail of the pool where it began to accelerate over the gravel bar. Nothing.

I let the thing dangle and then retrieved. Again, nothing.

I cast out a second time and swam the fly round. Not a thing.

I was beginning to have Doubts.

I cast into the current a third time. The fly swung round and was slowing as it got directly below me. And then the tail of the pool erupted. The small gold and orange double had taken the fatal fancy of a 2½-pound sea trout fresh from the tide.

If you can't trust a prefect, who can you trust? Thanks, Paul.

'Fish Gotta Swim,
Fishermen Gotta Fish . . .'

There are otters at the bottom of our garden. Nearly.

I live beside the River Cherwell at a point where it takes some nerve to call this small stream a river. For some years an Otter Project has been quietly encouraging the beasts to return to these tributaries of the Upper Thames. Streams have been restocked with eels, farmers encouraged to leave the river-banks well alone, artificial holts constructed in case any passing otter feels like setting up home. No one is sure, but all the signs are that the otters are back.

Otters, of course, are a Good Thing. One or two fish might give you an argument on this but, for the river as a whole, the otter is a Good Thing.

Exactly the same could be said of another predator: the fisherman. In fact, the fisherman is an Even Better Thing. When all is not well with a river, when fish are disappearing or dying from pollution, the otter just folds his tent and makes for somewhere else. He does not inform the Environment Agency: he does not write to his MP: he does not phone the Anglers' Conservation Association and have them sue the bejazus out of the polluter. Only fisher-men and otters notice when a river is in trouble and only fishermen do something about it.

This is not a question of morality: it is a question of practicality. Fishermen are vital to the health of our waters.

Fishermen catch fish – not as many as they would like, of course, but cer-tainly some. Fish are caught. If that fish is a trout or a salmon or some other tasty species, the fisherman then has a choice. He can kill the fish, take it home and eat it. Or he can return the fish to the water.

More letters-to-the-editor have been winged, more battles have been fought, more collars got hot under, on this subject of Catch-and-Release than on any other topic in game fishing.

The argument is commonly fought for the moral high ground. Side A says something like this:

'Man is a hunter. He has always hunted for food. The fish suffers in being caught but by killing it swiftly for the pot the angler is simply hunting as humanely as possible.'

Side B responds:

'Rubbish. No one needs to fish for food. It is cheaper in Tesco. We are rising above the base bloodlust of our ancestors. By releasing the fish we are showing mercy and respect for our quarry. Also we won't get shouted at by the wife for gutting the thing in the kitchen.'

Side A counters:

'Catching a fish and then releasing it is causing suffering just for your own pleasure. The worse sort of torturer.'

Side B:

'Hold on: if catching a fish is tantamount to torture, how does bashing the victim on the head wipe the slate clean? To kill or to release? I bet I know which way the fish would vote.'

And so it goes on. Cries of 'Torturer!' alternate with 'Murderer!' and pretty soon things get ugly – as they often do when people start worrying about other people's morals.

Please, let's leave morality to the individual. Catch-and-release fishing for game fish (it is the norm for coarse fish – most of them taste awful) is a practical issue.

Look: fishermen are vital to the wellbeing of our waters. Fishermen catch fish. That is the price the river pays for protection: it pays much the same for otters, kingfishers and herons. The fisherman can choose to charge less for this service by releasing some or all of the fish he has caught.

Some waters are better off than others. If trout are plentiful and fishermen are few then the water can easily afford at least one or two fish for any angler who wishes to play man-the-hunter-living-off-the-land. I sometimes like to play man-the-hunter: it is a good game.

There are other waters where the fish are few (but perhaps bigger) and the fishermen are many (because the fish are bigger?). Here the river simply cannot pay full whack. Either the fish must be released or the river continually restocked from a fish farm.

Personally, I would rather catch wilder fish and shop at Tesco.

27

Rubén's Restaurant

If it had been up to me I wouldn't have gone fishing that day. If it had been up to me, I would have stayed in bed. It was noon in early April, it was Spain and it was cold. Not a clear, crisp, last-one-to-the-bottom-of-the-piste-buys-a-round-of-schnapps sort of cold. It was grey-cold. A bitter wind was driving an endless drizzle into our faces and out through the soles of our feet. It was monotonous-cold: occasionally the rain would turn to wet sleet but, believe me, the change was not as good as a rest.

We were huddled against the northern slopes of the Cordillera Cantábrica, the spine of mountains that runs along Spain's northern coast. Behind us they rose above 7,000 feet, still muffled under the deep snow of winter which was melting reluctantly under this unending deluge. Twenty miles ahead of us the beaches of the coast were bathing in spring sunshine. But not here. Beneath us the River Nansa boomed in a thick brown icy flood of snow melt.

We weren't here for fun. We were here to catch fish.

It was Rubén's idea. I had met Rubén the evening before in La Jontoya, a bustling bar and restaurant in the small village of Luey near the mouth of the River Nansa. If you want to fish hereabouts, they told me, you must meet Rubén. And they were right. Rubén is a legendary hunter and fisherman along the Nansa and in the high *cordillera* above. Better than that: Rubén spoke French. After days of fruitless fumbling through a Spanish phrase book it was like meeting Livingstone. We could talk.

Up to a point. After a few baffling moments I realised that my French, which had seemed practically seamless in France, might not be all my fancy painted it. They make allowances in France: they can spot where I am heading and pitch in and help. There was a fair amount of spin on the stuff Rubén was giving me and, curiously, he seemed equally baffled at what I was serving up. In the end we hit on a sort of Desperanto – a lowest common denominator of our two versions of the French tongue. Once we had abandoned all pretence of conjugations and tenses and other such linguistic fol-de-rol we got on famously. At least I think we did. We jabbered and gesticulated through that evening; we were fellow fishermen; we were blood brothers; we were drunk.

And in this manner we had decided to go fishing the next morning. We left Luey in convoy. I followed Rubén's pastel-green Land Rover along a cinder track that plunged down through a heady plantation of eucalyptus trees, which certainly gives the sinuses a good pull-through on a cold morning misty with rain. We pulled up in front of a small farmhouse. The grey-brown waters of the swollen Rio Nansa glinted on the far side of a field of beans. I was ready to fish. I climbed out of the car in waders and waterproofs. Rubén swung open the door of the Land Rover. He was in carpet slippers. I had never before seen a man set off for a fishing trip in carpet slippers. But then I had never before been fishing in northern Spain where, God knows, they are used to rain and civilisation has reached its zenith. By civilisation I refer to a society that has solved the age-old problem of popping out to fetch coal or more wood or to empty the ashes at the bottom of the garden without having to kick off the comfy slippers, find a reasonably waterproof shoe from under the heap of wellingtons in the cloakroom, search for the other one, tie them up – only to go through the whole process in reverse on returning. The solution was sitting inside the farmhouse porch: *albarcas*.

Albarcas are a happy blend of clog and trivet. Like clogs, they are carved from a solid chunk of wood. Like a trivet, each *albarca* has three short legs, two under the ball of the foot, one under the heel, to carry the wearer serenely above the perils of a well-watered land where cows wander freely around unmade village streets. *Albarcas* are inspirational footwear. Dryshod and inches taller, Rubén was disappearing round the corner of the farmhouse. We had not, it seemed, come here to fish but to collect bait. The farmhouse, the field and a small but fecund dungheap beneath an apple tree belonged to Rubén. It was a day for learning new things: the secret of a really good wormy dungheap is paper and plenty of it buried in piles. Rubén dug into the heap, which peeled apart at a newspaper revealing appetising red worms burrowing between the pages. We gathered a boxful, collected rods, waders and something that looked uncomfortably like a keepnet from the farm and set off up the Nansa valley.

The Land Rover bounced down a track to pull up by a flooded stand of bushes beside the swollen river. Out from the back came the keepnet. This, I thought, was confidence. I was wrong. It was more bait. What I had taken for a keepnet was a *butron*. A *butron* is a collapsible fish trap. It is extended by a couple of springy hazel twigs and I won't go into much more detail. It is illegal. It is very illegal when used for trout – when it is baited with a white object: a hard-boiled egg, say. It is at its most illegal for salmon, when bait is unimportant and careful positioning is everything. Today it was only slightly illegal. We baited the belly of the *butron* with bread and Rubén sunk it in a grassy backwater. A few minutes later it was full of minnows. Some of the minnows were tumbled into a tin and we set off again, climbing ever upstream towards the grey snows of the *cordillera*.

It was getting colder. Rubén switched on the heater, not for warmth but to dry and toughen the small silver corpses he had spread on a sheet of news-paper between our feet. From Puentenansa the road climbs steadily and the mountains begin to crowd in from all sides. At La Lastra we swung off the road and rattled up to the gate of a small but unlovely hydroelectric plant. We had come to catch trout and with the river in full freezing flood, the quieter water behind the small dam at La Lastra was our only chance. Personally I would be happy to come back another day – say in June. But we are not here for fun, we were here to catch fish. And if we don't catch fish then La Jontoya does not have a fish course on its menu.

And so there we were, in the rain and sleet, at noon in early April. We had been standing there for three hours. We had caught nothing. We had tried everything. We had even tried 'Bingo'.

'Bingo' is a fishing method. It is prohibited in the waters of Asturias and Cantabria. It is always fascinating to see what is and isn't allowed. Flies that are now run-of-the-mill have, at some times and places, been banned for being too effective. Baits that one nation of anglers might dismiss are regarded by another as deadly. And perhaps they are – once they have been prohibited. And so it is with Bingo. Bingo is done with a dead minnow. The minnow is cast on a light ledger out into the turbulent pool below the hydroelectric plant. It can rest there, wafted by the current, and the law smiles upon the angler. It can be wound in again, inspected and recast and the angler remains in a state of grace. But if, during the retrieve, the angler should pause, allow-ing the dead bait to sink before it is drawn again towards the bank, well, then the angler is committing Bingo and is subject to the full rigour of the law. Bingo is just 'sink and draw' – which is a good method, but surely not that good. Not on that day in April at any rate.

An hour later I had had enough. Rubén agreed that it was difficult. Difficult? I would hate to see what he regards as unfishable. There is, he says, just one last chance. Rubén is playing his joker. There is a place he reserves for difficult times. This, he concedes, may be one of them. It is a place he has not visited for several years. If it is somewhere else, I am all for it.

As we scrambled stiffly back to the Land Rover, Rubén pointed to the corner of the small dam where a pounding maelstrom of water was visible in a narrow channel before it disappeared under a concrete cover which wound along the contours of the valley. We were off to fish in it.

As the Land Rover rattled down the Nansa valley, I could follow the course of the concrete channel as it clung to the mountainside high above us like a miniature Great Wall of China winding through the forest. After 3 miles we turned up an unmade track which hairpinned up from the road through the forest slopes. High above the road the Land Rover bumped across the concrete channel before the gravel track petered out in a small clearing. Here I could trace the overgrown remains of a track through the trees. It was the track used years ago when the channel was being constructed. Time has not been kind to this track: trees lean across it and the torrential rains have washed alarming portions away. I did not fancy walking along it. Besides, there are wild boar, bear and wolves in these mountains. To my horror, Rubén clambered back into the Land Rover and nudged it through the first of the branches. We were going to drive. I did not see any wild boar, bears or wolves during the 2 nightmare miles of that track but then I had my eyes clamped shut for most of it.

The view, when we lurched to a stop, was breathtaking. We were hanging high above the Nansa valley, the small village of Rozadio a thousand feet below us. Two green pipes hurtled the water from the channel straight down the slope to expend its energy in yet another hydro plant on the valley floor. Beside us was the unlikeliest and unloveliest fishing nook I had clapped eyes on. The mouth of the concrete channel debouched its chaos of currents into an oblong concrete tank. The water boiled and bounced to the far end, perhaps 20 yards away, where a large grille trapped the debris suspended in the turmoil before the water swirled away down the tubes. A large, arcane mechanical device slid down the grilles to scrape away the debris. It seemed unlikely that anything could live in those tumbling currents but during the drive Rubén had told me of fish he had caught here before. He set up another minnow on tackle with enough lead to hold the stuff down in the quieter waters along the edges of the tank. We had brought worms from the farm. Everyone I had spoken to used worms when they fish the Nansa in the early season before switching to flies and a bubble float in late spring. And then it dawned on me. Rubén was simply 'matching the hatch'. The trout that live in the turbulent water below the turbines grow fat on the stunned carcasses of turbined fry and minnows. Similarly, any fish that could live in the quiet corners of this tank might simply inhale a soup of creatures stunned by the turbulence and swept down the long, black channel. Rubén cast out into the confusion. The line was whipped away and swung to the side of the chamber. There, hard against the rotting concrete sides, tight back-eddies crept the tackle along the wall back towards the channel mouth.

It was not subtle when it happened. The fish took the morsel and panicked into the current, the rod-top dipping fiercely. All that was needed was patience and a very long handle on the landing net to swing a 1½-pounder up into the daylight. Neither of us had noticed that the rain had stopped. It was the first fish I had seen from the Nansa. A fish of bright silver and white, with large black spots: not a trace of the red and cream of our brown trout. And it had been feeding hard. That first fish had a small head and a body that bulged out behind the gill covers. A second fish, identical in size and shape, followed from that implausible pool. A young man arrived, panting from the climb up from the village. It was his job to operate the grille scrapers. He stared in astonishment at the gleaming brace by Rubén's creel. And then Rubén's rod-top lurched for a third time. I was becoming blasé by this time: I had seen large wild fish from mountainside settling tanks before. I walked round the side of the tank with the landing net and lowered it towards the water only to have it taken firmly from my hands by Rubén. We had only known each other a day or so: I was not to be trusted with whatever was dancing him around that confusion of currents beneath us. It was big. Rubén was trying to pretend it was just a fish like any other but he was fooling no one. At all costs it had to be kept from that main thrust of the channel where there would be no stopping it. The maintenance man and I danced about getting in each other's way as Rubén reached down for the last time – and then swung the fish aloft.

It weighed a touch under 5 pounds. As Rubén slipped the magnificent creature onto the grass and removed the minnow, a slightly chewed sala-mander slid from its throat. The low sun was shining in the narrow gap between the cloud base and the mountaintops and it was very cold.

*   *   *

On the way back down from the mountains to the warmth of the coast we stopped at a bar in Puentenansa for a little something to thaw and celebrate. The fishing aficionados gathered around and sympathised. Had we been out fishing? We had. Impossible! There was too much water, it was too cold. Did we catch anything? Well, just one or two. Any size? Well, not really. We all got up and trooped to the back of the Land Rover to admire the splendid fish once more. Rubén is surely a master, they all said. How does he do it? Where did he find such fish in such weather and water? I do not pretend that I understood every word of Rubén's directions – but it was nowhere near where we had been.

A Man Called Emma

My mother does not read *Trout & Salmon*. It is not really her speed. This is a blessing because it will be better if she does not find out what follows. Some years ago – it was the year that Bruce & Walker brought out their Hexagraph rods, I do remember that – I was on a little visit to a favourite river. I was on my own. I planned to be away for a week, so, rather than leave my wife without a car, I decided to borrow my mother's car for the trip. Mother was away on holiday. I packed the car with tents and kettles and all the stuff of camping down by the river.

Two hundred miles later I found the farm manager doing something hot and bothering with silage. I asked him where I might camp and he suggested Pillar Holme. The River Eamont beyond Penrith carves a course through the soft red sandstones leaving steep cliffs hanging over deep and interesting pools. And then the river wanders off and does something else. Pillar Holme is a magical little meadow enclosed between these ancient cliffs and a loop of the river. A steep track of loose boulders has been sliced down the eroded cliff. I didn't fancy this track – but then again I didn't fancy carting a car-load of camping gear down and then up the long, steep slope. Indolence won. It usually does. I tippled my mother's car over the edge and onto the track and gingerly jounced and slid downwards.

I knew it was a mistake after about 3 yards but that was about 2 yards too late. I carried on to the bottom. Pillar Holme, like the grave, is a fine and private place. At either end the river joins the cliff. There is only one way in or out. And, just like the grave, Pillar Holme is a damned sight easier to get into than out of.

I did not unpack the camping gear. I turned the car round on the short sheep-nibbled grass of the meadow and backed off for a run at the track. It is not easy to take a run at a boulder-strewn track. Not if you are attached to your sump. Or your exhaust system. I clanked and banged for a few yards up the track until the wheels started to spin, spitting pebbles against the underside of the car. I did this several times and then gave up. It was late in the afternoon when I trudged into the farmyard where the manager was still loading silage. Silaging goes on long into a summer's evening. It was almost dark when he could break off to help the idiot who had taken a Ford Escort down to Pillar Holme. His tractor went down the track easily enough. He hooked a huge steel chain onto a bendy bit underneath the car and, as the big wheels scrabbled to find grip, a volley of pebbles peppered the front of the car like grapeshot, cracking one of the headlights.

*   *   *

I mention all this because last Thursday I was sitting behind the wheel, one-and-a-half thousand feet up a Welsh mountain, and contemplating a steep hillside that fell away a bit sharpish from a boulder track that looked like it might have been made by the same firm that makes boulder tracks in Cumbria.

There was, however a difference: I had just come *up* this track. Cruised up, actually. Wafted up. And still had a sump and an exhaust. But then this time I wasn't in my mother's Escort. I was encased in a Vauxhall Frontera.

Now, you will understand that a Frontera is not my usual mode of travel. Frankly, my mother's Escort was a bit of a step up for me. So I will explain how I came to be smooching up a Welsh hillside wearing a Frontera. You will have spotted that this month is the fortieth anniversary of this illustrious mag. Also that to celebrate this event said mag is offering a brand-spanking-new Frontera as a competition prize.

'Take it,' I was told, 'or one just like it, and put it through its piscatorial paces.'

'The Frontera is a creature of the wilderness,' they said, 'take it to the wild places of this world, places where the hand of man has yet to tame this rampant earth: take it to where civilisation – and the tarmac – ends.'

I took it to Wales.

*   *   *

There is no point looking for Llyn Gwyddior in *Where to Fish*. It is not there. Llyn Gwyddior and its sister, Llyn Coch-hwyad, are two small lakes nestling on the high moors above Llanbrynmair. I found them in one of my dog-eared collection of old Ordnance Survey maps. There didn't seem to be a lot of civilisation round about, just an awful lot of contours. Would there be boats up there? It is little use travelling miles off the beaten track to a remote little lake only to find the fish rising another 40 yards further away from the beaten track. Us Frontera drivers are not daunted by little problems like these. I would take my own boat. It is not every car that you can bung a boat in the back of: but you can in a Frontera. Contrariwise, it is not every boat you can bung in the back of a Frontera: but the natty little Seahopper folding dinghy I managed to borrow could have been made for the job – which, I suppose, it was.

With a boat, rods, waders and an awful lot of space in the back, I headed west from Banbury towards the farther limits of civilisation. I could rapidly get to like this sort of driving. There is something about travelling a little higher than ordinary mortals. One is spiritually elevated; one feels the natural superiority of the man on horseback to the lowly pedestrian; one uses the word 'one' quite a lot. I got a bit lost in Shrewsbury. I wound down the window at the traffic lights to ask the driver of the car down beside me if I was on the right road. He said I was. He didn't exactly tug his forelock and I didn't exactly press a copper coin into his hand – but I think we both wanted to. It would have been even more impressive if I hadn't made such a dog's breakfast of winding down the windows. The windows are electric – naturally. I don't have electric windows in my car so I wasn't expecting the controls to be above the hand brake. I *did* find a little electric controller on the door where my window winder is and I pushed it. Nothing happened to the windows. It had little arrows so I pushed it again in all the directions offered and still nothing happened – until I noticed both wing mirrors rotating independently like the ears of a majestic hippopotamus after surfacing.

Mr Lewis is a large and rugged individual, as Welsh NRA men tend to be. I met him by his house in Llanbrynmair. He grasped my hand in a firm, manly grip and introduced himself as 'Emma'. You think twice before you call a large and rugged Welshman 'Emma'. It turns out it isn't spelt that way. Emir had a large and rugged Alsatian as a companion. So I was a bit put out when his wife mentioned that he didn't like to travel the track to Llyn Gwyddior alone. Good grief! What was up there? Sheep are up there. And to keep the sheep where they are, the long track to Llyn Gwyddior is gated. It is about as gated as a track can get. There is something about driving alone up a gated road that can drive a man insane. Getting out, opening the gate with whatever unique contrivance the farmer has cobbled together out of binder-twine to keep it closed, stopping it from swinging back while you get back to the car, drive 5 yards, get out, then get back in again and drive another yard because you hadn't left enough room to close the gate, closing the gate, getting back into the car and driving on to the next gate in the sure and certain knowledge that you will have to repeat the whole rigmarole on the way back down. Add a large farm dog of uncertain character at the point where *three* gates divide a farmyard and it is the stuff of nightmares.

The track steepened beyond the farmyard and the tightly folded valley fell away behind us. I switched self-consciously into four-wheel drive and we wound up the contours of the hill. The track itself is newish (there was not a hint of it on my old Ordnance Survey map), the residue of the recent forestry plantations that dot the old grouse moor. We went through a couple more gates, ground round another bend and Llyn Gwyddior lay below us.

Quite a long way below us actually. Between us and the water's edge was the long, steep hillside of slippery grass and the reedy gully that had prompted my memories of the Humiliation of Pillar Holme. On the other hand, it did look a long way to carry the boat that lay in the back of the car. And besides, we had come here to put the car through its paces. I engaged low ratio four-wheel drive and eased the Frontera forward, tipping down the steep lip and taking to the springy turf. At last I was Offroad. We parked with two wheels in the water on the slatey gravel of the margin.

Llyn Gwyddior was a dramatic place, on top of a bleak moorland world and rasped by ranks of leaden clouds that beetled up from the southwest throughout that afternoon. It is entitled to blow a bit at 1500 feet. We got into waders and tackled up. I lifted the slim package out of the back of the car. It didn't look much like a boat. It looked like a pile of plywood. The bloke who had lent me the thing had made it look easy. And it was: within one minute the pile of plywood had blossomed into a tight little pram dingy. Emir had disappeared. There was, it seemed, a boat on Llyn Gwyddior, housed in a tiny dry-stone boathouse tucked into the mossy bank. Emir didn't really fancy the Seahopper.

I cannot blame him. The Seahopper is a splendidly light little craft which scuds across the water as you row upwind to the start of a drift and scuds just as fast downwind as you try to fish. I had not thought to bring a drogue which would have cured the problem. As it was I was doing an awful lot of rowing and precious little fishing. No matter. I beached the Seahopper and fished the shore.

Emir was soon into a fish. A nice fish, not a huge fish. They do not run huge up here in the cold waters of the moor. The best fish up here is 2½ pounds; a pounder is a good fish. But then a pounder is a good fish in any of the waters I fish. It needs a good hatch of fly to bring the better fish up and a good hatch up here needs the warmth of summer. The best months are June and July with always the chance of a good catch in September. Then, when the fish are up on the surface, the dry fly is favourite, particularly a Heather Fly and a Hopper – black with red hackle legs or a Dark Claret Hopper. Earlier in the season Emir suggested I try a Harry Tom on the point, ringing the changes with a Mallard and Claret with a Bibio on the dropper. Any time in May or June a warm evening can bring out a hatch of the big red sedge, tumbling across the surface and dragging up the best of the dark fish of Gwyddior.

Even now, on a cold day in May, there was a little activity, one or two splashy rises off the reed beds that were just beginning to emerge in the shallower margins. I waded out within comfortable casting range of the last rise and soon enough there was a vicious little tug and a splash somewhere out there and I had a little Gwyddior trout of my own. Smaller than Emir's, perhaps 12 ounces. They are not born and bred in Gwyddior, these trout. One or two may hatch from a fortuitous spawning along the wave-wash of the shore but most are stocked as 4-inch fingerlings in the autumn. Emir's pounder would have spent three seasons up here on the moors before finishing up in the net.

And so the afternoon went on, as such splendid afternoons will. Emir picked up fish steadily from the sheltered waters along the windward shore. I had one or two more from the margins, fluffing the chance for better things when a movement in 3 inches of water just a yard from my waders caught my eye and a prodigious tail fin waggled through the surface. You have a choice in such circumstances: you can freeze stock-still and if you do this well enough for long enough, you will have a splendid view of a very big trout rootling for nymphs beneath the gravel. You will not, of course, catch it. Or you can make some sort of movement of a fishy intent, a gentle pulling of line through the rings, anything really. You will have a splendid view of a very big trout heading suddenly for deeper water. You will not, of course, catch it. I did a bit of both. I did not, of course, catch it. What I should then have done was to sit, very, very quietly, with a nymph resting on the bottom gravel or with a dry fly rocking on the surface, the leader draped across the grasses of the margin, and wait until the old trout returned on his circuit. I know what to do. I just don't do it.

Later on, the few rises stopped and the wind grew chillier. It was time to leave if we were to make it back to civilisation. Emir thought that there would be a splendid hatch of big red sedge that night. I hate it when people say things like that.

As we were packing the boat back into the Frontera, another car appeared on the horizon. Emir recognised it as the two fishermen who had been on Llyn Coch-hwyad, another 3 miles further into the wilderness. They had called at his house for tickets that morning. They had got chatting. They were both doctors from Hereford. They had fishing on the River Lugg.

I have given the Frontera back now, but one little bit of that day has stayed with me. The back of the Frontera was plenty big enough for me to leave my rod up and I had still not packed it away by the time I arrived home. I carried the thing into the house, meaning to pop it into the rod case the next morning. The next morning I remembered the hooks along the main ceiling beam in the living room. I had not used them for years. In those days I always kept a fly rod made up with a small black fly, hanging along the beam: every day or so I would take it down and irritate the dace and chub that live in the small River Cherwell alongside the garden. It was fun fishing no more, and I had given it up for grander things long since. I had forgotten how good it feels to see a rod made up, hanging over my armchair, to reach up and lift it down, to cast it over eager little fish of whatever species.

I hope I don't forget again.

Heavenly Hawthorn

Hagiology – I have just looked up the spelling – is not my strong suit. I know St David's Day (easy: first of the month – daffodils – probably March) and All Saints' Day (first of the month again – day after Halloween – must be November). I fancy St Stephen's must be around Christmas, the snow laying round about deep and crisp and so on, and I seem to recall the poet Keats remarking that it was fairly nippy on St Agnes' Eve so that must be around then too. The rest is a blank.

Except, that is, for St Mark. His feast day is 25 April. Fly-fishermen should draw a big black circle around this date on the calendar because it can herald the cream of the season's trout fishing.

Let me explain. The hawthorn fly is not much to look at. It is black and untidy with dangling legs and looks like a small housefly that has been on a prolonged diet. It flies a bit like that as well: it does not zoom. It dances feebly, sometimes in loose swarms, around the trees and bushes of a spring meadow. Its scientific title is *Bibio marci,* the last name reflecting its old country name of St Mark's fly. And all too often this little St Mark's fly is ignored by the fly-fisherman.

This is not surprising. Many never notice the thing. For a start, the hawthorn fly is not a fly of rivers and lakes; it is a creature of the land. Most of the insects of interest to a fisherman are aquatic: they are born, grow to maturity, lay eggs and die in or on the water. A fair number of these aquatic flies end up inside trout, and just occasionally one of these flies will be an angler's cunning imitation and the trout will end up inside the fisherman.

So what has all this to do with the land-loving hawthorn fly buzzing unsteadily over the meadows? They are swarming to find a mate. Now, we are all inclined to lapses of concentration when mating and the hawthorn fly is only a so-so flyer at best: it is hopeless in a clinch. Ardent hawthorn couples often fall to the ground in large numbers to squirm amongst the grass roots.

On a gusty spring day with a river nearby this is a mistake. Lovemaking and large amounts of wind are never a happy combination: in the case of the hawthorn fly it can be fatal. The hawthorn fly was never designed for the water. Where the aquatic flies ride serenely on the surface film before taking off or even dive through it to lay their eggs on the weeds and stones, the land-lubberly hawthorn fly struggles and gets glued into the surface tension and is trapped as a sorry mess.

Trout love hawthorn flies.

It may be the taste – but I doubt it. I have tasted hawthorn flies, in the interests of investigation you understand: they are nothing special. There are several other good reasons for the trout's partiality. The hawthorn fly is easy pickings: it is helpless in the water. There is no danger of it winging off at any moment like the olives and sedges born and bred in the river. These aquatic flies have evolved alongside the trout. They have strategies to help them cope with a predator the relative size of the Albert Hall. Many aquatic species emerge on the surface in bursts – for the same reason that bombers in the Second World War bombed in huge groups arriving at the target as near simultaneously as possible – by swamping the enemy there will be casualties, to be sure, but most will get through. It is the straggler who gets picked off. Hawthorn flies are stragglers.

And there are reasons why St Mark's fly should be a favourite of the fisherman. Its arrival on the water is an accident. It can splosh down in a heap or tumble onto the surface at any odd angle. This is strikingly similar to the way my artificial fly often lands on the surface when I cast. Once on the water the hapless beast struggles into an untidy mess and eventually sinks. Just like the flies I tie. All in all the resemblance is quite uncanny.

It is enough to fool a trout.

And that is why a fisherman armed with a small, untidy black fly can find some of the best trout fishing of the season during three breezy weeks in spring.

St Mark's fly got its old country name because it swarmed in greatest numbers around St Mark's Day. Last Thursday. Do not wring your hands and cry out, 'Why did he not tell us all this earlier?' You have missed nothing. These days, St Mark's fly swarms a little later, beginning around the saint's day and peaking in the first week of May. This has nothing to do with the balmier days and warmer springs of a bygone golden age: it has everything to do with England's adoption of the Gregorian calendar in 1752 when everything shifted by eleven days. Which is why mayflies mostly hatch in June.

Fishing With Frogs

'Going fishing' means different things to different folk. For some, it can mean lifting the rod and bag from the rack and walking down to the familiar stream. To others, it means a tramp across the wild moors accompanied by the plaintive cry of the heather and the restless rustle of the wind in the curlew. Or the other way about. Often enough it means a long, long drive in a car. On a day in August I was sitting in a deckchair, feet up on another, sipping a cold beer after a sumptuous meal and reading, not for the first time, *Last But One in the Sack Race*. In front of me was the steady blue of the Atlantic under the sort of sun we got last August. The only real problem was to keep the book in the shade so I wasn't blinded by the whiteness of the pages. It meant shifting position a bit every quarter of an hour to keep the book in the shadow of the funnel. I was going fishing.

It is important how you broach the subject of holidays with Judi. You have to come at it from the right angle. You might, for example, have a hankering to visit Béarn, a small region of the western Pyrénées – Basque country. Now, with some wives it would be enough to mention that Béarn has some of the finest trout fishing in France. Also the best salmon fishing. That would do it with some wives. With Judi it would be a mistake. On the other hand, it would be unwise not to mention the trout. It might look as though you had something to hide. Experience tells her that trout fishing will occur on this holiday: better to admit that Béarn has the odd trout. You have to dip something in all that Béarnaise sauce, after all.

Béarn does have the odd trout. It is hard for a Brit to get a grasp on some of the trout fishing in this part of France. Listen: for a day's fishing on a Hampshire chalkstream you may be master of a beat of perhaps 800 yards. A mile at the most. On the wilder waters of the north and west you may have several miles at your disposal. There are clubs and associations with 20 miles or so. In the department of the Pyrénées Atlantiques there are over *a thousand miles* of pristine trout and salmon rivers and streams. And what's more, all this lot is available to the summer visitor, including fishing licence, tax, the whole kit and caboodle, for about £17 for a fortnight.

There is one problem with a thousand miles of trout fishing. It is a nice problem, though: I had no idea where to start. So I asked a man who did. He was called Lilian. In England any chap finding himself christened Lilian by an unthinking parent would look to a career in interior decoration or possibly aromatherapy. Lilian Carli is a fishing guide. I will tell you what Lilian told me.

There are four famous rivers of the region. Well, three-and-a-half actually. The half is the most westerly and the smallest, the Nivelle. The other three are all tributaries of the Ardour draining the mountains of the Pyrénées to the south. The next river, travelling east, is the Nive, which joins the Ardour near the coast at Bayonne. Fifteen miles further inland the Ardour is joined by the waters of the Gave, which is really a combination of two famous rivers, the Gave d'Oloron and the Gave de Pau. The mountains of the Pyrénées rise gradually from the coast, so the waters of the Nivelle in the east trickle down from 2,000 feet or so and the waters of the Gave de Pau in the west melt from stuff at four times that height. All this has a profound effect on the fishing. The little Nivelle fishes well from the start of the season in March, but by the end of May it is past its best. The Nive and its tributaries start a little later in April and are at their best in May and June. The Gaves are unfishable in the early season and afternoon snow melt can affect the fishing late in the spring, but these cold waters are still fishing well in July.

Unfortunately, I arrived on these beautiful waters of Béarn and the Basque country in mid-August. That first evening we stood and looked at a splendid stretch of the Gave d'Aspe. Many of the headwaters and tributaries of these rivers share the name 'Gave de Something-or-other'. Often the something-or-other is a town (as in Oloron and Pau); often it isn't. The Gave d'Aspe is typical of these rivers. The road to Spain climbs slowly, winding between conical peaks. The river runs alongside the road with long riffle sections interspersed with slower, deeper glides over a bottom of rounded pebbles. Casting is easy across the broad, shallow river into the deeper run along one bank. You could sit down and design a trout river and not come up with anything better. Occasionally there is a narrower neck, a rush of water and a deeper pool scoured beneath. And down there, through the crystal water, you can see huge trout, anything up to 6 pounds, holding the bottom, tilting a fin to glide across the sand to intercept some morsel.

It was a depressing sight. Lilian took me to such a pool on the Gave d'Aspe. Fishing guides the world over do this in August. It means you are not going to catch anything. They know you are not going to catch anything and, not wishing to be blamed for this inevitable failure, they bring you here to a pool where you can see that there are huge fish in the river and lots of them. *Alors, mon ami* – now you go and catch them.

I did not catch them. Nor did he. Neither of us thought we would. It was the height of August. Lilian said I should have been here in May. Or June. With this painful little ritual over we got down to cases. It was a broiling August in one of the finest trout regions of France. Where would *he* fish if he *had* to catch a trout tomorrow? Lilian thought. There was a place, he said, but he did not think I would like it. The fish were not so big as the fish in the Gave d'Aspe. It was high up in the mountains where the water is cooler and the stream is smaller and more shaded. The fishing was not so easy and no one goes there but Lilian. It sounded perfect. We would meet at seven the next morning.

I pulled into the small market square of St Etienne de Baigorry. Lilian was tying flies and sipping coffee at a small table on the vine-shaded terrace outside a small café. The old poseur. More coffee and croissants arrived and we had our breakfast surrounded by the pyramid peaks of the Pyrénées, 5 miles from the Spanish border, whilst Lilian spread great dollops of silicone grease on his fly line. I took a closer look at that fly line. The word for a fly line in French is *soie* – silk – and that's what Lilian's line was made of. Now, I haven't seen a woven-silk line in England for many years, but in France that summer I was to meet several guides, some of them amongst the finest fishermen I have met, and most of them use natural silk lines. Lilian was the first so I asked him why. He told me to feel the silk line.

The first thing you notice is that a silk line is thinner than a plastic line. This is inevitable. A floating plastic line is less dense than water – that's why it floats. A silk line is denser and floats in the surface film by greasing in just the same way as a greased leader. This slimmer, denser line has two advantages, claimed Lilian: the thinner line cuts through the air better and is less affected by the wind. It is also less obtrusive on the water.

The second thing you notice is that the silk line is very supple and, it seems, a line that twists and bends to each nuance of current creates less drag. Hmmm, I don't know. But I do know that some very, very good French fishermen take the superiority of a natural silk line as self-evident.

Lilian's leader was another surprise. For a man concerned with delicate presentation, it was very thick and level for perhaps a metre then stepped suddenly into very fine stuff. It looked a little makeshift to me. And then he got a small bottle from his tackle bag. It was a bottle of luminous yellow paint, the sort of stuff you might use on the tip of a quill float. He painted the thick leader just above the joint to the thinner stuff. The paint dried in a few seconds and he wiped line grease on the thick part of the leader. 'Nymph,' he said. And, by golly, it made perfect sense. The thick, greased leader lies in the surface: the fine tippet dips below the join and the fisherman watches the bright yellow painted portion of the leader for a hint of a take. Neat and quick.

We climbed the road towards Spain. The river beside us was the Nive des Aldudes, a tributary of the Nive. Gone were the broad reaches of the lower Nives and Gaves: high above St Etienne de Baigorry the mountain river had narrowed into a wooded stream beside the hairpins. We set up the rods and made our way down the steep grassy slope and into a green tunnel of a river.

The Nive des Aldudes is an unspoilt wooded headwater like unspoilt wooded headwaters anywhere. You do not have to take the long, luxurious ferry to Spain and drive back into the French Pyrénées to find such a thing. We have them in the hillier bits of England, Wales and Scotland. And, in truth, fishing one UWH is much like fishing a British UWH. The cool waters bounce between the rocks, through bright rapids, small falls, under dark roots, eddy into deep pools and babble on to the next run or rapid. It is this endless variety of dappled light and dense shade as the sun moves through the day, of speed and depth of current, of shingle, stone and silt on the bottom together with the cold fresh water bursting with oxygen that ensures that on the hottest day of the most languid season, somewhere fish will be moving and feeding.

You do not wait for a rise on such waters. You hear them, an unseen 'plop' above the babble of the stream, but as often as not that is just another hazel-nut falling from the canopy. You look for depth and current where a fish can feel secure and a fly will swing past without too much time for scrutiny and you fish each miniature run and pool, working upstream, not worrying too much whether the fly floats or sinks as it bounces down towards you. Usually nothing happens. And sometimes it does. Sometimes the fly just disappears as it has done a dozen times before but this time there is a fish on the end. Sometimes a fish porpoises over the fly, grabbing on the way past, or then again a nose will just appear and then engulf the thing. You do not get a 'kidney-shaped whorl' on this sort of water. You get something and you strike. And we got things. Not the huge fish of May and June on the lower

Gaves and Nives. But nice wild mountain trout. Less than a pound most of them: and more than a half-pound. A perfect day in the Pyrénées.

*   *   *

Noon on another sunny day and we were standing once again beside a pool on the Gave d'Aspe. The same pool as before. The sunlight illuminated the pale sand of the bottom and the same huge fish were hanging in the depths, betrayed by their shadows. Another guide was pointing them out to me. Christian Paris is a professional fishing guide. I had met him in the bar of the hotel the night before. He had heard we had been up on the headwaters of the Nive. How did we do? I told him of the fish in the cold headwaters. What size? Up to 400 grams, I said. There are fish five times that size here on the Gave d'Aspe. I know – but can we catch them? Of course!

Standing there at noon the next day I did not see how. The pool is close to a layby on the main road south to Spain. By August the fish in its depths must have seen imitations of everything natural and unnatural under the sun. They had seen a few of mine two days before without a touch. They were deep, probably 10 feet down, but the clarity of the water was deceiving. I had some pretty hefty nymphs in my box and cartwheeled them into the neck of the pool. It was hard to pick up the path of the fly. On the first run-through a fish or so might make a move towards where I thought it might be. On the second run it was ignored and if subsequent casts were lucky enough to bring it onto the nose of a fish the thing would disdainfully swing out of the way as if it were avoiding something unpleasant on the pavement. And yet they were intercepting something. From time to time a fish would slip aside to grab a morsel and then return to station.

Christian said it could be done. He showed me the answer on his palm – somewhere. It was a minute nymph – size 28. But how can something as small as that be delivered to a fish 10 feet down? I was fascinated. Christian tied on a dropper and attached a large conventional leaded nymph. This would get the rig down to a working depth where that tiny unweighted titbit could drift naturally in the currents across the bottom of the pool.

It did not happen at once: the miracle is that it happened at all. We had been there an hour, Christian patiently swimming the tiny particle into the path of one of the monsters of the Gave d'Aspe. I was forlornly fishing the broken water above the pool when I saw Christian's line tighten, the rod tip raise and bend down. Christian stepped gingerly into the tail of the pool and edged into deeper water. You do not horse a fish on a size 28. It did nothing spectacular. I have my doubts that it knew it was hooked. It may just have felt rear-end heavy, like its wellingtons were full of water, because it simply held station in the bottom of the pool and then circled slowly, the line taught behind it. And then it wasn't. The tiny hook had pulled out.

Funny thing: I felt a curious sort of relief when that fish got off. If anyone deserved to catch it, Christian did, but if ever I really believed it was possible to catch one of these 5- or 6-pounders, 10 feet down on a size 28 nymph in August then I might have felt obliged to stick at it. National pride and so forth. As it was, I felt free to leave them until the easier days of some other May or June and go explore the odd thousand miles of sparkling headwaters.

This Other Eden

The story so far: Our stocky hero (a crooked smile but straight teeth) has caught nothing all day fishing the long, still flats of the Eden under a summer sun. Spirits further dampened by a short but nonetheless unpleasant shower, they fish on into dusk – which also produces no fish. The river has grown quiet and they are about to leave and take up golf, which at least works no matter what the conditions, when in the near-blackness of the still pool behind them something stirs. Now, read on . . .

The noise was of something big sucking something else big down through the surface. The nearest I can get to it is the sound of a plug pulled quickly out of a washbasin containing 1½ inches of water. (I have just been experimenting in the bathroom – it's not *quite* that but near enough.) It is *not* a sip.

More of these noises were coming from the far bank of the flat where the deep channel ran past trees rapidly disappearing into the night. The fly on the end of my tippet had a black parachute hackle tied around a tuft of white calf's tail. Its principal advantage at dusk is that it is visible: the white scud of a wing shows up well against dark water. It got no reaction. Meanwhile, the noises increased and heavy rings of disturbed water caught the odd vestige of light as they spread out from the blackness under the trees. Whatever they were taking was big and it was on the surface.

I have a fly in my box that is kept for just these occasions. It is not a fly I am inclined to discuss but it can, from time to time, be very effective when the light is failing. I put this down to the fact that although it exudes all the right signals for 'struggling insect' and, heaven knows, exudes enough of them to interest the most sated trout, if a trout were to catch sight of it in the full light of day, that fish would run screaming from the field of play. It has that effect on me a bit.

It is a sort of Griffith's Gnat. Now, a Griffith's Gnat is an entirely respectable pattern for imitating the smaller midges and suchlike. It comes from the

United States where they grow the finest grizzle capes and it consists of nothing more than a long, short-fibred, well-marked grizzle hackle palmered the length of a peacock-herl body on a small hook. The hook size is usually in the low twenties: John Roberts in his *River Trout Flies* suggests sizes 16–28.

My variation differs subtly. I use a size 8. The hackle is proportionally larger and it has to be a good quality hackle indeed to retain any stiffness and marking at that size. It is grotesque – but it has taken two of my three largest Usk trout and is disconcertingly effective at dusk. I cannot bring myself to call something that big a 'Griffith's Gnat'. It is a Griffith's *Bat*.

Tying on a size 8 hook in the gloaming is not difficult: the eye is large enough to pull a small hawser through. Pretty soon we were in business. There was still a steady background of sucking noises from across the way and I cast the Bat over in their general direction. Still nothing for several casts and then, after a sucking noise in the region where I presumed the fly had reached, I began to retrieve and encountered a resistance that became a fish which bore off downstream. I cannot honestly claim to have played much part in the hooking of that fish.

You can take liberties with a size 8 hook. There is little weed to worry about in the Eden but to have the first fish after a long, long day weaving about in the dark is unnerving. I pulled it up to the surface and skidded it towards me and into the net.

A dry Griffith's Bat is an airy thing of movement and sparkle. Wet, it is a bedraggled dishrag of a thing, sinking like a stone under the weight of all that iron. I dried it as best I could and cast out again into the darkness, but it seemed to have lost what little effectiveness it had once possessed on the midnight trout of the Eden. They were still slurping across the way.

When a man wants something to float, his thoughts turn to deer hair. In my box were a few dry flies with bodies of spun deer hair, tied to be bounced down the waterfalls and broken water of steep and stony becks: 'Irresistibles' – another fly from the United States. As such, they had not proved an unqualified success. In the small sizes needed for such streams it is difficult to clip the deer-hair body sufficiently to stop it masking the hook point. But I had one Irresistible, my first attempt to tie one, on a size 12. The effect of the deer-hair body is to make this look much larger than a 12, much too large to fish on a beck but every bit as meaty as the defunct Bat.

It is not often, on the sort of waters I fish, that a change of fly produces a dramatic change of fortune from blank to bonanza. This was one of those rare occasions.

At first I tried to fish a conventional dry fly, slightly upstream and with no drag. By tightening when a slurping rise was heard I found another fish was on the end, but I have no idea how many I had missed like this. Then a rise heard downstream prompted me to cast down and across. There was no way of avoiding drag in the darkness – and, as it turned out, no need! The sound of the rising fish coincided with a sharp pull out of the darkness and a third fish was sawing upstream and down. It is exciting stuff, this landing of big fish in the dark – for all of the fish we took that night were around the pound, a prodigious average for wild fish.

This was the beginning of a purple patch, with a fish almost every cast for a brief period. The dragging of the dry fly, far from scaring the fish, seemed to attract them to the fly so that it was sufficient only to cast into the general direction of activity and then to draw in on the fly to keep in contact: the slight current does the rest.

Three fish later, the Irresistible became entwined round the barbed-wire fence on the bank behind my head and I heard it part company with that unmistakable 'ping' of goodbye.

Changing flies by the light of a small torch held between the teeth is by far the best way to appreciate the density of fly life over the Eden after dark. Within seconds the pool of light containing your hands becomes a soup of small insects that must be breathed in – there's nothing else to breathe. Occasionally something much heavier slaps into the back of your neck or into your face, a large moth or sedge that is the cause of all the activity on the water.

My remaining Irresistibles were size 16. Even so, the fish were prepared to latch on to one, but after the third one had just as rapidly wrenched itself off after a few seconds, it was clear that the crowded gape of the hook just wasn't up to the business of hanging on to these big, wild fish.

I was frantically playing the torch over my fly-box, trying to distinguish the living from the artificial, when it dawned on me that the activity in the darkness was slackening and then within just a few minutes it had stopped. We had probably been catching fish for less than twenty minutes. It had been a good twenty minutes, to be sure, but I was now determined to come back again when I had more than just the merest toehold on what I should be doing out there in the dark.

*   *   *

If you have turned your back on duty and responsibility and are determined to live for pleasure alone, you will come to Appleby by the Settle and Carlisle railway, probably the most beautiful, certainly the most dramatic, railway line in Britain. From Settle to Appleby it picks its way across the high moors of the Yorkshire Dales, burrowing through eight tunnels and flying across nine viaducts over some of the great rivers of the north country: the Ribble, the small headwaters of the Lune and, from Shotlock Hill tunnel, over the southern becks that feed the upper Eden before crossing the Eden itself at Ormside just before Appleby.

From Appleby station, the dedicated sybarite should get himself wafted to the Tufton Arms in the market square. There are reasons for this. They will become apparent.

Appleby is surrounded by Eden. Literally. The small stone town sits in the centre of a large meander so that any stroll from the market square, north, east or west, brings you up against the Eden. This is the Town Water: free fishing for residents and that includes visitors to the town's hotel.

The Eden around Appleby is trout fishing of the highest quality. In a pollution incident a few years ago on the town water 1,200 fish over 7 inches were collected from every 200 metres of the river – a staggering density of trout up to 5 pounds. Now, of course, nobody knows this better than the anglers of Appleby, who have cornered almost every portion of the river that is not irrevocably private. Appleby Anglers do not issue day tickets. Almost. Two day tickets *are* available for the 18 miles of Appleby Anglers' water to residents of the Tufton Arms.

And there's more. In the centre of the market square is an island of old buildings including a shoe and tackle shop on the southeast corner. Now, a shop that sells fishing tackle and something else entirely unrelated is always worth a visit: the proprietor is usually a fanatically dedicated fisherman. John Pape is no exception. He is a master of the North Country style of fly-fishing and runs a series of classes on his private 4 miles of the Eden above Appleby. When it is not needed for one of his classes, John lets this fishing to a maximum of four rods per day – and it was on this water that I had started my belated education into the ways of the trout of the middle Eden. Mastering a trout river is all a question of choosing the right tactics. In my case the tactics were obvious – arranging to have my next crack at night fishing on the Eden in the company of John Pape.

Preparation is everything in night fishing. Ours began in the bar of the Tufton Arms at seven on a warm evening in early August.

With John was a renowned local angler who had spent a lifetime fishing on and around the Eden. Hugh Eggleston looks every inch the weather-beaten local fisherman. He only needed a pint of 'Thrapstons Old Particular' to complete the picture. Somewhat of a disappointment, then, when he asked for a gin and tonic. I had just had my first lesson in night fishing on the Eden – and had missed it entirely.

The bustard fishing on the Eden takes its name from the original material from which the large flies used after dark were made. The great bustard is the largest European bird. At one time it was common in England on the wide plains of the south and on the bleak fells of the north. It was far too large (the male could be over 30 pounds) and tasty to survive and it disappeared with the improvement in sporting guns during the last century. By a curious twist of fate, its name survives now in the common name for the large nocturnal moth the fishing fly was supposed to imitate. Perhaps in times to come there will be hatches of Tups or Wickhams. Bustard flies have not been tied with bustard feathers for a long time. Owl feathers were popular for a time, but now the wings are usually of mallard or grouse.

Hugh produced a packet of flies a quarter of a century old. I had been expecting something ornate and elaborate: I found myself looking at what could easily be modern still-water flies with bodies of chenille in various colours in sizes 10 to 12. Anyone with a fly-box for any still water would have no problem tackling up for bustard fishing on the Eden.

John then produced the two night flies he recommends for such fishing, one pale, the other dark: one on the point, the other on a single dropper, the order to be determined by experiment. The dark fly is an Alder with wing of grouse, a body of peacock herl and a black hackle. The pale fly is, to all intents, a Silver Sedge with a body of pale hair or wool, a tail and hackle of tan and a wing of pale mallard.

At nine it was getting dark. We were wearing chest waders. Although it is perfectly possible to fish some of the flats in thigh waders, or in wellingtons for that matter, the flat we were heading for, the long 'fishless' expanse I had previously noted above the town, has tall tangled banks and is best fished from the water. Hugh's wise choice of gin and tonic now became apparent. It is hard to relieve oneself of several pints of 'Thrapstons Old Particular' whilst wearing chest waders.

This night fishing is a thing of July and August. The sport becomes patchy as the latter month goes on and is over by September. It was growing darker as we crossed the river beneath the sandstone crag of Clint Scar. John does not disturb the river before dark, before 'you can't discern blades of grass on the far bank'. There were fish rising in the glassy glide at the tail of the pool. But these were not the rises we were waiting to hear, the sucking 'plops' of the big fish of the flats.

In fact, we were to wait for these rises in vain. For whatever reason, a falling barometer perhaps, there was none of the surface activity that had started me on this Eden night fishing. I was prepared to go home again. Again I was quite wrong. Hugh and John began casting their flies directly across the river to where a now-unseen channel ran beneath the overhanging vegetation on the far bank. Within a few minutes Hugh was into a fish which John matched before the first was in the net.

It feels foolish at first. Casting into the dark, lengthening the line with each cast until the rattle of foliage is heard or a hook is treed on the retrieve. The line is shortened a fraction and the flies recast. When there is nothing doing on the surface, everything is by feel. As soon as the line is shot the slow retrieve is begun to keep in contact with the flies. The rod tip is held lowish and pointing towards the flies so that any take is felt as soon as may be.

It is a shock when it happens. An unseen, silent hand tugging at the line out in the darkness. Often, as in sea-trout fishing, which this closely resembles, that is all and the fish is off or there is a run and then the line goes slack. (But these are not sea trout with their 'soft' mouths. So is that all hoohah? I wonder.) But often enough they stick. Occasionally there is a bright splash as they jump in the night, but usually these magnificent trout of the Eden bore down into the deep pool time and again before they can be worked gently, gratefully over the net.

This is exciting stuff, no question.

But it does prompt a few (questions). If the trout do this on the Eden, do they do it everywhere there are deep flat pools? Should we all be out casting flies after midnight (if the local rules allow such behaviour)? Why is there no tradition of such fishing elsewhere? Or is there?

Fishing With Alice

It was Mick Jagger who sang, 'You can't always get what you want.' How wise the old sage was.

Ten years ago, perhaps five years ago, the arctic char would have needed a little introduction to most British anglers. Few anglers knew of their existence in these isles; fewer still had seen one. Nowadays, you can buy arctic char over the fish counter at Tesco: great silver things with tiny, neat scales, like a salmon in evening dress. These are farmed fish from Iceland, but wild arctic char still run most of the wild, stony rivers that border the frozen seas of the North. The seas round the British Isles were once every bit as chilly, and arctic char would return to the barren, tundra lands of Scotland, Wales and the North to spawn in the meltwater of the glaciers and icecaps. The glaciers retreated and disappeared, the ocean currents changed, the shores of these islands were washed by the warm waters of the Gulf Stream, waters too warm for the cold-loving char to swim. But not all the char left. Some individuals remained, trapped in the frigid glacial lakes. These isolated remnants adapted to their enforced freshwater life, running the feeder streams to spawn or making do with the rocky wave-washed shallows, and they lost the instinct to migrate to the rich feeding of the sea. As Europe warmed up, these char took to life in the depths where the temperature rarely rises above 4°C. And there they remained, waiting for the inevitable return of the ice, unseen and unregarded by anglers to this day.

Almost unregarded. On Windermere and Coniston a tradition of spinning for the char had grown up in the last century. It is a sophisticated form of trolling for an elusive quarry that must be found in three dimensions on big waters. It is an arcane practice carried on with tackle that resembles the rigging of a small but complex sailing vessel. In brief, it consists of two 'sides' of 'baits' (see what I mean?). The baits are small, hand-made spinners in brass, copper – even silver or gold, highly polished before each fishing session and then untouched lest a fingerprint dulls the shine that must reflect the glimmers of sunlight deep in the lake. The baits (usually eight a side) are trailed from very long droppers, spaced along the 80 feet of the main line which is weighted with a 2-pound lead and suspended from the end of a rod which resembles nothing so much as a spindly bamboo clothes prop cantilevered over the water. That is one 'side'. There are two of these and hence up to a score of spinners twisting and winking at intervals from the surface to 60 feet or so below. It is not the sort of rig you can tuck into a waistcoat.

So why were we doing just that – loading motors, fish finders, lines, baits, bells and plumbs, not to mention four 18-foot poles onto the Sealink-Stena ferry for Ireland?

Well, the search is on for char. Imagine a brown trout of 80 pounds or a 16-pound grayling, or 240 pounds of Atlantic salmon. These are the sort of sizes you would need to approach the revolution in record British char. Before 1982 the record had hovered for many years below 2 pounds. Then, in October of that year, a fish of 3¼ pounds was taken in Dubhlochan in western Scotland. Now, 3¼ pounds is worth having in any species. Before long, another, rarer species appeared amongst the waters between the Great Glen and the sea – big char fishermen. Loch Garry produced a fish of 4 pounds 13 ounces in 1987; Loch Arkaig then came up with one of nearly 7½ pounds in 1990. Then, just a few months later, a fish of over 8 pounds took a worm suspended 300 feet below the surface of Arkaig. The record of the 1970s had been quadrupled. And if that has been beaten by the time you read this I will not be one jot surprised.

Curiously, many of these char fishermen had not been fishing for char. They had been after ferox, the huge and elusive fish-eating brown trout found in the depths of some big waters. The fact that ferox trout may be taken by deep trolling is interesting in itself: what are they hunting down in the chilly depths? The indigenous brown trout are much more plentiful up near the sunlight. The answer of course is 'char'. This link between an unseen population of char and the large ferox is very interesting – and there are some very big ferox taken in the loughs of Ireland. Could the next leap in the record come from there? We were going to find out.

First, find your char. Now, Ireland has more loughs than you can shake a stick at, even a very big stick. But many of these loughs are relatively shallow, less than 30 feet, and unsuitable for char; even more unsuitable for the 80-foot traditional char tackle we had brought along. Deep lakes are usually surrounded by steep mountains tumbling down to the water. We were heading for the mountains of the west, of Leitrim and Donegal.

Lough Melvin straddles the border between Northern Ireland and the Republic, close to Donegal Bay. Lough Melvin is a special water. It is home to at least three varieties of brown trout. The sonaghan, gilaroo and ferox trout of Melvin look very different, feed on different sorts of prey and breed in different parts of the lough and its streams. More significantly, a seven-year study by Dr Andy Ferguson and his co-workers from the Queen's University of Belfast found that these varieties were *genetically* distinct. And the netting and sampling during this study had confirmed the presence of char.

Near the western end of Melvin, in Lareen Bay, the lough is drained by the Drowes River. Thousands of salmon run the 5 miles or so from the Atlantic to Lareen Bay: around a thousand each year never make it, falling to the flies and lures of the anglers that fish this prolific fishery. The char of Lough Melvin, unlike those of Coniston and Windermere, had never been deliberately fished. Several years ago, Tom Gallagher, the owner of the fishery, offered accommodation and boat hire to the first experienced Lakeland char fishermen who would come and ply their recondite trade on the waters of Melvin. None had come. Until now.

Time to introduce the team. There were three and a half of us. Jeff Carroll and Bill Gibson are char fishermen. We first met on a cold dawn last year beside the colder waters of Coniston. A few hours, seventeen char and one 2½-pound trout later I was fascinated by char fishing: the handmade tackle, the technique, the fish, the whole thing. They have fished and found char in most of the waters of the Lake District and elsewhere in Britain. It was their first attempt in Ireland. I was invited along to fish with them. And Alice came too. Alice is my four-year-old daughter. We couldn't find a babysitter for a week and so, with much maternal misgiving and solemn assurances that she would wear a lifejacket at all times (in the boat, in the car, even in bed it seemed), Alice was to come on her first fishing trip with dad.

It had been raining for days, for weeks, since the beginning of time. Melvin is a biggish lough and it was getting bigger with every drop. So it seemed, as the rain poured down and the wind blew on that first day. There is something magical about trying a technique for the first time on a virgin water. The fish, all unsuspecting, are just waiting beneath the keel. It is going to be great. You think. To the south, the high, bleak fells of the Dartry Mountains came and went in the rain; to the north, the burly shape of Woody (or Maguire's) Island receded as we rowed west and re-emerged as we rowed east along Roosky Shore. This area is a deep trench of 90–150 feet. Just the spot where the char should lie. But they didn't. Or if they did then they were not eating.

Or if they were then they weren't eating anything that resembled a Lakeland spinner. We did not see a char on that first day.

No matter. On the second day we were old hands, we knew the place. We fished along Roosky Shore and down into Rossinver Bay, shortening the tackle as the bottom shallowed to its usual 30–40 feet. And round and round and round. A brown trout that had lost the will to live attached itself to the tackle at some time during the day. It was not the bonanza we had been banking on.

On the third day a brief but frightening look at the waves outside Lareen Bay sent us scuttling back to the safety of the dock at the top of the Drowes River. There was little sympathy to be had from the salmon fishermen who gather at this favoured spot. The salmon had been running well; small contented knots of anglers were walking up the lane to the cottages, a fish in each hand.

The tackle had been fishing for a fishless hour on the morning of the fourth day when the bell on the starboard pole rang violently. A second later the surface exploded behind and a fish hurled itself from the water. So what – many trout leap when they are hooked. So they do, but this one, remember, was trailing a 2-pound lead weight! In the normal run of things, when a fish is hooked on one side of the char tackle, the other side is left fishing as the side in question is pulled, bait by bait, to the surface and the fish netted. This was not the normal run of things. A fish that could shift thus with a 2-pound weight could make a fine mess of two sides of tackle with its total of 340 feet of line and sixteen spinners. The spare side was pulled in as the fish careered hither and yon behind the boat. With the problem halved the active side was gradually worked, kicking and screaming, into the boat. The trout was big, 22 inches from nose to the fork of the tail: a dark fish with black spots and no relieving colour. And as it came into the boat it disgorged its last meal: a brace of 3-inch fish. They had a ferox.

But no char. The ferox gave hope – until we examined those two fish carefully and found that he had been dining on small brown trout or salmon parr.

It was make or break on the fifth day. The weather forecast was bad but things were calm at dawn and we dragged ourselves down to the lough to get in what fishing we could before the wind came up. Eighteen-foot char poles and so on are not the things to be playing with in a lively wave. By 2 o'clock that lough had us beaten. In six hours nothing had rung the bells. We were losing faith in the char of Lough Melvin. You need faith in this business.

Sean Smyth, a retired bank manager and Melvin veteran, was helping us search for the wretched char of the Lough. Had he actually *seen* a char here?

No. Of course, that meant nothing: you could fly-fish for a lifetime on a lake with a thousand char and not see one or even suspect their presence.

Just north of Melvin, in the mountains of Donegal, lies Lough Eske. We *knew* that had char for there was a customary orgy of catching the things when they came into the spawning shallows in November. In desperation we dismantled the tackle and packed up the car for a last-ditch attempt on Eske. In the face of the direst forecasts, the weather had stilled and warmed by the time we found Harvey's Point Hotel down endless leafy lanes by the lough-side. Eske sits in a stunning bowl of wild hills with the Blue Stack Mountains towering over all. Harvey's Point is not a fishing hotel, though they have one or two small dinghies for residents and there are fish in the lough to be caught. We begged. Yes, we might hire a boat for the tail end of the day. In fact we found two.

Jeff and Bill got to work improvising the rig onto a small plastic boat with clamps and string. Sean and I launched another in which to follow the fishermen and record their triumph. We would not be fishing. That is not strictly true. Half of us was fishing a bit: Alice (remember Alice?) had brought along a tiny 5-foot spinning rod that I had given her. Its tiny Mepps twinkled at the surface as the small flotilla set off for the deep water across the mirror of Lough Eske. In the improvised char boat Jeff and Bill began the intricate task of setting the sixteen baits on their long lines and downriggers. In our boat Sean rowed steadily in a wide turn around the char boat as I stood to photograph the mesmeric scene.

'Daddy, something's pulling my line.' It was not an urgent request, just an observation. I looked. Something was pulling very gently. Alice has never caught anything bigger than a minnow. This was her first trout. I held the reel with her and we wound in the trailing line. There was a gentle tug and the little fish came unresisting towards the boat. And then the little fish began to overtake the boat. Not hurrying, just going somewhere else, you understand. Which was strange because little trout don't usually do that.

It is around about this time that one remembers that the nylon on the reel is 4-pound test and at least six years old and that there is no net in the boat. People have asked since: 'I bet Alice was excited, wasn't she?' Well, only for the first twenty minutes and then she tired of the game. Which is a strange coincidence for it was almost exactly the same for the salmon. I don't believe it knew it was hooked until then. After that it was a game of keeping the fish moving against the gentlest drag until it began inevitably and slowly to tire.

Getting a net was exciting. A char boat cannot stop or the spinners become irretrievably entangled. Contrariwise, the last thing one needs close to a lively salmon on weak nylon is a rig of sixteen spinners, 26 feet across, ploughing through the vicinity. As the boat swung past a small char net was hurled and we waited for the fish to snag on one of those spinners. It didn't. I doubt if a fish has been played so gently as that salmon. When, after three-quarters of an hour, a 9-pound salmon was finally threaded into the net by Sean there were emotional kisses all round. Alice got one or two. The fish got several. Sean and I were shaking. It was a most magical moment. And out on the stillness of the lough the char fishermen fished on.

We never did catch a char – but we had a miraculous salmon and you'll find that Mick Jagger goes on to sing:

'Sometimes . . . you get what you need.'

Fishing With Father

I have always envied people with eccentric relatives. I have a friend whose Aunt Rosalind shot a postman because she thought it was Thursday. That sort of thing. What stories I would have to tell if only my father had had the foresight and consideration to have been potty – not crouching-in-the-corner-and-drooling potty but interestingly potty in a retired-Indian-Army-colonel-using-curry-flavoured-trout-flies sort of way. This will not be that sort of story. My father has retained his marbles to this day.

Nor will it be a story of angling lore learned at my father's knee, passed down during enchanted days of childhood scrambling up the trickle of a Highland burn. In fact our angling lives have converged only slowly over the years until now we find ourselves fishing together as we might have done thirty or more years ago.

I do not say that we never fished together in those days. The first trout I ever saw hooked and landed was caught by my father. The occasion, though isolated by so many years from our more recent fishing expeditions, carried many of the hallmarks that characterised our subsequent enterprises – disaster, deliciously mingled with just enough meagre success.

The family was on holiday in Scotland, in a guesthouse on the shore of Loch Eil, west of Fort William. The previous evening we had been walking over the hillside when we passed a local lad carrying a string of trout he had wormed from 'the Black Pool' They looked enormous to eyes used to the small roach and perch of the Grand Union Canal in Hertfordshire. Father promised that we would catch some of these creatures.

The next morning we drove to the mouth of a small river that drained into the loch over miniature sandbanks. With a tempting of fate that now makes me wince, we took out a frying pan ready to receive the catch. Father announced that we would spin. From an ancient box, unopened I suspect since his childhood, he gingerly pulled out a Devon minnow. It was beautifully painted with eyes and translucent flanks of mottled green. It looked deadly – as well it might, for, in addition to the first treble-hook I had seen protruding from its rear end, there was another treble on a short length of wire sticking out from behind each of the two spinning vanes. These nine barbed hooks, whirling gaily, would carve a swathe through the Highland fauna like Boadicea's chariot through a Roman legion. What it would have done through a shoal of grayling I shudder to think.

We took excited turns pulling this offensive weapon through the runs and cleaning the masses of weed it collected at every murderous pass. In due season something livelier than weed was jerking at the end of the line and the first small trout was landed. I can't remember which of the hooks it fell to: I cannot believe the trout was trying to catch a minnow only marginally smaller than itself and even if it was I don't see that it had a hope of getting to the tail treble without first being mown down by the other two. It didn't seem to matter at the time.

Galvanised by this first success we spun all the harder, grapnelling a second beautiful but tragic fish before a wetness in the wellingtons alerted us to the fact that Loch Eil is a sea loch and that we were on a shrinking sandbank in midstream. I scrambled up onto Father's back and he splashed through the deep channel that separated us from mother and sister. We were both soaked from the waist down. Damp but delighted.

There is a sort of something on the faces of womenfolk when triumphantly presented with a haul of two small trout. It is something less than a sneer but rather more than a smile. Anyway, eked out with a pound-and-a-half of sausages, those fish made a good meal for the four of us. It had been a good day. And as we drove off that afternoon we crushed the frying pan that had been left under the car to cool.

Our fishing paths diverged at this point. Father was increasingly busy at the Helm of Industry and I returned to real fishing, to the roach and perch of the Grand Union Canal. I was never a fishing fanatic. I continued to fish in a desultory, even furtive way into my teens, but, if the truth be told, I thought the image clashed somewhat with my prospective career of blues singer.

But at around this time I met someone who was a fanatic. Where I was under the sway of Blind Lemon Jefferson and Spider John Koerner, Paul Richardson was under the sway of Mr Crabtree and young Peter. Paul was a school prefect at the time. In fact nature had fashioned Paul for a prefect: he was a stickler for the propriety of things like the wearing of school caps and such. When, after university, he settled in the Derbyshire Dales, it was inevitable that he would wallow in the fly-fishing that he had only been able to dabble in before. And, given that streak of fanatical puritanism that marks a natural-born House Captain, it was equally inevitable that he would fish the dry fly.

I had never seen it before. We went to the Derwent at Darley Dale above Matlock. There were thick beds of ranunculus growing up from the cool depths of gravel and towing downstream into a sparkle of white flowers. I had never seen a fly dropped into a channel and a dark shape rise from the shade to sip it down. I had never seen a man smack his rod on to the water in the frustration of missing a third rise in a row, or seen that top section shatter under such abuse. This was stirring stuff. I was captivated.

I was shown the rudiments of casting and given a Tups to drop into a tumbling run where ineptitude and arm-waving would count for little. An obliging grayling hurled himself onto the fly and hung on until towed into the shallows of the lower pool. His job of captivation complete, he slipped off and disappeared. But one of us was still firmly hooked.

It was fly-only for me from then on. This is considered eccentric on the rich waters of the Lincolnshire fens. The names of those streams I plied, the Maud-Foster Drain, the South Forty-Foot Drain, had little of the magic of the Test and Itchen – and none of the trout. But they had rudd by the million which would come at a tiny black dry fly and later, as I progressed, could be taken on a Pheasant-Tail Nymph worked along a reed-bed. It was an excellent school for the lightning rises of the small wild trout I found on visits to wilder regions. I was starting my fly-fishing at the bottom.

Father, meanwhile, had come to fly-fishing by a different route. Steering the Ship of Industry is, by all accounts, something of a strain. A fellow captain of industry had, on retirement, acquired an interest in a famous tackle manufacturer and dealer. Father had helped in the negotiations and had taken some of his reward in a comprehensive array of tackle, mindful perhaps of the pleasures he had enjoyed fishing for trout on the soft waters of Somerset during the war: also, perhaps, mindful of the tax benefits of goods over cash. If fly-fishing were to become his hobby then he would do the thing properly. He had taken casting lessons and later a rod on the serene and expensive waters of a carefully managed millstream and lake. He was starting his fly-fishing at the top.

Years later we met again, somewhere in the middle.

In the intervening years he had moved from Hertfordshire, I had moved from Lincolnshire and we both ended up within 3 miles of each other in the north of Oxfordshire. We met, we chatted, we splashed about on a mile of the upper Cherwell that a benevolent fate had dropped in our laps; we got to know each other. And then, a few years later, when Father relinquished the Helm of Industry, we celebrated with the first of our fishing trips.

Uncle John had bought a house with frontage on the River Eamont in Cumbria. I have written before about the delights of the Eamont and I will no doubt do so again, for it has, in my opinion, some of the best brown-trout fishing in England. But I knew nothing of that on this first trip.

It did not start well. It had been raining steadily on the long drive up from the South. Each brook and then beck that we crossed was fuller and dirtier than the last. On the flanks of the Pennines we spotted the silver streaks of torrents tumbling down each gully.

We were cold and wet and slightly daunted as we stood beside the River Eamont for the first time. The Eamont is a big river when you are used to the softer streams of the South. Full of admirable restraint we decided to walk the water before fishing – but we would carry rods 'just in case'. And a landing net. And everything else. The lower Eamont twists between cliffs and steep slopes. On the first of these slopes, barely 100 yards from the car, I slipped and fell onto the hand that was holding the rod and the landing net. The rod crunched like a stick of rhubarb over the net handle. The only rod I owned had shattered an inch above the butt. The rain stopped.

In Penrith I bought Araldite, doweling and sandpaper and spent the afternoon whittling, sanding and then gluing a doweling plug to join the two sections. The sun came out.

The whipping of the keeper-ring was extended to cover the scars of the breakage and the whole shooting-match left on the radiator overnight. The rod survived a tentative first cast next morning. We were back in business.

The river, thanks to the gigantic settling tank of Ullswater, was full, but not flooding, and carried just a tinge of colour from its two tributaries. It was dry-fly perfection. Each walk up the river revealed rising fish in ever more lies: all, so it seemed, prepared to put on a real show for our first visit. We have fished the same spot many times since then, but never with that volume of water or with that reckless rising of fine fish. But we learned. Now we always look eagerly for white water cascading off the gaunt hills beside the M6: we always carry Araldite, dowel and sandpaper somewhere in the car – and I have given up handled landing nets for trouting.

Another trip took us to Wensleydale and the River Ure. I had visited the dale years before with a party of students and retained a vivid memory of stone-walled fields, each with its square barn, stepped waterfalls in a river flowing over smooth pavements of limestone, and really alarming pub opening hours. As befits responsible staff members, we had prised our students out of the pub before eleven and sent them back to the hostel. We had thought to grab a quick one ourselves just before last orders. If we finished it quickly, we might get another one in before 'time'. The flaw in this plan was that 'time' was never called. We continued having just a last quick one until around 2 o'clock, when some of the students found a spare set of keys in my luggage and fetched us back in the college van. In truth, we could not have walked. We couldn't stand.

I told this story to Father on the journey to Wensleydale: I'm not sure he believed me. I'm not sure I did. We arrived at the Rose and Crown in Bainbridge, HQ of Wensleydale Angling Association which controls 6 miles of this beautiful river around the village. Father had just booked a room and I was studying the map of the association water hanging by reception when a man, chuckling heartily and wiping away tears of laughter, led another chap out of the office. The second chap wore the modest grin of one who has just told a cracking good joke.

'Heh, listen to this one, dear,' said the landlord to his wife, who had just booked us in. 'Mr Riley here says he'll be staying another week, now that we've moved him out of the punishment cell. D'you hear that? The punishment cell! Guess what room he was in?'

His wife shifted uncomfortably, but the landlord was having far too good a time to notice. 'Room Three – the punishment cell! That's a good one, eh?' He shook his head and chuckled: it was a good one, all right. We had just booked Room Three.

The meal was outstanding. Rack of lamb consisted of half a ribcage of succulent stuff that melted as we chatted far into the evening, relishing the fishing to be done the next day. We lingered over it, the kitchen long closed and the tables set for breakfast around us. It was well past midnight when we tottered upstairs and opened the door to Room Three. Inside, the noise was deafening. Room Three was directly over the packed bar whose ancient exposed beams supported our uncarpeted floor. Lying in bed I could clearly follow a three-cornered conversation below: A was standing under my bedside table; he was telling jokes to B, who was on the other side of the bed; C was slightly to the south of B. Animated chatter from other knots of noisy dalesmen was coming up through various portions of the floor space. We laughed – at first – and then the awful implications of my earlier story began to dawn on the two of us. I do not know what time that bar closed: around 2.30 I suggested to Father that we might as well go and join them, but I couldn't make him hear above the noise. So we lay there. I think A's jokes bored me to sleep in the end.

We didn't really do the fishing justice that next morning. But we were still learning. Father bought a camper van before the next season.

There is great joy in rolling the camper van down a farm track and into a field beside a tumbling river. The gentle sounds of running water lull you to sleep and sunlight reflected off the rippling water dances about the roof as you wake. As you lie there you know you have only to sit up to see rises dimpling the surface of the lovely River Petteril. You are wrong. In fact, you can't see a damned thing. Every window is covered with a thick, translucent, sticky smear of cow dribble. They have coated every inch in their frantic efforts to lick God-knows-what from the bodywork. It is wonderful stuff this cow spit: if left to dry, it can glue the wipers to the screen or be peeled off in a tattered sheet from the glass. When we opened the side door for an alfresco breakfast, a chorus line of boisterous heifers jostled in to join us. We learnt from that, all right: we now carry in the van, as essential fishing tackle, an electric fence. Connected to the battery, it means we can enforce a 200-inch exclusion zone around our riverside residence.

It was on the River Petteril in Cumbria that we had our briefest fishing trip. The Petteril is a charming tributary of the Eden. Its source is on the northeast slopes of the Lake District and it runs for most of its length between the M6 and A6 to join the Eden at Carlisle. We had visited this stream several times but always, it seemed, during a drought, not uncommon for streams in the northeastern rainshadow of the Lake District. But on our route north the hills had been shining this time and we knew we would find the river at its best. Two hundred and fifty miles is ample time for two fishermen to wind up their fevered anticipation but, as old hands at the game, we knew how to play it cool. No frenzied scramble for tackle with us: first we would have a cup of tea and plan our campaign with cool heads. I boiled the kettle, stumbled, and tipped the whole thing down Father's leg and foot.

A dash to Carlisle General for emergency treatment and then the long drive home again. Two hundred and fifty miles is ample time for a silent, severely scalded fisherman to reproach his son.

We haven't visited the Petteril since then. But there have been other trips to other rivers, sometimes in the West Country or Wales or wherever we can find wild brown trout willing to come out and play.

We started from different places, Father and I, and though our tastes and tactics have converged through many miles of discussions and shared experiences, the different roots of our fishing are still visible through the later growth. Father casts better than I do: his leader unrolls and straightens in copy-book fashion to lie like a line drawn across a still pool – if you like that sort of thing. On the brooks where I first hung out you made a score of sideways flicks for every classical overhead cast: my leader always bends a lot – I call this 'creating slack to delay drag'. Father calls it something else. But we both catch fish. And, by and large, I am beginning to enjoy fishing with Father.

Look, it shouldn't be true, but it is true: we find it hard to say what we mean. What I have been saying is, 'Thanks, Dad.'

Factfile

Fishing With Mr Crabtree

The Carnarvon Arms Hotel, alas, has closed and the fishing has been sold off. If you want to make local enquiries, contact Lance Nicholson (tel: 01398 323409) in Dulverton.

Educating Douglas

All the rivers Douglas and I fished are available on day tickets.

River Otter. Free to rod licence holders for 1½ miles below Clamour Bridge (footbridge below Otterton).

River Coln. The Bull Hotel (Judy Dudley), Fairford, Gloucestershire (tel: 01285 712535) has a mile of single-bank fishing on the River Coln. Catch-and-release fly-fishing for brown trout and grayling (barbless hooks, please). No wading. Day ticket (non-resident) £24, half-day ticket £17 (grayling DT £14). Booking recommended.

Wylye. Two- or three-day tickets are available on the Sutton Veney water on the River Wylye. Contact The Sutton Veney Estate Office, Warminster, Wiltshire BA12 1BT (tel: 01985 212325). DT £50 (grayling £25). Booking essential.

Lyd. The Arundell Arms. Lifton, Devon PL16 0AA (tel: 01566 784666) has 20 miles of fishing on the Tamar, Carey, Wolf, Thrushel – and the Lyd. DT: salmon and sea trout £18–£25; brown trout £18 (half-day £9).

Just A Closer Walk With Three

Archie MacGilp runs Fyne Tackle, 22 Argyll St, Lochgilphead, Argyll PA31 8NE (tel: 01546 606878). He can supply tickets for the local angling club hill lochs and Loch Awe. He can also give very valuable advice on all the local fisheries.

David Hay-Thorburn runs Brenfield Activities, Brenfield, Ardrishaig, Lochgilphead, Argyll PA30 8ER (tel: 01546 603274). David organises and can arrange shooting, fishing, riding, sailing and other sporting activities in Argyll.

Fishing on the hill lochs of the Ederline estate can also be arranged through David. There are hundreds of such lochs to explore in the hills of Argyll. If you fancy having Dougal along to carry your stuff, David will arrange that too.

Hobbs's Leviathans

Trout of the Thames by A. Edward Hobbs, published by Herbert Jenkins, 1947.

The Swan at Radcot Bridge (A4095 between Witney and Faringdon) has several specimens of Thames trout.

The A.E. Hobbs, Valley Road, Henley (Bill Thurston, tel: 01491 573628) has several information displays including extracts from Hobbs's book.

Things have changed since I came across the Hobbs collection in the brewery. The complete collection is now available to public gaze at the River and Rowing Museum, Mill Meadows, Henley-on-Thames (tel: 01491 415600) and a grand sight they are too.

Troutes Directions

Things have changed. For the past few seasons fishing has been much easier and cheaper for the visitor to France. A *Carte de Vacances* costs around €30 and buys the national licence and club membership for fifteen consecutive days between 1 June and 17 September on Category 1 (trout and salmon) waters.

In most of France this allows you to fish the waters of most of the other clubs in the department because most clubs have reciprocal arrangements, and very sensible this is too. But for historical reasons there is more private water in Normandy than most places, so you must choose your club carefully. See below.

The Chateau des Pêcheurs, La Bussière, is open from the end of March to 11 November, 10.00–12.00 and 14.00–18.00, every day except Tuesday (every day in July and August).

The APPMA de Dieppe has water on six trout rivers around Dieppe, most on the Eaulne and the Béthune. This is an awful lot of water but the club does not have reciprocal arrangements with any other clubs. Many of the small clubs on the upper reaches of the Eaulne (e.g. APPMA Le Pêcheur Eaulnais at Londinières) and the Béthune (e.g. Le Pêcheur Brayon at Neufchatel en Bray) and other rivers share their waters with each other. When you join one, you join them all. This may be vital: some clubs only allow fishing on certain days of the week.

Tackle and tickets from M. Piedefer, 4 Place de Lombardie, 76880, Arques La Bataille (in the middle of the village, you can't miss it). Tel: 00 33 2 35 85 87 79.

There is a very useful fishing guide available from: The Normandy Tourist Board, The Old Bakery, 44 Bath Hill, Keynsham, Bristol BS18 1HG (tel: 0117 986 0386).

The Passing of the Peugeot

The Llanidloes and District Angling Association has about 20 miles of fishing on the Upper Severn, Clywedog and Dulas. The season permit for these waters costs £3.50. Available from Mr Gough, The Travellers Rest Restaurant, Llanidloes, as well as from the two newsagents in the town. DT £1.50.

The club also controls the fishing on Llyn Clywedog, for which a separate permit is necessary: DT £8.

An Ice-Hole in the Arctic

Ice-fishing in Swedish Lapland: to the British and most Europeans, ice-fishing appears to be a minority sport for a few lunatic enthusiasts. This is quite wrong. In Finland, Norway and Sweden – not to mention vast areas of North America – ice-fishing is huge. Lakes here may be frozen for half the year: ice and snow is the norm. There are advantages for the fisherman: every area of the lake can be fished and explored to find the fish. Ice-fishing competitions are common throughout the winter. Up to 10,000 fishermen compete on a single lake in Finland, although the thought of standing on an ice sheet riddled with 50,000 holes (several are drilled by each fisherman) gives me the willies.

My ice-fishing in the mountains was nothing like that. I stayed with Mikael and Vanja Linder. They have built two or three cabins in the forest overlooking the Upper Juktån. They are for visitors to this forgotten valley who want to sample the life of the Laplanders. I was their first customer. It was a magical few days in a magical world.

Contact Mikael and Vanja Linder, Prästgatan 28D, 920 70 Sorsele, Sweden (tel/fax: 00 46 952 12027; mobile: 00 46 010 6922 942).

There are many lakes famous for big trout in Swedish Lapland. Some have fishing camps with luxurious cabins and restaurants, all the trimmings. The fish, of course, are just as big in winter. After my visit to the high mountain lakes I fished at Sandsjön, a famous big-fish water with trout up to 8.9 kilos (19½ pounds) and arctic char to 4.9 kilos (11 pounds). How you get such creatures through a hole in the ice I cannot imagine. They drill bigger holes in Sandsjön. One of the blokes I fished with caught a trout of 4 pounds and considerably longer than the rod he was using. How many of us can claim that? All clothing, equipment and advice is available on site – as well as toasty cabins and a sauna overlooking the frozen lake. Fishing and accommodation from around £250 per person per week.

Contact Alf and Birgitta Andersson, Sandsjön, 92072 Blattnickelse, Sweden (tel/fax: 00 46 952 500 29).

Anyone interested in doing something similar to my trip should contact Norvista, 227 Regent Street, London W1R 8PD (tel: 020 7409 7334).

Permits: Fishing is surprisingly cheap and simple in Sweden. There is no national licence: you just need a permit. These are available from the contacts (above) or from the tourist office in Sorsele, the centre for all fishing information – the tourist chief is married to the head fisheries officer.

Contact Inger and Tommy Stenlund, Vindelälvens Turistbyrå, Stationsgatan 19, 920 70 Sorsele, Sweden.

Seasons: March and April usually give the best combination of weather and fishing for char.

The Lone Ranger Turns Fifty

Every fisherman should be a member; it costs just £15. Contact the Anglers' Conservation Association, Eastwood House, 6 Rainbow Street, Leominster, Herefordshire HR6 8DQ (tel: 01497 851611).

Bubblegum and the Boardmaster

The Scourie Hotel (Pat and Judy Price), Scourie, Sutherland IV27 4SX (tel: 01971 502396). The hotel is open from April to October.

The Caledonian Sleeper service to Inverness is far and away the most civilised way to get to these parts from Euston. For further information and train times call National Rail Enquiries, tel: 08457 484950.

Back-End Blues

Denford Fisheries are run by Nigel Wilson of 'Tucketts', Lower Denford, Hungerford, Berkshire RG17 0UN (tel: 01488 658539). The fishery consists of about 2 miles of main carriers and a short stretch of the River Kennet. The water is stocked with fine rainbow trout from the Berkshire Trout Farm. Any brown trout are wild – as are the grayling.

There are day tickets during the trout season on Fridays (£50) and other days by arrangement. Day tickets for grayling fishing (£20) are available from November to February.

Once Upon a Time in the West

Launceston Anglers Association has around 9 miles of salmon, sea trout and trout fishing on the Tamar, Carey and Inny. All tickets from The Fishmonger, 16 Southgate Place, Launceston PL15 9DY (tel: 01566 777287). Day ticket (trout) £7.50, weekly ticket £25. Salmon DT (before Sept) £15, (from 1 Sept) £25.

Fishing on the De Lank River on Bodmin Moor has generally been permitted from Bradford Bridge downstream to the next road bridge. Elsewhere, local landowners may give permission – if you can find who they are and where they live.

Ode to Melancholy

Sweden: The landlocked salmon fishing on the Klarälven is very special. The fishing is fly-only from 20 May to 30 September. Visitors cannot fish two days consecutively. Day tickets: 150 krona from the general store in the village. These are best booked beforehand by the tourist-fishing office in Karlstad via Angler's World Holidays in Chesterfield, tel: 01246 221717.

The Ogmore: a good little sea-trout river with a fair head of brown trout stocked each year. The sea trout come from June onwards. The Ogmore Angling Association has 14 miles of the river and its tributaries. Weekly tickets £25 from the club secretary, Tony Protheroe, 'Henllan', Coychurch Road, Pencoed, Mid Glamorgan (tel: 01656 861139).

A Winter's Tale

The regulations governing the use of maggots and other baits on game rivers, particularly those with a run of salmon, varies from region to region and river to river. It also depends on what you are fishing for. And when. And then each fishery may have its own rules.

For grayling: On the Wye and tributaries maggots can be used from 16 September until 14 March. Worms (natural or artificial) *cannot* be used upstream of Boughrood Bridge (near Hay-on-Wye) between 30 September and 1 November.

The fishing at Llangammarch Wells has, alas, changed hands.

Rocky Mountain Breakdown

Martin and I flew to Edmonton with Canadian Airlines and from there to Fort Nelson with one of their subsidiary airlines, Calm Air. In Fort Nelson we were met by a rather plush minibus from the Highland Glen Lodge and were driven another 160 miles (3 hours) down the Alaska Highway to Muncho Lake.

Highland Glen Lodge is run by Marianne and Urs Schildknecht, a Swiss-Canadian couple. From Muncho Lake, Urs runs the only two float planes in northern British Columbia, the only way into this vast mountain region. Marianne sees that the cuisine is mercifully Swiss. (The draught beer, Warsteiner, is imported from Germany. Two other fishermen were staying at the lodge with us. When they left they were seen off with a feast of whole roast suckling pig.) The lodge has cabins for travellers on the Highway and two lakeside lodges for resident fishermen (a maximum of eight). Fly-fishing is best during July and August when the rivers run clear after the peak snow melt in May and June.

There are several ways of getting to Muncho. A good place to start is Angler's World Holidays, 46 Knifesmithgate, Chesterfield, Derbyshire S40 1RQ (tel: 01246 221717).

A River Runs Through It

Sweets Fishing Tackle (Jean Williams), Porthycarne Street, Usk, Powys (tel: 01291 672552). Jean Williams writes the *Trout & Salmon* river reports for the River Usk, stocks everything a fisherman could want and ties all the flies he could need.

Gliffaes Country House Hotel, Crickhowell, Powys NP8 1RH (tel: 0800 146719, fax: 01874 730463). Gliffaes has been run by the Brabner family for half a century. It has 2½ miles of wild brown trout and salmon fishing on the River Usk.

A Better Mousetrap

As far as I know, the Italian-made Vivarelli is the only lever-wind reel available in Britain. It costs £115 and at present is only available from Sportfish, Winforton, Nr Hereford, Herefordshire HR3 6EB (tel: 01544 327111).

Fishing in the Forest

The Inn at Whitewell, Forest of Bowland, Clitheroe, Lancashire BB7 3AT (tel: 01200 448222). The Inn has four rods for residents only on the Whitewell Fishing Association water on the River Hodder from Burholme Bridge downstream, beyond Doeford Bridge (5–6 miles, half of that double-bank; on the single-bank sections the other bank is, for the most part, unfishable).

The Hodder has fishing all the year round.

March 15–July 31: DT £17 (WT £84).

August 1–October 31: DT £37 (WT £216).

November 1–March 14: DT £10 (grayling only).

A Man Called Emma

There are two lakes in the high moors on the slopes of Carnedd Wen. Both are about 25 acres and accessible only by rough forestry track from Llanbrynmair. Llyn Gwyddior is the closer, southerly lake, Llyn Coch-Hwyadd is another 3 miles or so further north. Both are controlled by Llanbrynmair Angling Club.

Day tickets: £8 (limit two brace), available from Mrs D.R. Lewis, 'Bryn-llugwy', Llanbrynmair, Powys (next to the river, opposite the caravan site). Tel: 01650 521385. Bank fishing is good but there is a boat on both lakes (£4 per day). Boats can be booked up to 48 hours in advance.

Llanbrynmair Angling Club also controls 5 miles of double-bank fishing on the River Twymyn (major tributary of the River Dyfi or Dovey) from the village to the junction with the Dyfi. Good salmon and sea trout, June–October. DT £6.

The Seahopper folding dinghy is far and away the best folding boat I have tried – and I have tried a few. It can be sailed, rowed or outboard-powered. The smallest (6 feet 8 inches) carries three adults. Kits (completed hulls with all fittings and instructions for finishing) start at £580, completed boats start at £628, sailing gear (mast, sails, dagger board, rudder and rigging) £500. From: Seahopper Folding Boats, 37a Waterloo Road, Wellington, TA21 8JQ (tel: 01823 665151, fax: 01823 660740).

Fishing With Frogs

Brittany Ferries (tel: 01752 221321) sail from Plymouth to Santander in northern Spain: two sailings per week late May–mid-September; one sailing per week at other times. From there it is about a 3-hour drive to the French Pyrénées.

Guides. The Brits are not used to using guides for their fishing. Nobody else can understand this. I can – I like to explore for myself; however, I learnt a lot from fishing with my two guides and it does save precious time.

Lilian Carli, Centre Régional Loisirs-Pêche, 4 avenue du Grand-Jean, 40220 Tarnos, France (tel: 00 33 5 59 64 23 21).

Christian Paris, 64570 Feas, France (tel: 00 33 5 59 39 01 10).

This Other Eden

John Pape, Long Cast Cottage, High Wiend, Appleby, Cumbria CA16 6RD (tel: 01768 352148). Five miles of the Eden and tributaries. Four rods only, DT £15.

Tufton Arms Hotel, Market Square, Appleby, Cumbria CA16 6XA (tel: 01768 351593). The owner, Bill Milsom, is a keen angler for salmon and trout. Two day tickets are available to residents on 18 miles of the Eden. Salmon fishing on the lower Eden can be arranged. One mile of town water is free to residents. The hotel also offers fishing courses in conjunction with John Pape.

The Sandford Arms, Sandford, Nr Appleby, Cumbria CA16 6NR (tel: 01768 351121) has 4 miles of double-bank fishing on the Eden, downstream of Blacksyke Bridge. DT £8.